OFFICE AND OFFICE BUILDING SECURITY

Ed San Luis

Security World Publishing Co., Inc.

TABLE OF CONTENTS

SECTION I: THE INVADING FORCE

SECTION III: THE SECURITY FUNCTION

SECTION I

THE INVADING FORCE

Chapter 1

OFFICE SECURITY YESTERDAY AND TODAY

Someday in the distant future an office employee or managerial student may ask when security became an important office function. The reply will probably be that office security evolved as a necessary staff function in the 1960s, a response to rising crime, violence, and terrorism, compounded by drugs, unprecedented urban crowding, labor (and criminal) mobility, and the "revolution of rising expectations."

Prior to that decade, the office could have been said to be a safe place for business and for employees. Historically, offices had needed little protection; limited (and recognized) numbers of persons arrived via elevators manned night and day by long-time building employees, while inquiring—and experienced—receptionists were a second line of defense.

While these factors clearly limited crime in the office, the single most important reason for the low office crime rate was probably even simpler; there was little worth stealing. Offices were drab. Walls were painted in "institutional" green or gray; desks, chairs, and filing cabinets were wooden, worn and scarred. Office machines were few, heavy, manual in operation, and frequently old. Finally, more often than not the worker lunched at his desk. What, why, and when would a thief steal from yesterday's office?

But times change, and offices (and office buildings) changed with the times. Salaries rose, tasks became more sophisticated, and "keeping up appearances" entered into the considerations of management. The office environment was upgraded to provide a better image of the company, while practical economics dictated providing employees with more and improved equipment with which to do their jobs.

No longer drab and shabby, today's office is designed for beauty and efficient function. It is rich in furnishings, atmosphere, and expensive (and highly portable) equipment. Since the employees are better paid, they have more —and therefore more to lose—in their purses and wallets. At last offices have become profitable targets for thieves, ripe plums ready to be plucked. And they are—every day. The thief has clearly identified his target and has taken dead aim.

As a result of this growing attention of the criminal community, the security of offices and office buildings is today becoming an integral part of office operations and of the world of the white-collar worker.

In addition, the modern office is confronted with a multiplicity of other security problems—fire, explosives, drug abuse, espionage, riot, internal theft, vandalism, and terrorism.

Office Security—A New Challenge

The introduction of security to the office and in building management, a function which will never be easily reduced to a routine, represents a real challenge to today's management. Already burdened with an information explosion on every subject, management is asked to understand a new professional field that must differ with each company and, often, each office of that company.

Equally competent security can be provided quite differently by different security programs, while each program—however successful—must remain open to constant change in order to respond to shifting risk and new loss experience. Only the satisfaction of profitable operation and a stable, responsible work force could reconcile management to a responsibility so fluid.

The Security Professional and the Security Amateur

While more and more security professionals are being drawn into office and building security, many office and building management operations will develop their own security professionals from interested administrators who accept the assignment while it is still less than a full-time job for the company. If these administrators choose to throw themselves into learning and growth for their new assignment, they will add to the usual job satisfactions that of an unusually constructive personal involvement where satisfaction is in losses that never happened and tragedies that never occurred.

That is not to say that the road to contemporary security is not—necessarily—strewn with painful instances of learning the hard way, but that the security function well handled is a source of satisfaction both to an enlightened management and to the responsible administrator and his staff.

YOUR DESK
IS NOT A SAFE
MP
AND OUR OFFICE IS
NOT FORT KNOX
SECURITY

Chapter 2

OPEN-HOURS CRIME

PART I: ROBBERY, LARCENY AND ACCESS CONTROL

Very few offices and probably no office buildings can be open for business while closed to the public. Clients, salesmen, messengers, delivery men, service personnel, visitors—a steady stream of outsiders is essential to the operation of almost every business.

This traffic is the vehicle or cover for the criminal few who enter to prey on the office and its personnel. They may enter in any guise and, because they know their way around today's office, they're rarely spotted.

The crimes which can be laid to these relatively few are many and serious.

Theft

Theft (larceny) is the most common crime committed by outsiders while the office is open for business. Type-writers, calculators, purses, and wallets disappear constantly, virtually regardless of the kind of office, its location, or the number of employees present.

The great frequency of theft gives this problem top priority in office loss prevention. Since the procedures which reduce theft are generally those which deter other "open-hours" crimes, preventive measures are discussed further on in this chapter, after the entire risk has been examined.

Assault

Less common in an operating office, but far more feared, are the crimes against persons, which include robbery and rape.

In many offices such crimes may seem impossible, but they do occur, as does murder in the course of a robbery. Rape has occurred in a women's restroom in the Senate Office Building, on the fire stairs of a Los Angeles building, and in offices left unlocked from the corridor when late workers were putting in overtime. Robberies have occurred everywhere; in restrooms, corridors, elevators, and in subterranean garages. No one and no place is immune from these attacks.

The fear that such attacks create is infectious. Everyone feels victimized. Personnel leave for jobs in "safer" places. Employees who remain are reluctant to work overtime. An entire office can be demoralized by an attack on one of its members. There is also the possibility that liability for injury or damages may be placed on the employer or building management.

Preparation for Crime

Freedom of access to the building and the individual office is very important to the criminal. It permits him to "case" the office for a burglary. Taking advantage of his freedom of movement, he can identify the most attractive targets and check out escape routes. He can locate hiding places, such as air conditioning machinery rooms or accessible crawlspaces, where he can wait for the building to close. He can get into telephone equipment rooms where he can identify alarm connections or where he can install a "tap" on a phone without the risk of approaching the target office. He might even tap a computer telephone line to record incoming or outgoing data. (*See Chapter 8.*)

Criminals enjoy even more freedom of access if they appear as "pseudo-servicemen." They enter as "typewriter repairmen" who have come to "pick up the machine"; as the electrician come to fix Mr. X's desk lamp when he's away on vacation (and check his desk and files between lamp fixing); or as a telephone serviceman who wanders freely from desk to desk "looking for the trouble in the phone." These wolves in sheep's clothing are rarely challenged, and hardly noticed by a busy office staff .

As long as the thief has freedom to roam the premises, the odds are in his favor. He will, in no time, familiarize himself with the rooms accessible from the public corridor, find out how (or if) the doors to the fire stairs are secured against re-entry from the stairwell, and whether or not there is an escape route over the roof. He may enter a great many offices on the "oops, wrong office" routine—and in doing so check each one for the quality and quantity of its office machines, and the alertness of office personnel.

We must also consider authorized visitors. Deliverymen and messengers have been known to have taken up larceny as a side line. Few offices bother with receiving deliveries at their entrance; most of them actually encourage messengers to find their own way to and from the department they say they are seeking.

The Geography of Security

Neighboring tenancies, the neighborhood, even the city where the office is located play important roles in determining the security needed by an office.

If all other factors were equal, the office crime experience would vary directly with that of the city and the neighborhood in which the office is located. It doesn't work that way. Other factors are *not* equal and can materially affect the crime risk for the individual office.

Among the elements that affect crime risk for a specific building are: the kinds of tenants in a multiple occupancy building; the size and makeup of the working population of the building; the number and kind of outsiders legitimately present during business hours; and the amount of pedestrian traffic outside. All or any one of these factors can be enormously important in determining the crime potential facing your office. An example of just one of these factors: A downtown building in Los Angeles had the same infrequent incidence of crime as that of the neighborhood generally. Three firms of bail bondsmen moved into the building as tenants. The authorized visitor traffic changed character significantly, and so did the rate of thefts from offices in the building.

Open Is Not Public

The security of office buildings by day is an area of protection which, in spite of its paramount importance, is all too often neglected until a serious loss or a tragedy occurs. Such an event brings on a rash of security measures and directives, many of them effective and overdue, and most of them aimed at the necessary control of building traffic. It should be remembered that access to a building is not a right—it is a privilege subject to control and refusal.

Offices and office buildings are *not* open to every casual visitor who happens to stroll by. Building traffic must be controlled if you are to hope for any degree of security. It can be controlled courteously and economically, but it must be controlled.

There are many ways of effecting this control; some involve security measures built into the building; others are devised to fit specific needs and may involve equipment added to older buildings; all of them are designed to safeguard personnel, their assets, and the office environment itself.

PART II: SECURITY FOR THE OPEN OFFICE BUILDING

What you can do to solve your security problems forms the balance of this chapter.

The first step in the security of the office begins with a careful, realistic examination of the building and its environment. Even if you feel your own office is secure, there can be no security for your employees or your assets if building corridors, restrooms, elevators, and the adjacent streets are crime-ridden. You should, therefore, familiarize yourself with every aspect of your building or the building in which you are planning to lease space in order to plan your security program.

Pedestrian Traffic and Interior Traffic

One veteran security administrator makes a practice of visiting the neighborhood of a proposed lease several times and at all hours to watch the flow of traffic and to observe the activity. This technique, which borrows from the police stake-out, can be a valuable tool for evaluation of the neighborhood.

This is not to suggest that offices should never be located in high risk areas; rather that the risk must be weighed and both office and office building security structured accordingly.

An example of the weighing process in security decision-making is represented by Manhattan's subway entrances. On one hand, the nearness of the subway entrance to the building increases the number of "floaters"—idlers wandering through the building, often looking for an opportunity to steal. To them, the subway entrance is an effective escape route. On the other hand, office personnel also regard the subway entrance as an "escape route"—because they don't feel safe on the street, they look on the proximity of the subway entrance as a plus for *their* security. (Here the protection equation would appear to balance at securing the building against casual traffic, thereby maximizing the advantage which the nearness of the subway represents to personnel while minimizing the less recognized risk it offers.)

In checking a building as described above, the traffic within the building is not as readily observed, but observing the lobby during both heavy and light traffic periods and riding the elevators will give you a good idea of the kind of population the building has.

Off-Hours Security

If traffic is freely permitted in the building at unusual hours due to the needs of some office, is there a means of securing uninvolved floors of the building from traffic?

Certainly the use of a lobby guard with a sign in/out log will discourage the casual criminal or the eager amateur. Such a log will also serve as a continuous profile of the building's after-hours traffic pattern.

The supervised off-hours lobby is more effective, of course, if there is a closing-hour building check of office doors, stair doors, and unsecured areas. Where fire stairs are secured against re-entry at office floors, such a search has some assurance of flushing hide-ins out of the building.

If, as in New York City, it is illegal to lock roof and floor fire stair doors, they can be alarmed to sound locally and at a manned remote point in the building if opened. Also, or alternatively, the stairwells themselves can be alarmed at various levels. In either case thought must be given to the response the alarm will receive; an unanswered alarm offers no protection.

Day Traffic Control

There is little that can be done to regulate ordinary traffic under ordinary circumstances while the building is open. It is important to building tenants that the flow of traffic be unimpeded. The presence of a daytime uniformed lobby guard, unsupported by communications and back-up, in no way regulates traffic though his presence seems to offer a deterrent to less determined thieves. The guard will have no effect on the professional office thief, but he can present an image of order to the general public.

Unfortunately this image can actually be damaging to the security of the building. Far too many people think that a guard constitutes security; they feel a sense of security which may not be—and usually is not—justified by the real circumstances. Tenants, as well as building management, are prone to feel that the presence of the lobby guard during open hours means that the building is "secured" and that they can be excused from taking those basic precautions dictated by good sense. No building security system, however practical and complete, can relieve the tenant of the responsibility to take reasonable security precautions on his own behalf.

The assumption that *any* security equals *all* security is so common that, to the security professional, "a little security is worse than none." Where there is no security at all, management can see the risk and take appropriate steps; where there is token evidence of security, management often takes outrageous risks which are in no way provided for.

You would be wise to be constantly aware of this tendency to infer more security than exists, and to guard against it in all phases of security planning and administration.

Building Security Service

With the growing crime rate the offer of security has become an attractive sales feature for any building seeking new tenants. The thought of a secure environment for employees and assets is certainly a comforting notion to the management of any company and one which undoubtedly enters into the evaluation of any building being considered for its new offices.

Unfortunately, although more and more attention (and publicity) is being given to security in the planning and development of multi-story office buildings, too often the security advertised is more apparent than real.

A classic, though hopefully rare, instance of the depths to which advertised security can fall is a much-publicized "security building" which places a guard in the main entrance lobby, while tenants park in subterranean garage levels to which access on foot or by car is not only open but unobserved. Anyone who can walk and push an elevator button may enter this "security building" at tenant floors. On the other hand, if the trespassers prefer not to go further than the garage, they can wait for the tenants in the cul-de-sac which must be entered to reach the elevators.

In another instance, a "security force" of unarmed guards is provided. Their instructions in the guard manual include (1) "Guard personnel are not to respond to requests for help from tenants," and (2) in the event of a felony committed in their presence, they are directed to notify local police and to "observe from a distance."

Only an unusually knowledgeable tenant can distinguish between real and apparent security, whether in the original evaluation or in the periodic reviews of status which are so important. It is interesting to note that these reviews can be valuable in more ways than one; it has been held that where the level of security has been reduced below the level advertised, the lessor is guilty of a breach of the lease, even though security was not an article in the lease.

It is frequently true that inadequate security is simply the result of the lack of experience of the building operators. The natural solution, both for building management and for responsible tenants, is the employment of a qualified security person on staff, or a security consultant, or a combination of the two.

Building Security Systems

In spite of the difficulties inherent in "open-hours" security, a growing number of high-rise office buildings have developed security systems which have shown themselves to be effective in reducing problems.

The common denominator in all these systems is the presence of a guard or an attendant at a security station in the lobby. This station, which is either the primary or a secondary security communications center, is usually centrally located and highly visible. The communications network may be simple or elaborate, depending on the needs of the building, but whatever it is, it communicates with back-up support which can be in the lobby within moments.

Where this back-up is located is a confidential feature of any building security system, for none are overstaffed and any emergency which brings men to the lobby on the double necessarily leaves other areas unmanned and thus temporarily vulnerable.

It must be emphasized that neither here nor in any security plan can the police be considered to be this kind of immediate, on-call support. Police response will always be dependent upon police problems. Their assistance should only be requested in cases of unavoidable arrest or where the situation seems to be potentially serious. The "best" and the "worst" police response times should be calculated, and emergency planning based on a holding action for the probable length of time required for the police to arrive.

Most lobby problems, however, can be handled by unflaggingly cheerful determination and persuasion without any need for back-up personnel. The daily role of the lobby security center is to serve as a building information and directory service. Many building managements feel that this public relations role is of prime importance and they stress the role of "attendant" rather than "guard." Other buildings are convinced that the public relations role is implicit in the function, and use guards in the belief that the presence of a uniformed guard additionally displays the intent of management to discourage crime in the building. Still another alternative places both a receptionist and a uniformed guard on duty in the lobby.

Communications

Another necessary feature of a building security system is some method of communication to and from the security station.

This may be a transmitter communicating with hand-held two-way radios, or a telephone-to-pager system, and/or equivalent systems all having in common the ability to reach building personnel wherever they may be in the building. Normally this communication system includes building engineers and emergency maintenance, as well as security personnel and their supervisors. Personal pocket paging systems are surer and less disturbing than public address systems, and offer the advantage of reaching only those being sought.

The "Electronic Guard"

An increasing number of high-rise office buildings are setting up closed-circuit television surveillance systems to permit full and regular inspection of key points without the necessity of increasing the guard force. Exterior fire doors and emergency stairwells are alarmed and flash a signal at a manned console from which they may be viewed by television. In addition, particularly in the newer buildings, closed-circuit television cameras provide visual surveillance of all stairwells, key corridors, and other areas attractive to office thieves.

After-hours access identification and admittance are sometimes controlled remotely from television-equipped security consoles (which, in these applications, are usually located away from the lobby in order to protect the confidentiality of the building security operation.)

Where the lobby console is not the primary (and protected) communications console, a closed-circuit television camera is sometimes installed to view the lobby desk area, for the protection of the lobby man. At the security console or a lobby panel are also located inconspicuous coded lights, supplemented by an audible signal, which are alarm terminals for fire, intrusion, and air conditioning alarms from throughout the building. A considerable number of alarms can terminate in a relatively small console panel.

Elevators

Traffic indicators, emergency communications, and emergency controls for the elevators are frequently located at the lobby security station. Elevator traffic patterns may be switched for an evacuation, for example, or all elevators brought to the first floor and secured against automatic operation, to make them available to firemen.

Further Systems

The capabilities we have discussed here are fairly standard in existing security systems in the newer multi-storied office buildings, but the possibilities of equipment utilization for security go beyond those detailed here.

In one high-rise building authorized personnel entering during low traffic hours give the guard their identification cards for insertion in a computer-linked reader at the security console. The card, which also admits them to their office area, authorizes the guard to give them access to a specific floor, while their name, entry and exit times are automatically recorded. Any card may be cancelled on a moment's notice, and the system can incorporate such distinctions as for what hours of what days irregular entry is authorized for each tenant employee. The guard at the console activates an elevator for the employee, and the elevator will open only at the authorized floor, or back at the entry level where the guard is stationed. Such a system can also be put into virtually immediate effect in an emergency in which it becomes necessary to close the building to visitors and even to some but not all employees.

Smaller Office Buildings

Security systems for the small one- or two-story building are correspondingly simpler and cheaper.

Lobby security becomes the receptionist at the entrance. Fire exits are alarmed. CCTV, if used, is more likely to be used to watch the parking lot. In problem areas it may become necessary to fence the employee parking area and lock it except during heavy use periods.

In these small buildings, good building security practices become office security and are essential to it.

PART III: SECURITY FOR THE OPEN OFFICE

The final responsibility for security rests with the individual office; it cannot be delegated. In order to arrive at an effective security program, each office must evaluate its specific problems and needs in light of its specific exposure. Office policy and procedures follow from that.

Employee Cooperation

Cooperation by employees is, without doubt, the first essential for security. Rules are useless without it. And this cooperation must be continuous, just as any security procedure must be to be effective, and it must be gained by persuasion. To threaten employees into protecting themselves, their belongings and the company's property by frightening stories would produce much the same effect on morale and employee retention as would working in a crime-ridden environment. This is hardly the goal of security, which aims for tranquility and the safety of the office. Posters, coasters, scratch pads—security reminders with a light touch—are some of the techniques used to remind employees of their personal responsibility to prevent the crime of opportunity.

Employee Property

It would seem hardly necessary to remind employees to exercise reasonable care of their property, and yet self-protection must be a continuous campaign. Purses are left on top of desks or on the floor beside it, jackets with wallets and checkbooks in them are hung in unoccupied offices. These are attractive targets and thieves are lured by the easy pickings. Not only are they looking for the money left so carelessly, but for credit cards which bring fast cash, and the checkbooks and personal identification needed to facilitate forgery.

Carelessness with purses and wallets brings thieves back again and again until eventually they may raise their sights from purses to office equipment, the single largest source of loss from offices according to insurance statistics.

The Thief's-Eye View

What does the thief see in your office when he looks in from the corridor door? Does he see a one-desk reception area which is usually—but not always—occupied? Or is it always occupied by a receptionist or her relief?

The reception area is the office's first line of defense during open hours. In many offices it is the only defense. Despite this, more typewriters are stolen at this point than from any other. A company located in a single two-story office in a low-crime area ignored four separate open-hours thefts of new executive typewriters from the front office reception area, despite the fact that their insurance was cancelled after the second loss. At last report they had just lost their fifth new typewriter from that desk—along with six more, in a nighttime smash-and-grab. This company's controller is aware that there are office equipment locks which will withstand a surprising amount of attack. He doesn't believe it would be "wise" to drill holes for the locks in the typewriter extension of the office desks, although the company's loss in typewriters is now approaching $10,000.

Executive decisions such as this have everything to do with the "why" of office security. The big question that is so hard to answer is, why are so many offices operated as blatant invitations to theft?

Unfortunately the office thief or criminal tipster may be an employed opportunist; he may be a messenger or a deliveryman. Does he learn that what he brings will be received at the reception area, freight entrance, or freight elevator, or will he be directed by a wave of the hand in the general direction of the department or office to which he says he is going? We met this type before and we'll meet him again, because he is the most common type of impostor, and one who can easily break through the office's defenses unless effective systems are established to keep him out.

Making sure that the reception area is never unattended, meeting and escorting visitors, and receiving deliveries at the entrance may seem like simple measures, but their effect on open-hours theft and burglary is substantial. Such open-hours measures can also reduce burglary by concealing attractive "targets."

Security Equipment

Not only typewriters, but adding machines, desk calculators and desk-top computers can and should be locked in place, particularly if they are valuable, or if the office or nearby offices have had machines stolen.

Any machine adequately locked in place can be readily unlocked for movement but, once the lock is fastened, it cannot be pried, wrenched, or battered loose from the desk. Even the lock's keyhole is protected against picking. Less secure locks will prevent *surreptitious* removal of equipment, as they still require considerable force, but the security lock of choice for equipment would seem to be the one which also resists the relatively more leisured attack of burglary as well as the "fast snatch" of larceny.

Low-Traffic-Hours Security

Except during business hours, office entrance doors should be kept locked, regardless of the number of employees who may still be present.

The reason for this is that the hour immediately before or immediately after regular business hours is recognized by the thief as a time of unusual opportunity. Too, it is these hours—when traffic in the halls and in the office is lower—which attract the criminal whose specialty is crimes against persons; robbery and assault. The presence of a receptionist in an office from which the majority of workers have left is no protection for the office—or for the receptionist.

The responsibility for locking the entrance doors (and for alarming the fire exit doors, if necessary) should be assigned "in depth." The primary responsibility should be assigned to one person, while the responsibility for checking that it has been done should be assigned to another.

Where employee keys are issued for the corridor entrance, the doors should have a latching lock which can be set to automatically lock behind each arriving and departing employee, until it is put in the handle-operated latching position for business hours. This measure will reduce the human error factor and—almost as important—will require fewer morale-squelching lectures on *why* the doors must be kept locked.

These are also the hours in which employees may be least safe in building corridors, or in unlocked restrooms opening off halls accessible to visitors.

There is no excuse for unlocked restrooms in today's office building. They are not designed for use by the general public and can be extremely dangerous if they are so used. Office keys can be loaned to clients. Public facilities, if needed, are usually located on the lobby floor and are clearly marked.

For the same reason—but 24 hours a day—equipment rooms should also be kept locked. Frequency of access to such rooms is very low, and keeping them unlocked invites their use by hide-ins or muggers, or as a place to conceal a bomb. They should always be kept locked and/or alarmed. In addition, these rooms, to which access should always be limited, should be separately mastered.

Even stairs and elevators offer opportunity for robbery and assault, a situation which all concerned regard as intolerable.[1]

Even when the building is secured at the close of business, with a lobby guard with a sign-in log on duty, the problem remains to some degree. The loitering criminal who entered during open hours may still be in the building looking for an opportunity.

Where the building has a security force, and where floors can be secured against re-entry from elevators or fire stairs, a sweep-search will move loiterers out. Even when floors can't be secured against re-entry, the sweep-search— although not as positively effective—may be enough to send the criminal loiterer on to other, greener pastures. Few employees, however conscientious, will continue to work outside of working hours once they have had a frightening experience, even if it is only finding a stranger well inside the office, and no one within call.

Office Security Systems

In lieu of, and sometimes in addition to, building security systems, office floors may be secured much as a building can be, by a combination of personnel and equipment.

In one such installation, doors from the elevator foyer into the office area are unlocked and locked at the opening and closing of business hours, automatically and remotely. Outside of business hours, entrance from the elevator lobby at each floor is activated by the employee's identification card, and each such entry and exit is logged by computer. Elevators will not rise to the protected floors unless activated by an authorized user, and fire stair doors, already locked against re-entry, are placed on alarm.

During business hours, the visitor to these floors finds a receptionist always on duty just within the doors. Out of

[1]*It is for this reason that elevator "alarm" buttons should be separate from elevator "stop" buttons.*

sight at her desk is a "panic button" for use in the event she has a troublesome visitor, or if strangers refuse to stop. Plainclothes security personnel quickly and quietly respond to her silent alarm signal. Restroom facilities are within the protected office area, and the building's freight elevator is manned by a building guard, to prevent its use for access or escape.

A second example is an installation which meets the special problems of Manhattan in a manner appropriate to the occupancy. Some nine floors of an otherwise unsecured building are occupied by a single tenant, whose personnel use the fire stairs to travel between their floors. Day or night, alarms signal if anyone goes up or down the 14-story stairwell into the protected nine-story area. Signs warning that this will happen prevent accidental use of the stairs.

Visitors leaving the elevators at any of the nine floors send a signal as they step out, alerting a communications center. The floor's small elevator lobby is designed to direct a visitor toward a point where he can be seen by a closed-circuit television camera and can be responded to on a monitor. The women operators responding are "on camera" also, to avoid a totally impersonal response. If the person arriving is an employee, however, he simply walks to one of two doors opening off the elevator lobby, and punches a code which releases that door. If he is a frequent authorized visitor, or an employee from another location, he may have an identification card which he shows to the camera. The door can be released from the communications console. In other cases, the person the visitor seeks is notified by telephone of his arrival, and it is then his responsibility to dispatch someone to bring the visitor in. If an attempt is made to force the door, it will alarm.

In planning this installation, careful consideration was given to the amount of authorized-visitor traffic to be expected and the electronic receptionists are on those floors having the least visitors. Where there is more traffic, or a department head decides he would prefer a receptionist, the camera and monitor can be removed and replaced by a receptionist's desk in less than four hours.

Within these offices, employees work with a lack of concern rare for their part of Manhattan, particularly in an unsecured building.

Few Rules and Much Thought

Security of the office during business hours is the application of a few standard rules and much thought. Each building and its traffic offer different problems, and the application of original thinking to the tactful solution of security problems is probably at no time more necessary than in the protection of open buildings.

Most or all of the rules discussed above will be touched on again in other contexts, for these rules are the very basics of office defense.

If an office is not a pleasant place in which to work, it cannot retain the best employees; the security of the office plays an important role in how employees feel about their work, their company and its leadership.

Chapter 3

AFTER-HOURS BURGLARY

As offices became equipped with more portable and readily resalable office machines, burglars turned their professional attentions to the office. Typewriters, adding machines, calculators and dictation equipment all found a ready market.

Today, some theft operations are so well organized and selective that offices are burglarized for "pre-ordered" merchandise!

While businessmen who acquire late model business machines at "cut-rate" prices profess to be ignorant of their source, a significant number of these "businessmen" are not gullible. (In fact, a veteran police officer estimates that 90 per cent of office equipment seized in bookie raids can be proved to be stolen.)

The obvious goal of the ordinary office burglar are those items having the highest demand, the best resale value, and—to facilitate the theft—the least weight or bulk. Modern office machines accommodate him in every particular, and there is a steady increase in the demand for "bargains" in this equipment.

In addition to the more obvious examples of office equipment, postage meters and check protectors also attract the burglar, as do such accessories and amenities of the modern office as radios, stereo systems, and digital clocks.

Paintings and other art objects are not immune, although this is less common so far—the office burglar is not a connoisseur and lacks a ready outlet for art.[1]

The smart professional burglar also looks for an accessible cache of company checks and the company checkwriter. These sell at a handsome profit to professional checkpassers. Indeed, the "ambitious" burglar may try to pass the checks himself, tempted by the much larger return possible, but the two "professions" require different criminal skills.

If check-*signing* equipment is stolen, not only are the false checks more easily passed, but the burglarized company is itself liable for all checks cleared by its bank prior to formal notification from the burglarized company.

Can you imagine what *your* company could lose if a burglar made a Friday night foray on your premises and fraudulent checks were cashed all weekend long?

Why Pick an Office?

In the decade 1960-1970, burglary in the United States increased 142 per cent, reaching a reported total of 2,-169,300 burglaries in 1970. Of this figure it is officially estimated that some 42 per cent, or almost one million burglaries, took place in non-residential occupancies.

An office is a natural target for a burglar. He can anticipate what he'll find there. Or, if he has a more meticulous approach to his work, it is easy for him to get a "preview" of the office during working hours by posing as a misdirected customer, as a "lost" messenger, or using any of a thousand pretexts to assess the office's assets.

Beyond the obvious appeal of easily transported equipment is the attractive schedule followed by businesses. Few offices are occupied at night or on weekends. They are rarely alarmed and even more rarely guarded. Locks

---

[1]*However, future theft-to-order of art items cannot be overlooked as a risk so long as publicity is freely given about the value of such features. One bank, for example, publicly values the paintings and small statuary displayed in its headquarters at over $1.5 million.*

and doors are frequently woefully inadequate against illegal entry. And, if this weren't attractive enough to the burglar, most offices are located in buildings and commercial areas which are generally empty outside of nine-to-five working hours.

What Is the Risk?

There is little chance the office burglar will run into effective security measures—and even less chance of his being detected while at work.

Burglars will usually go to some pains to avoid running into an overtime worker. Unfortunately, "usually" is not "always," and cornered burglars have been known to make vicious attacks.

But except for accidental discovery—which is rare— most office burglaries are a thief's dream of ease and safety.

What Is Burglary?

Under old English common law, burglary was "the breaking and entering of a dwelling place in the nighttime." But burglary today is more correctly defined as occurring when a person "knowingly enters, or without authority remains within" premises "with intent to commit a felony or a theft therein."

This modern definition extends to sneak thieves who enter the office to steal during the regular working day—a far cry from the traditional idea of the burglar with mask and bull's-eye lantern entering in the dead of night.

In this chapter, however, we are not concerned with the sneak thief, whose activities are discussed in Chapter 2, where we deal with the problem of office "traffic" and access control during business hours. In this chapter, however, we must be concerned with that aspect of the legal definition that says, "without authority entering *or remaining within.*"

The hide-in burglar is an example of remaining within. It is a technique growing in popularity which has, therefore, been recognized in the broader scope of the law. This hide-in burglar steals—and then breaks out with his loot.

Perhaps fortunately for the success of available and appropriate security precautions, however, most office burglaries are still committed by breaking *in*.

Assessing the Risk of Burglary

The most effective approach to burglary prevention begins with the recognition that each office *building*—and virtually every *office* in the building—is different in operation, in construction, in exposure, and in ease of access. Each occupancy presents a different problem and each represents a different risk.

One office may be small, well-insured, without irreplaceable equipment or information, and keeping no cash on hand. It may be housed in a low-rise building, and located in a low-crime area frequently patrolled by police.

Another office may be located in a high-rise building in Manhattan, and accessible to building visitors around the clock. This particular office may have negotiable securities on hand, or vital confidential material and trade secrets in its files.

From a security point of view, virtually the only common ground between these examples is that both are "offices." Beyond that one similarity, even though both might be offices of the same company, their security needs are totally different. The security measures adequate for the former would be completely insufficient for the latter.

In determining our defense against burglary, then, we must ask: *What* should we defend, *where* (or how) shall we defend it, and what should we defend it *against*?

Any office can be burglarized. Indeed, burglary occurs on military reservations and in prisons, even though both are considered to be under heavy guard and constant surveillance. An absolutely burglar-proof office is possible, but the cost would be prohibitive—and cost is an essential consideration in security planning.

Furthermore, the "ultimate" burglary-proof office would necessarily have to be built in such a way as to compromise life safety in the event of fire, and anti-crime measures must always yield to life safety whenever the two are not compatible.

Costs and Consequences

Many companies regard a burglary as a nuisance; a matter of no great concern.

This attitude is more common in offices that have so far been spared. Managers holding this attitude are aware that a burglary will cause insurance premiums to go up, but they overlook such considerations as the fact that repairing the damage caused by forced entry may prove a greater cost and nuisance than the theft itself. (Under almost every standard lease the tenant is liable for all such repair work, and the building has no responsibility in the matter.)

Arson, often used to "cover" a burglary, can inflict a far greater loss. Too, if the burglar has "dumped" desks and files in his search for valuables, the interruption suffered by the business while files are being reorganized or duplicated may, as in the case of fire, represent a serious business interruption.

Offices holding negotiable securities or jewels, or those that must have a considerable amount of cash on hand, are obvious targets. Such offices present substantial risks—both from the consequences of a successful burglary and from the higher probability of attack by experienced and skilled professional burglars.

Insurance Recovery

Many office managers sleep soundly—secure in the knowledge that they are "insured" against burglary. But often this sense of security is not justified. Insurance policies are very specific both in what they cover and in what they specifically exempt. All too frequently management overlooks the import of these exceptions. Let us consider:

- It is usually stipulated that *proof* of burglary must appear. This generally requires visible evidence of forced entry or forced exit.
- If a loss occurs through negligence, such as an unlocked door, or by key—even if the key must have been in the hands of an unauthorized person—most burglary insurance policies will not pay.
- There must be *proof* of the nature of the property, and of the amount stolen.
- If the means by which the theft occurred are unknown, failure to recover is almost certain under standard policies.

Clearly, it is as important to understand the definitions that govern insurance recovery, and the provisions of the specific policies in force, as it is to understand the principles of loss prevention.

The Protection "Equation"

In setting up appropriate security programs to counter the burglar's attack, it is vital to begin by considering how the thief *could* steal.

Each countermeasure considered must be evaluated in terms of cost, feasibility, protection offered, and convenience lost.

No preventive security arrangement can be absolutely secure. The "best" security protection will always be a special case; that is, the most appropriate measures feasible for that specific risk in that specific environment. Beyond that level of security, insurance is the means by which management "completes" its protection and safeguards against the improbable and unavoidable.

From the Outside In

Security planning against burglary begins with the first-line defenses—the perimeter of the premises to be protected. In an office building the perimeter is the *com-*

plete exterior of the building, since entry is possible at virtually any point.

Entrance Security

The central entry point of any building is, of course, its main entrance. Today most of these entrances are of aluminum-framed glass set into plate-glass facades.

Ordinary quarter-inch plate glass can be easily broken; in practice, however, these entrance facades are rarely attacked. Main entrances are usually well-lighted, and they are generally located on well-traveled streets. Such an exposed location is unattractive to the burglar seeking an unobtrusive entrance.

Plate glass is attacked from time to time, but—except for vandalism—this is done almost exclusively for "smash-and-grab" burglaries, where valuable merchandise can be scooped up and carried away faster than any response can be effected.

"Burglar-Stopping" Glass

While many new office buildings have no glass at street level except at the main entrance, there are enough exceptions—and certainly enough older buildings with easily accessible glassed openings—to justify consideration of the security offered by the use of UL-listed burglar-resistant glass or plastic glazing materials in such exposures.

Unlike tempered glass, a safety glass designed to protect people from dagger-like shards of broken glass, laminated UL-listed[2] burglary-resistant glass resists heat, flame, extreme cold, hammers, picks and axes. It would take a most determined criminal, working under highly unusual circumstances, to make a man-sized opening in such glass. Practically speaking, it can't be done.

---

[2]*The term "UL-listed" means the material has met certain standards of Underwriters' Laboratories for burglary-resistance. Unlisted laminated glass can be as vulnerable as plate glass, and no insurance premium reduction can be gained by its use.*

UL-listed burglary-resistant glass is considerably more expensive than plate glass, however, and is generally used only in situations where an attack through glass is likely, or where the risk (or premium reduction available) is such as to justify the added expense.

UL-listed burglary-resistant polycarbonate or acrylic plastic glazing materials also resist blows that would shatter plate glass and destroy tempered glass. These plastics are less expensive than the glass laminates (as well as lighter), but are more readily defaced and scratched. These plastics are useful above the street level in areas where vandalism such as rock-throwing is a problem.

If you are planning exterior metal gates across an entrance you might want to pause for a moment and consider burglary-resistant glazing. It's true that it is more expensive; but the added security—as well as better appearance—might offset the difference. It's worth looking into.

Entry by Lock

As a security device, the average lock only insures privacy. "It keeps honest people out" is the common explanation.

Well-chosen locks *can*, however, defeat most amateur attacks and force even the skilled professional to make some effort to gain entrance, resulting in the visible signs of forced entry required to satisfy insurance requirements.

There are many ways to attack a lock, its cylinder, and its surroundings, and the experienced professional can accomplish them with astonishing speed.

Forcible Attacks

When a door is locked, a metal bolt extends from the door into the door frame. If this bolt can be disengaged from the door frame by any means, the door is open and entrance has been achieved.

If the lock has a short bolt and the unreinforced jamb is lightweight and flexible, as is the case in some modern construction, it may be possible to "pop" the door open. Unfortunately, in such cases this can be done in such a way as to leave no sign of forced entry. If the jamb is a little stronger, and/or the bolt a little longer, the jamb must be pried away to release the bolt. Even where the lock is properly equipped with a long-throw bolt, if the soft aluminum jambs are unreinforced they can be "peeled"— which is the accurately descriptive word for the way in which the aluminum frame of the jamb is ripped away from the bolt. Peeling can be prevented by a reinforcing section within the door jamb.

A less common but effective method used to force entry is sawing through the bolt. This method is used in untrafficked locations where the burglar has plenty of time and little fear of being heard. Entry by sawing can be prevented by use of locks having special ceramic inserts in the bolts.

"Pulling" is the technique whereby the lock cylinder is ripped from the door, after which the lock can be operated through the opening left in the face of the door.

Special hardened-steel cylinder guards prevent this type of attack.

Undetected Illegal Entry

Two highly professional (and virtually undetectable) means of entrance are "picking" the lock and making a key by impression. In the former method, metal "picks" are used to operate the lock as a key would, by turning the cylinder. Making a key for the lock by taking impressions is an even more skilled technique requiring repeated trials. Because these methods may take time, they are more commonly used to attack interior or little-used exit doors than on building entrances, which are more often observed.

Both these methods are thwarted by special pick-resistant, impression-resistant lock cylinders, which are more expensive than standard lock cylinders.

Here again, as in every security system evaluation, we must weigh all the factors in the "security equation." We must consider the cost of better lock cylinders both in light of the risk (the potential for loss and the caliber of attack which can be anticipated) and in view of the associated equipment and procedures. These special cylinders are extremely effective and can play an important role. On the other hand, they are only as effective as the lock they operate, the strength of the door and jamb, and the adequacy of the key control system. (Keys for such cylinders are not readily duplicated; the greatest risk is of loss or theft of a key.) If any element of the total locking combination is weak or inadequate the purpose is lost.

All too often companies economize on one or more of these elements and thus compromise the security of company assets. Locks, cylinders, door and frame construction, key control are all inseparable elements in entrance security.

Entry by Key

The most efficient "burglar tool," of course, is the key that fits the lock the burglar wishes to open. This can be a stolen key, an unauthorized duplicate key—even an authorized key in the hands of the keyholder, or loaned by him.

Entry by key is doubly harmful because not only does the burglar make off with your property, he leaves no evidence of forced entry; however much "evidence" of burglary he may leave within the office, his entrance by key prevents you from recovering your loss through insurance.

The risk of misuse of keys is enormous. This necessitates the most careful consideration in selecting the basic keying system (see below) and requires vigorous continuing supervision of a well-planned key control system.

Both of these aspects of security are illustrated in one example: The grand master key for an 18-story office building was reported stolen, and rekeying was considered.

An estimate of $10,000 was received for re-keying all the locks operated by that master key. Building management choked a little and decided to pass. As a result, the locks have never been re-keyed. None of the tenants are aware of their vulnerability.[3]

Any master key system is vulnerable. And any system wherein one key can open all locks in a building is unjustifiably insecure, particularly against "picking" and making a key by impression. For a related reason, tenant office keys should not open the main entrance to the building.

Depending upon building hours and access policies, separate entrance keys should be issued upon tenant authorization or, more desirably, no entrance keys should be issued to tenants, with entry before and after hours controlled by a building employee or guard. Where entrance keys must be issued to tenants, the lock cylinder in the entrance should be changed and new keys issued to authorized tenant personnel every few months, and whenever an entrance key is reported lost for any reason.

Keys for Maintenance Staff

To avoid issuing exterior entrance keys to janitorial services, with their high personnel turnover, it is best that cleaning personnel be admitted by building employees. Appropriate interior keys should be passed out to each shift upon arrival, and returned to the building representative before the janitorial employees leave the premises, whether at the end of their shift or any other time. This reduces the possibility of unauthorized duplication.

The Watched Door

Although, as we have pointed out, attacks on building entrances are not common, they have occurred—and we

---

[3]*In a happier case, the grand master key was known to have been lost by an employee of the building's maintenance service. Their insurance covered the cost of re-keying the 30-story building. In the process, building management discovered many unknown master key holders, who showed up to complain that their keys no longer fit the locks.*

cannot assume that they won't happen to us. In many instances, some kind of entrance surveillance is necessary or desirable. This might be supplied by a guard, a closed-circuit TV camera observed from a nearby point, or even by alarms that bring a fast response.

A lobby guard and a sign-in/sign-out log for "closed hours" traffic are the most common and the most economical positive protection, particularly in existing buildings. Some new office building construction, however, is incorporating alarms and CCTV to protect various sensitive areas through the building.

Entrance Security Summary

Main entrances of office buildings are a prime example of the workings of the security equation in evaluating burglary risk. The risk-versus-cost computation indicates that, except in special instances, the standard plate-glass facade and entrance—assuming the adequacy of the locking unit and the effectiveness of key control—is the best bet in most areas, in most cities.

Exterior Security

The modern high-rise office building is the ultimate in security, when we think of traditional kinds of forced entry.

Air conditioning alone has served to virtually "button up" the building. In modern construction, street-level windows are omitted, windows admit light but cannot be opened, and the enclosed fire stairs terminate in steel doors with heavy-duty latch locks.[4] It is common for these new buildings to be separated from their neighbors, thus avoiding the danger of common walls as well as forgotten connecting doors. Delivery of merchandise and supplies and removal of refuse is taken care of at supervised loading docks.

There can be no question but that such buildings are

---

[4]*However, these sturdy doors are even more subject to key compromise, lock-picking, etc., than main entrance doors are, and may be ill-lit and located out of sight of traffic. Entry in the Watergate case was through a fire exit door.*

more secure from direct assault. But they are packed with the desirable, resalable goods so dear to the heart of the burglar—and he still has his eye on them. So the very security that protects the modern office from easy forcible entry on the building's perimeter makes *surreptitious* entry —access by use of keys, lock-picking and hide-ins—more likely.

Older Construction

Older office buildings present different and more difficult problems. Exterior fire escapes, operable windows, older (and worn) locks, common walls, unused and forgotten connecting doors and windows, windows at street and basement level—all increase the exposure of the building perimeter to burglary.

In crowded urban locations, the adjacency of similar buildings exposes fire escapes to entry at any level. In such cases, accessible windows can be protected by burglary-resistant glazing, if they are properly locked; or the windows can be barred. In either case, fire safety must be a primary consideration. It is axiomatic that you must check your local fire codes before taking any step that would eliminate or obstruct any openings that might be thought of as emergency exits—whether so designated or not.

Window air conditioning units are frequently used in these buildings and entry can often be gained by removing the unsecured air conditioning unit. Such windows should be alarmed when they are accessible from ground level, exterior fire escapes, or adjacent windows. Other accessible windows should be barred, alarmed or secured in position so that they cannot be opened far enough to permit entry.

Commercial Buildings

Many smaller offices are located in one-story buildings, either connected (as in shopping center construction) or free-standing.

These buildings normally have the characteristic glass

entrance, a single rear exit, and one or more accessible rear windows. It is important that the rear door be solid, steel-framed, and secured with heavy duty locks, and that the rear windows be treated as suggested for accessible windows in the section above—again in compliance with local fire laws or good safety practices.

A very common means of entry into these adjoined occupancies is through a common "crawlspace" above the ceiling, or through common walls, while the free-standing single-story building is vulnerable to attack through the roof. Roofs can be easily chopped open, an activity rarely detected by passers-by or patrols. In addition, a roof entry bypasses perimeter (door and window) alarm systems. Obviously, breaking through a common wall is done from an office or store having little to lose (and, hence, poorly secured) into a high-risk occupancy that is otherwise protected against direct access.

If the risk factor is significant you have two counter-measures that can be used singly or together, depending on your assessment of the situation: You can secure your nego-tiables, records, or goods *within* the premises in burglary-resistive safes or vaults; and/or you can alarm the interior in whole or in part with a motion detection alarm. (*See Chapter 13.*) Obviously, the high-risk office should use both measures, and might well consider others.

Summary of Perimeter Protection

Clearly, some precautions should be common to all construction, particularly heavy-duty tamper-resistant locks, strongly-framed doors, good key control, and the securing of accessible windows. In many instances alarms are inval-uable, and certainly alarm, guard, or CCTV surveillance of vulnerable and/or high-risk areas can be important in your defense against burglary and other crimes.

Much more can be done—and in many cases it should be—depending on your own situation. But office buildings aren't fortresses and cannot be as long as you must continue to conduct business in them. Nevertheless, you can prevent casual, unskilled burglary—the crime of opportunity—by a careful evaluation of your situation and the application of a reasonable and practical physical security program.

The Interior Office

The second line of defense against burglary is the suite or floor of offices within the building.

Modern interior office construction is standardized. The decor varies, but the construction is much the same everywhere. Fire codes spell out the requirements for corridors and the doors that open from them. Corridor ceilings are fixed, and fire resistance requirements for corridor doors have the effect of insuring that these doors will resist most prying if locked with adequate hardware.

On the other hand, we must remember that the modern office itself is essentially an open-top box. It is walled, has a relatively solid door hung in a steel frame, and a concrete floor. But nothing on top. What appears to be a solid ceiling is, in fact, tiles lying loose on suspended runners at the top of partition walls, which end well below the concrete slab of the floor above. In the space between the "ceiling" and the next floor run power and telephone lines, and air conditioning ducts.

The net effect is that virtually every room and every occupancy is accessible through the ceiling from any other office on that floor, particularly those adjacent. It is possible to extend the office walls up to the slab above, but this is merely "drywall" construction and must still allow for passage of all the utilities. Such wall extensions are effective as sound-proofing, but are expensive in cost and can offer no total security, as "drywall" construction can be broken through with singular ease.

Older buildings have a distinct security advantage in this respect in that heavy, permanent, floor-to-ceiling walls cannot readily be breached. Unfortunately, this advantage is usually offset by older, less adequate locks, worn cylinders, and the many, many unrecovered building and office keys floating around "out there somewhere."

Elevator Security

Another measure available to add to interior security is the incorporation of "lock-out" features on the elevators.

Stairways are (or should be) locked against entry from the stairwells, leaving the elevators as the only ready means of access to the upper floors. These elevators, however, can be programmed to "lock out" all but authorized personnel during "closed hours." An elevator control panel can be provided which has locks for each floor. Once the floor is "locked off" for the day or weekend, the elevator will not stop at that floor unless a keyholder arrives and uses his key to reach the secured floor.

Another form of floor control of elevator use is badge (or card) actuation. In this, like other badge access systems, a badgeholder inserts his badge into a "reader" at the lobby level. The elevator will then travel to the floor authorized for that badge. Coupled with a computer, this "reader" can also record the time and identify the employee. However, this system is only as secure as the holders' control of the activating badge, unless other controls are incorporated in the system.

Portable Items

A simple and generally desirable method of reducing the attraction of office equipment, both to the after-hours burglar and to the thief who enters while the office is open, is to secure valuable typewriters and adding machines by means of locking mounts. There are several different makes of such mounts on the market and comparative evaluation of these locks, and the utilization of the best of them, could pay off in a substantial decrease in equipment losses.

Safes, Files and Vaults

In protecting company property by burglary-resistive safes, files, or vaults you must bear in mind that you are guarding against the specific problem of burglary; you are not providing adequate protection against fire by using these particular containers. In the same sense, don't make the mistake made all too frequently by cost-conscious office managers who use their fire-resistive safes to store high-value assets which require protection from burglary. It won't work. Each type of equipment has a specialized job. The point cannot be overemphasized. It is true that new safes becoming available are designed to resist both risks, but these are too expensive and heavy for general use.

Burglary-resistive files are secure against all but the most sophisticated surreptitious attack. On the other hand, they can be pried open in less than half an hour if the burglar isn't concerned with the noise he is making. Such files are adequate for non-negotiable papers or for proprietary information, the kind of target which attracts surreptitious attack.

Burglary-resistive safes (Class E through H) are secure in varying degrees against all but the most experienced safecrackers. This further risk can be protected against by a silent central alarm on the safe. The principal disadvantage of a burglary-resistive safe is that, in addition to its lack of fire-resistiveness, it is expensive and has a limited holding capacity. You will be well advised to look very carefully at the physical volume of negotiables you wish to secure, and to weigh that against the cost of obtaining a safe of such volume. If you find you have a large quantity of negotiable papers and other burglar-attractive material which you must keep on the premises, you might be better served by a burglary-resistive vault protected by an appropriate alarm system. Such a vault entails reinforced construction and is, generally, speaking an expensive venture. Once again, the risk must justify the expense.

On the other hand, if you are protecting non-negotiable paper and business records which are essential to your daily operation and must be kept on the premises, you would be interested in a fire-resistive safe or vault which contains a burglary-resistive money chest for the relatively small amount of cash, negotiables, etc. that must also be kept on hand.

If you use this combination, you must educate your people in the different roles of the different parts of the unit. It is all too common for company personnel to assume that the fire-resistive safe or vault is also burglary-proof and vice versa. You must continuously educate your staff in this matter if you are to avoid being the unhappy victim of this misconception.

Physical Security Summary

Nowhere is the protection-versus-cost equation so apparent as in the consideration of office security against burglary. The office location, the age of the building, the building management, the quality of building security, and the specific risks of your company must be included in pre-planning. Only after the most painstaking evaluation can a responsible and practical security plan be developed for your office.

mable materials, either as decor or as a function of the business. The degree of fire exposure in any office is dependent upon its fire-loading; the amount of flammable materials within the office, in adjacent offices, and in offices and occupancies elsewhere in the building.

Materials which have proved dangerously flammable alone or in combination include carpeting, carpet padding, acoustic tile, wood paneling, wall board, finishes, drapes, insulation on wiring bundled in uninterrupted cable runs, upholstered furniture, plastics, and such miscellaneous supplies and decorative pieces as accumulate in every office. And every office has some or all of these materials. Unfortunately, few managers know whether the materials in their offices are properly self-extinguishing or if, once ignited, they will support and spread fire, sometimes almost explosively.

Good News and Bad News

In spite of the constant potential for tragedy and the steady increase in office population, the 1971 incidence of fires in offices and banks as reported by the National Fire Protection Association was less than 1.5 per cent of the national incidence of all building fires, though the dollar loss these represented was in the millions. There was a decline in incidence of 4.9 per cent from 1970 to 1971. If this decline continues, the threat of fire is diminishing in numbers, if not in severity.

However, with 11,850 fire deaths occurring annually, as well as 996,000 building fires representing a dollar loss of slightly over $2.25 *billion*, the problem can hardly be considered either solved or minor; these figures would indicate that each month over 1,100 office fires are occurring, at an average *monthly* cost of $3.5 million. That's something to be concerned about. And $3.5 million is only "the tip of the iceberg," reported direct losses. It omits unreported losses, and the very real losses from business interruption, destroyed records, lost customers, unemployment, etc. It is clearly of the greatest importance for management of offices and office buildings to acquaint themselves with the rudiments of fire prevention and protection, and to establish precautions and procedures accordingly.

Prevention and Protection

For the knowledgeable consideration of office fire safety, we should understand the significance of two related but different terms, "fire prevention" and "fire protection."

Fire *prevention* is the more familiar term, and represents the prevention of the occurrence of fire. This embodies the control or abolition of the well-known common sources of fire, such as careless smoking, overloaded or inadequately insulated wiring, accumulation of combustibles, improper storage of volatile liquids, and careless use of open flames or heaters. Indeed, so much emphasis is placed on "fire prevention" that there is a very real risk that its equally or more important companion, "fire protection," may be overlooked.

Fire *protection* incorporates not only the means by which fire is extinguished or controlled, but also the factors which will protect the buildings, its contents, and its occupants in the event of fire. Fire safes, fire files, sprinklers, adequate and accessible water supplies, inflammable rugs, furnishings, and finishes, and fire detectors, fire exits, and emergency lighting are as much "fire protection" matters as are fire-fighting equipment and measures.

Fire prevention can never be 100 per cent effective all the time. Ignition may occur from causes not only never contemplated, but never likely to occur again—for example, the fire resulting when an airplane struck the Empire State Building. In every office, however, there must be a degree of fire protection proportionate to the value of the contents and to the risk to personnel.

The Nature of Fire

It is essential that we understand the nature of fire itself if we are to be able to deal with it.

The classic triangle of fire consists of heat, fuel and oxygen. If all three exist in adequate quantities, there will be fire; take any one away and the fire is controlled or extinguished. If oxygen (air) can be excluded, the fire will go out. When heat is reduced below the ignition point by cooling the burning fuel, the fire disappears. If the "fuel" can be reduced or eliminated, the fire extinguishes itself.

Virtually without exception, only heat, the igniter, is missing from the office environment. Air is in plentiful supply from giant air conditioners, while a high percentage of the office interior represents high grade "fuel." While smoking and electrical wiring are the most common causes of fire, there are limitless other sources of ignition to complete the triangle. Sparks from office machines, overheated fluorescent fixtures, and even fire bombs have ignited serious office fires.

Fire Prevention in the Office

A basic consideration of fire prevention in office occupancies must be control of the fire-loading factor—the reduction of combustible materials in the office and in the office building to a level which will restrict and prevent the spread of fire.

As a matter of fact, not only management but many vendors do not know which products are highly flammable. For example, polyurethane foam used in upholstered furniture melts and burns as a flammable liquid and, even in sprinklered occupancies, is capable of continuing to burn, producing killing amounts of dense, noxious black smoke.

The Products of Fire

Contrary to popular opinion, the flames that disfigure the body are seldom the actual killers. Most deaths occur from smoke or heat, from gas or from panic. In addition to flame, every fire is accompanied by:

Smoke—will blind and asphyxiate. In a controlled test, billowing smoke filling the corridors of a hall reduced visibility to zero within two minutes after ignition; a staircase two feet from a tester could not be seen by that person.

Gas—mostly carbon dioxide and monoxide, the by-products of burning, will collect in pockets under the roof and the upper floors of a building. As the temperature increases, explosion can occur.

Heat—in its intensity, will explode gas, ignite materials and create more expanded air.

Expanded air—fantastic pressures will shatter doors and windows and travel through every passageway, hole or crack in the building.

Each of these elements is lighter than air and will therefore—building construction permitting—travel upward. This determines safe and unsafe areas, and permits us to control the direction of the fire if we have planned for that emergency.

Ventilation and Fire

Control the direction of the elements of a fire and you control the fire; a chimney is an example of this kind of fire control. Unfortunately most older office buildings failed to make allowances for the controlled escape of the elements of fire; each element—smoke, gases, and overheated air— becomes trapped in the upper reaches of the building. Explosions often follow. Since smoke cannot exit, its build-up becomes a very difficult fire-fighting problem since, without visibility, fire-fighters cannot move effectively or with speed and efficiency in knocking down the fire. Worse, office workers become disoriented and may not reach the safety of the fire stairs.

Recent fires in high-rise office buildings have emphasized the lack of ventilation and directional control features in such structures. With centralized air conditioning systems and solid glass windows, the building is engineered to retain its internal atmospheric environment. While this is fine under normal circumstances, it can be disastrous when a fire occurs.

In addition, conventional central air conditioning will circulate smoke throughout the air-conditioned interior. Various solutions have been developed to prevent this. Smoke sensors in ventilating ducts can automatically close dampers and block the passage of smoke. The air conditioning system can be designed to automatically vent to the outside of the building, or to have the air conditioning system shut down except for venting fans, when smoke is sensed.

"Pop-out" windows that can be easily loosened by firemen have been incorporated in some buildings to hasten venting of smoke. High winds, however, have dislodged some of these lightly framed panes.

Personnel Training

Just as the most common causes of fires are people, so fire prevention must begin with a program which teaches fire prevention and fire safety. Ignorance and carelessness are the cause of most fires, and much loss of life. A fire safety program will inform building and tenant employees, increase their safety in the event of fire, and help to keep them aware of the always present, very real danger of fire.

Such a program would ideally include practice evacuation or "retreat" drills. Since such drills require shutting down office operations for a period of time and lead to the loss of many man-hours, office management is understandably cool toward such exercises. Where practice evacuations cannot be held, indoctrination sessions for new employees and periodic up-date sessions for all personnel become doubly important. In these, the potential for danger as well as the building's safety systems are presented. Such sessions need not be lengthy (in fact, they are more effective if they are brief and well-organized) and they should involve only a small group at each session, in order to encourage and accommodate questions. A clear summary of your system of reaction to a fire, the responsibility of the employee, and the means of evacuation to be used, should be handed out to all employees. This, together with a clear map of evacuation routes for the specific floor, should be posted in office areas and corridors throughout the office building. The summary must be brief, direct and specific.

Responsibilities

Before detailing the educational program, the responsibility for education, for fire prevention, and for evacuation must be assigned. Where a security department exists, this would be a natural place for this responsibility.

Tenants should require that building management at least provide a plan for evacuating the building in the event of any emergency, whether for fire, bomb scare, or power failure.

Education

Educating employees and designated tenant representatives about fire prevention, protection, and evacuation should be a continuous program. Any structural changes or interior layout changes must be incorporated as they occur.

The following guide may be useful in establishing a fire-safety indoctrination program.

- Show all employees where primary and secondary fire exits are located and demonstrate, if necessary, how such exits may be opened. Explain the purpose of closing exit stairwells and the importance of keeping doors from the corridor closed at all times. If possible, employees should walk down these exits.
- Explain procedures for reporting fires discovered by employees or tenant personnel. Always emphasize

importance of reporting *first*, before any effort to extinguish the fire.

- Touch doors before opening them. Opening a hot door is usually deadly.
- Distribute summary with all points and procedures reviewed.
- Explain the building emergency alarm or notification system.
- Explain that elevators are *never* to be used as a means of emergency exit.
- Explain the need to react quickly and emphasize the need to remain calm and avoid panic.
- Demonstrate available fire-fighting equipment or show manufacturer's film on the equipment. Few employees know how to use extinguishers or corridor fire hose.
- Explain what should be done if all escape routes are cut off by fire or smoke. In explaining such an extreme and rare emergency, point out that they may:
  - Move quickly to a point farthest from the fire, closing doors between them and the smoke.
  - Enter a perimeter office with a solid door.
  - Move readily inflammable material out of that office if time permits.
  - Since air pressure may expand and exert enormous pressure, barricade the office door with heavy non-combustible furniture. (Assume that all upholstered furniture is combustible.)
  - Open top and bottom of a window in the office. (The elements of fire will exhaust through the top while fresh air will enter through the bottom.) Break window if necessary.
  - Stay by window and keep low where the air is cooler and purer.
  - Hang something from window to signal firemen.

Classes of Fire

An aspect of employee education, as well as a factor in the selection and distribution of fire-fighting equipment, is a familiarity with the classes of fires that are apt to be encountered.

Fires are classified in three groups.

Class A: Fires in ordinary combustible materials such as waste paper, rags, drapes, etc. These fires are usually and most effectively extinguished by large quantities of water or water fog. It is important to cool the entire mass of burning materials to below the ignition point to prevent rekindling.

Class B: Fires in substances such as gasoline, oil, grease, and volatile fluids. Such fluids are used in type-writer cleaning, art work, multilith printing, and some copy machines. Here a smothering effect is more effective than cooling with water.

Class C: Fires in live electrical equipment, such as switchboard insulation, generators, computers or electric motors. The extinguishing agent must be non-conducting (water is conductive) to avoid danger to the fire-fighter as well as unnecessary damage to the electrical equipment.

Class D: Fires involving certain combustible metals, such as magnesium, sodium, potassium, etc. These fires can be extinguished only by a smothering or coating effect. Dry powder is usually the most effective and, in many cases, the only effective extinguishing agent. Such fires are not, of course, a source of lively concern in this discussion, since such combustible metals are rarely found in offices or office buildings.

Fire-fighting Equipment

Many tenant offices forego the purchase of fire extinguishers, relying instead on the "Class A" fire extinguishers or water hoses located in the corridors of the building. Generally speaking, this is a short-sighted attitude, since time is lost in going for such connections and, in the event of a fire other than "Class A," the use of the extinguishers could be dangerous. There is also the problem of reach; in today's business world, offices are newly-partitioned overnight. The hose, whose length was originally determined by the size of the uninterrupted floor which it was to serve, may not reach many areas of the office, since it now must be snaked through a maze of partitions to reach the blaze. Also, the proper use of these hoses must be taught if they are to be effective.

Almost every office should purchase some portable fire extinguishers. Departments such as duplicating, supply, art, and computer services, to name a few, should be carefully studied to evaluate the risk and determine the needed number, kind and placement of extinguishers. Obviously any other departments that are particularly vulnerable by virtue of the presence of glues, paints, lubricants, volatile cleaners or chemicals, or simply (and particularly) the accumulation of combustibles, should be surveyed for protection.

Extinguishers

There are many different types of fire extinguishers and each one has certain specific values. Extinguisher manufacturers and distributors will happily supply you with all pertinent data on the equipment they handle. The selection to fit your particular needs is not difficult, but should be made only after a careful consideration of your exposure to fire in all areas of the office.

It is important to know the general types of extinguishers most commonly used and to be familiar with the purpose for which each is designed. The following list will give you a brief outline of agents and applicators which are in the widest use.

Soda and Acid Extinguishers

These water-base extinguishers are effective on small fires ("Class A") in ordinary combustible materials such as wood, paper, drapes, rubbish, etc.

Dry Chemical Extinguishers

These were originally designed for "Class B" and "C" fires. The newest models, however, are also effective on "Class A" fires since the chemicals are flame-interrupting and in some cases act as a coolant.

Dry Powder Extinguishers

Used on "Class D" fires. Smothers and coats.

Foam Extinguishers

Effective for small "Class A" and "B" fires where blanketing is desirable.

CO_2 Extinguishers

Generally used on "Class B" or "C" fires, they can be useful on "Class A" fires though the carbon dioxide has no lasting cooling effect. Particularly effective with "Class C."

Carbon Tetrachloride Extinguishers

These extinguishers are still in fairly wide use, though they are no longer recommended in the National Fire Protection Association Extinguisher Standard. They are usually rated for use on "Class B" and "Class C" fires. The liquid carbon tetrachloride vaporizes when exposed to heat and smothers the fire by oxygen exclusion. Great care must be exercised in the use of these extinguishers in closed spaces, however, since the fumes are very toxic and can be dangerous to the operator.

Water Stream

A solid water stream can be used on all "Class A" fires.

Water Fog

Fog is one of the most effective extinguishing devices known for dealing with "Class A" and "B" fires. It can be created by a special nozzle on the hose or by an adjustment of an all-purpose nozzle much as a garden hose nozzle is. It might be useful to examine briefly the advantages fog has over a solid stream of water.

- It cools the "fuel" of the fire more quickly.
- Because it uses less water for the same effect, water and fire damage are reduced.
- Because fog reduces more heat more rapidly, atmospheric temperatures are quickly reduced. Persons trapped beyond a fire can be brought out through fog.
- The rapid cooling draws fresh air in.
- Fog reduces smoke by precipitating out particulate matter as well as by actually driving the smoke away from the fog.

Adequate ventilation is, of course, necessary in order that smoke and gases may be exhausted ahead of the fog.

Once extinguishers have been selected and installed, a program of periodic inspection and maintenance must be set up. A good policy is for security to visually check all devices once a month, and to have your extinguisher service company inspect them twice a year. In the process the serviceman should re-tag and, if necessary, recharge and replace defective equipment.

Fire-Preventive Containers

Where highly combustible chemicals, glues or other materials are used, protective containers should be employed to house the main supply. Small amounts for individual use can then be distributed to persons who need to use such materials.

Fire-Preventive Waste Receptacles

In areas where discarded waste presents a fire hazard, waste receptacles designed to prevent fires should be employed. This is particularly necessary where solvent- or oil-saturated waste is discarded. In simple terms, these receptacles are engineered to create a smothering effect in the event of a fire in the container. Duplicating, art, and other departments that generate appreciable amounts of highly combustible trash are prime areas for this type of equipment.

Fire-Resistive Safes and Vaults

It has been estimated that 40 per cent of U.S. companies which suffer a major fire go out of business due to the loss of irreplaceable records. In spite of this frightening thought, it has been further estimated that 70 per cent of American firms either do not have, or do not properly use, adequate fire-resistive safes and vaults. In many offices the only essential assets are company records. When accounts receivable or accounts payable records are destroyed, a company is vulnerable to denial of liability on the one hand and unjust claims on the other. Irreplaceable drawings, notes, contracts, and plans can go up in smoke. Insurance rarely covers reconstruction of records, and customers are lost due to delay.

And any piece of paper can burn. Paper can withstand temperatures up to 350° before ignition, but fires reach temperatures of 1,000° or more in minutes. Unless papers are stored in a suitable fire-resistive container, such a fire will char them beyond recognition. Computer tape and microfilm are even more vulnerable; heat and moisture damage magnetic tape and film at 150°, a temperature lower than the setting for many sprinkler systems.

In order to protect records against fire, Underwriters' Laboratories-listed fire-resistive safes in three classifications are currently available.

Class A safes will withstand a temperature of 2,000° for at least four hours before interior temperatures reach 350° and thus destroy any paper documents stored within; Class B two hours at 1,850°; and Class C one hour at 1,700°. These safes will additionally withstand a severe impact test which consists of dropping a pre-heated chest 30 feet onto a brick flooring, after which it is returned to an oven where it is again subjected to the prescribed test temperatures. It is further tested for resistance to explosion by placing it in an oven preheated to 2,000° where it is held for 30 minutes. Only after all three of these tests is a safe rated by the Underwriters' Laboratories as a Class A, B or C fire-resistive safe.

Data safes (for tape or film) maintain a moisture-free interior temperature of below 150° by suspending a sealed compartment within a Class A fire-resistive outer safe.

It is important, however, to remember that these safes are for the protection of papers or tapes or film from fire; they cannot protect their contents against burglary.

Your choice of a safe will be dictated by the type of building you occupy, the kind of work your office performs and the materials present to perform it, the number and the importance of the records, the efficiency and response time of fire-fighters and equipment, whether the office and building is wholly or only partially sprinklered, and other factors specific to your operation.

The one element that those with irreplaceable papers cannot afford to overlook is that a *new* fire-resistive safe is necessary. Modern fire-resistive safes are made with a layer of a hydrous compound such as gypsum plaster between two layers of sheet steel. When the safe is subjected to high heat the gypsum gives off water, which is instantly converted into steam. This steam is forced into the interior of the safe as well as out around the safe door. This action absorbs enormous amounts of heat and will, within the rated period, keep temperatures down to acceptable levels.

Once a safe has been through a sizable fire, however, the insulation has been expended. Although a secondhand safe may be refurbished to appear like new, its hydrous insulation cannot be replaced.

Detection and Alarm Systems

There are many systems designed for fire detection and warning. And they are available at a wide range of prices. In this area it is very important to consult with manufacturers, the company's insurers, and the local fire department to get the best possible advice on the kind of alarm protection best suited to your office.

Generally speaking, fire detectors fall into four categories:

- Ionization detectors respond to the combustion particles generated during the incipient stages of a fire. This is the most rapid system of fire detection in general use.[1]
- Photoelectric detectors respond to visible smoke obscuring a light beam. At this smoldering stage, there may as yet be no flame or significant heat.
- Thermal detectors respond to accumulated heat and are of two types, fixed-temperature and rate-of-rise.

Since a fire can develop from ignition to searing flame in minutes or even seconds, advance warning in the earliest stage can be invaluable.[2]

Fire detectors can signal in any of a variety of ways, depending on the needs of the installation. They can sound a local bell or siren, light up a central control panel, signal a remote station, or any combination of these.

---

[1] *Critical areas in the U.S. space program utilize micro-second response systems based on detection of infrared in the flame of explosions.*

[2] *Where a building has a sprinkler system, "water-flow alarms" are usually (and should be) incorporated. These signal whenever a sprinkler is activated, or if the system is damaged. While water-flow alarms are considered to be "fire alarms," they are slower than most fire detectors and may be indicating only a break in the sprinkler system.*

Sprinkler Systems

According to the NFPA, in the last 66 years sprinkler systems have successfully suppressed fires in office buildings in 97.8 per cent of known cases, a very impressive record. Sprinkler systems are generally agreed to be the most effective method of automatically controlling building fires available today. The inclusion of sprinklers throughout in new construction also provides substantial reductions in insurance premiums.

The cost of such an installation in existing office buildings is usually prohibitive, but worth investigating. (In manufacturing buildings, however, the cost of sprinklering can often be recovered from insurance premium reductions within a few years.)

Fire Exit Signs

In most office buildings you will see a sign over each fire exit door worded "Fire Exit" or just "Exit." The sign will be painted red or illuminated by a red bulb, or both. Local building fire codes usually "spell out" the size and type of sign required. These signs are there even if you haven't noticed them—and most people do not.

Part of the "exit visibility" problem is lack of adequate indoctrination. Another is appearance. Fire exits, except for the sign, are usually painted to blend in with the surrounding walls. While more conspicuous exits may detract from the overall building decor, for life safety we must be primarily concerned with making their presence known. One way is to clearly label each exit with signs. Positive statements should be used such as:

THIS IS A FIRE EMERGENCY EXIT

Signs should be lighted, and have emergency standby power to keep them illuminated in the event of a power failure. Additionally, on large floors, and particularly floors having many partitioned passages, smaller signs should point the way to fire exits. Additionally, elevators should be labelled, at eye level, "In case of fire in this building, use Exit stairways. Do not use elevators." In fact, such warning signs are now required by some city codes, as are smoke-containing elevator lobbies in new high-rise construction.

Well-lighted emergency-powered signs have also been installed on each landing of fire stairs, to reassure emergency users.

Fire Danger Signs

Signs warning of fire danger are essential in sensitive areas. If certain areas are off-limits to smokers, highly visible signs should so state. Whatever or wherever the signs, they should always be kept clean, neat, free of graffiti and —obviously—visible.

Internal Public Address and Signaling Systems

One of the most valuable elements of building equipment for life safety in the event of fire is an internal public address or signaling system. The larger the building, or the larger the space you occupy as a tenant, the more reason you have for installing this equipment. Telephone notification, the common alternative, has proven too slow for large buildings.

Too, in a fire emergency, the public address system, properly used, could save lives by suppressing panic and directing people away from the fire and smoke-filled areas. Recent fires and other problems in New York City's subway system have pointed out the tremendous importance of being able to communicate with people during emergency situations. Now, partly as a result of these occurrences, most of New York City's subway trains have a public address system as standard equipment.

In office buildings, especially very tall ones, a simple bell or siren alarm provides a potentially dangerous minimum of information. Various systems have been proposed whereby bell codes would inform the building's occupants of given situations, but such codes require more indoctrination of building and tenant personnel than is reasonable to expect. Lamp annunciators located by the fire doors and activated by the alarm system have also been suggested to instruct people as to whether they should go up or down or use a different exit. This system, of course, presupposes that the lamp annunciators will be readable through smoke, and that all possible situations can be dealt with by a few pre-printed instructions.

A public address system, on the other hand, is instantly responsive to any given situation at a cost which need not be excessive. Once installed, such a system might pay for itself by increased efficiency in the operation of the office or building, since it can be used for paging, general announcements and background music.

If a public address system is not possible, setting up a system of notification by phone must be established. A list of office areas and the names of several people in each area would be posted by the switchboard or call director. In the event of an emergency, each area would be notified and appropriate instructions would be given by phone.[3]

Building Safety

Much can be done to prevent office building fires, which is the first essential in fire protection planning. Among these are:

- Reducing the fire load in each office and throughout the building.
- Use fire-resistive furniture. Remove any upholstered furniture and cushions incorporating polyurethane. Use fire-resistive drapes, and fire-retardant finishes.
- Keep combustibles from accumulating, particularly in refuse areas, chutes, and receiving areas.
- Reduce the amount and control the handling and storage of highly flammable chemicals throughout

---

[3]*In many large companies a "floor warden" and an alternate are designated whose responsibility it is to see that their floor or office area is properly evacuated in an emergency. In such cases, fewer persons need be reached by phone from a central point.*

the building, including offices.

- Identifying less-obvious fire risks.

Most wiring insulation materials burn when exposed to fire, giving off a great deal of smoke. Wiring should be encased in metal conduits or ducts. The area between the suspended ceiling and the concrete slab above frequently contains fuel sources such as nonmetallic ducts and conduits, cable and wiring with many insulated conductors, catwalks, duct connectors and coverings, etc. Such combustibles should be reduced or eliminated.

- Preventing the spread of fire and smoke.

Where the floor is concrete, its integrity must be maintained. The over-all fire-resistive integrity of a concrete floor can be jeopardized by cutouts. Look for trouble spots such as:

- Vertical flues. Fire barriers equal to the fire-resistance of the floor should be installed where these exist.
- Wire connections between floors. These should be covered and the openings sealed with a thermal insulation to prevent the transmission of smoke and heat between floors.
- Air conditioning ducts. These and other floor openings should be treated and sealed with fire-resistive materials and positive fire-stop seals.
- Fire and smoke venting systems should be incorporated in all new construction.
- Sprinkler systems should be installed in new construction and in high-risk occupancies and adjacencies.
- Fire detection and alarm systems, both manual and automatic, should be installed throughout the building.
- Each office building, as well as each tenant, should have fire emergency plans and training programs to insure the safe evacuation of building occupants.

These are just some of the recommendations being

made in cities that have high-rise office buildings. The ones mentioned here are among the most important. While we hope such risks can and will be eliminated, fire protection planning cannot wait until they are. We must, in the meantime, be guided by the need for fire prevention and life safety, and stay always on the alert for new problems arising in our offices or the buildings they are located in.

Air Conditioning

In today's "sealed" high-rise office building there are few, if any, places for the smoke occasioned by a fire to vent itself naturally. This can be accomplished by the design of the building air conditioning system, but in most cases closed-system air conditioning only contributes to fire problems by flooding other, non-affected floors with smoke. The usual "solution" is to cut off all air conditioning during a fire to avoid the distribution of smoke. In fact, many air conditioning systems are equipped with smoke detectors which automatically respond to the presence of smoke by cutting off all or part of the air conditioning system. Unfortunately, this means that people outside the fire area, but within the area serviced by that air conditioning system, are without a fresh air supply, and smoke in the fire area is building up without a means to vent itself. As has been pointed out, this build-up of smoke can be more dangerous than the heat and flames of a fire.

It is unfortunate that there is as yet no uniform system for smoke removal from the modern high-rise. It would seem that the use of air exhaust ducts in fire-resistive shaft enclosures would be a good start in the battle of smoke removal. There is, however, disagreement about this.

Suffice to say that while the smoke removal controversy rages, it is a matter for the experts. Until a solution is found, the rule must be "stand by to evacuate at the first sign of smoke in or around the office."

Elevators

In the event of a fire, elevators should never be used by building occupants and visitors. Cars may stall in the shaft for any number of reasons. Cars may stop at the fire floor, thus subjecting passengers to lethal heat and smoke, a situation which has claimed many victims. The elevator hoistway, being vented, is a natural flue by which smoke ascends to enter and asphyxiate the passengers.

Signs should be prominently displayed at each elevator warning that elevators should not be used in the event of fire.

It is also important that every building establish procedures or elevator controls by which all elevators can be brought to the lobby nonstop in the event of fire and prevented from further automatic operation. During a fire all elevators should be manually or key-operated by fire-fighters or designated building personnel acting at the direction of the fire department.

Evacuation

Evacuation plans involving an office or office building must be based on a well-considered system, thorough and periodic education or indoctrination, and as few leaders as possible. Adults do not respond to being lined up like children at a school fire drill and trooped downstairs. Whereas children are psychologically inclined to follow a leader, adults will revolt or even panic if they are restrained or confined or regimented in their efforts to leave the building. People should be assigned to educate personnel in safety and evacuation procedures, but for psychological reasons these persons should be drawn from security or from the personnel department.

What is most important is instructing all personnel in evacuation procedures. They must be familiar with the fire stair nearest to their office, as well as the alternate stair in the event of smoke or other obstruction between them and their primary exit. There must be a clear, simple, thoroughly familiar *plan*. Building management has the major responsibility to establish a workable plan, and to organize an emergency control organization which has active tenant cooperation.

In reviewing building and office plans, you should ask yourself these questions:

- Are floor diagrams conspicuously posted?
- Are routes to exits well-lit and fairly straight and free of obstruction?
- Are elevators posted to warn against their use in an emergency? And do these or nearby signs point out the direction of fire exits?
- Are all handicapped persons identified and their evacuation provided for?
- Is lighting adequate? Do corridors have emergency lighting against power failure?
- Who will notify personnel of decision to evacuate? Who will make the decision to evacuate? Who will operate the communication system? Who is assigned to provide information on the progress of the emergency, and by what means?

Summary

With over a thousand office fires occurring each month in this country, building and office management share a problem that needs thought and care. Fortunately the majority of these fires are relatively small, at least in terms of the monetary damage suffered. But each has the potential of being a major disaster—in any terms. We can never let down our guard in our constant fight with the ever-present threat of fire.

"ONE OF THESE THINGS DON'T BELONG WITH THE OTHER."

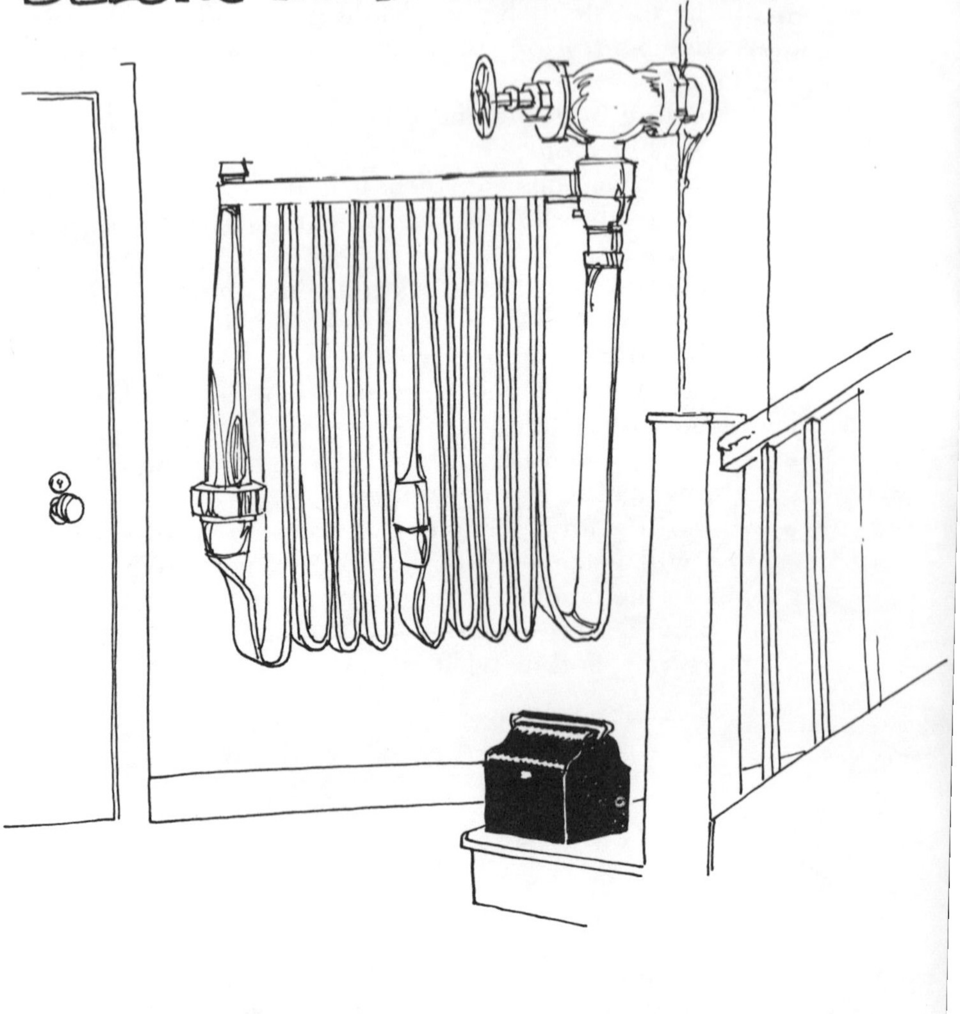

WHILE THE ABOVE CAPTION IS PART OF A SONG ON A CHILDREN'S EDUCATIONAL T.V. PROGRAM, IT IS A METHOD OF SEARCHING FOR BOMBS IN THE OFFICE.

IN SEARCHING FOR A BOMB WE LOOK FOR SOMETHING THAT IS FOREIGN TO THE AREA.

SECURITY

Chapter 5

THE THREAT OF VIOLENCE

Every office is subject to invasions of many different kinds. In other chapters we examine the dangers of fire, theft, burglary, assault, and the various ways of countering or overcoming, or even preventing, these attacks. As difficult as it may be to develop security against these known threats, it is even more so when the threat is potential violence, the "faceless enemy."

In the broad area of what we think of as acquisitive crimes we can, to a great degree, understand the motivation of the criminal, and, in understanding, prepare our defenses. Even in the case of unpreventable fire we can, by being constantly informed and vigilant, prevent destruction by fire. But in the face of the mindless violence of terrorism, of the bomber or the arsonist, or caught up in a riot or a labor dispute marked by violence, or if by sabotage or circumstance we are the victims of a power failure, we are all too frequently caught with our defenses down. We find it difficult to recognize and identify the "enemy" in this area of non-acquisitive or coercive crimes.

In this chapter we will try to define these uncommon and elusive threats so that you can more readily come to grips with the problems of prevention, control, and —if necessary—prosecution.

Contingency Planning

In preparing in advance for all eventualities we both reduce the likelihood of encountering them, and diminish their potential effect. Without advance planning, however, we are defenseless and risk the safety of employees, visitors, and the building and tenant companies.

No businessman can afford to consider his office immune from vandalism or terrorist attack. While it might be pleasant for him to feel secure from violence as he reads about it besetting others, he cannot afford such a luxury. He must plan for such eventualities, and the plan developed for each risk must be comprehensive, cover as many foreseeable eventualities as possible, and must be carefully distributed and rehearsed. All personnel involved in the response plan must be thoroughly conversant with his or her role in the plan. And each contingency plan must be kept up-to-date by regular review and rehearsal.

This chapter will help you in formulating your contingency plans. And—and this cannot be overemphasized—to handle the emergencies dealt with in this chapter, comprehensive pre-planning is a *must*.

BOMBS AND BOMB THREATS

Between January 1, 1969 and April 15, 1970 a total of 4,330 explosive and incendiary bombings occurred; of these, 1,000 involved explosives and the remainder were fire bombs. Altogether, they caused 40 deaths, injured 384 persons, and cost $22 million in property damage.

In addition, there were another 1,475 attempted bombings, and 35,000 reported bomb threats.

These, of course, are only statistics. Translate these figures into pain, fear, bereavement and loss—both personal and financial—and the true extent of the problem begins to come alive.

The National Industrial Conference Board, in a report released in the summer of 1971, stated that 90 per cent of major U.S. firms have been threatened with bombing. The report added, "On the average, a bombing now takes place in the U.S. every two hours. While bombings have eased in the first half of 1971, most law enforcement agencies expect bomb terrorism to continue."[1]

The Bomber

"In 1969 a study was made of known bombers in an attempt to determine if there were certain characteristics that were peculiar to the bomber and which would assist law enforcement agencies in identifying a potential bomber. The resultant report proved to be of value in one sense only. It was determined that a potential bomber could not be identified by any detailed characteristics, but the composite characteristics indicated a young white male of upper middle class or wealthy background."[2]

However, looking for group affiliation or motive provides very little to lead us to the potential bomber, for his motives are more varied than those of the criminal; he is indeed "faceless."

The Bombs

For bombs of the explosive type there are two classifications: "Low" explosives with relatively lower explosive power, such as the smokeless powder used in small arms ammunition, or black powder used in a number of applications. "High" explosives having a very fast rate of detonation include dynamite, PETN, TNT, Primacord, etc.

Low explosives produce pressures of approximately 30,000 pounds per square inch, while high explosives can produce pressures as high as one million pounds per square inch.

This is not to say that low explosives are unimportant or can be ignored. Black powder, the most commonly used

---

[1]*Release #2488, August 16, 1971, National Industrial Conference Board, 845 Third Avenue, New York, New York 10022.*
[2]*Major Joseph Stoffel, Explosives and Homemade Bombs, 2nd ed. (Springfield, Illinois: Charles C. Thomas, 1972), p. 3.*

low explosive, is the usual staple of the pipe bomb—a deadly homemade device put together from easily obtainable materials. It consists simply of a piece of pipe threaded at both ends, capped, and filled with black powder. It can be triggered by a number of means all well within the capabilities of the amateur bomb maker.

Effects of Explosion

All explosions follow the same basic pattern. Their effects may be described as follows:

- Fragmentation
- Blast or pressure
- Heat (flame)
- Vacuum

Fragmentation

Fragmentation will always take place to some degree upon explosion. Even when placed on a flat surface a bomb will throw off pieces of its own construction, as well as give projectile force to surrounding particles or debris.

The pipe bomb described above is particularly effective as a fragmentation bomb. It is lethal, rather than destructive; a weapon against people, not against structures or other property.

Blast or Pressure

Blast accompanies any explosion. It consists of expanding gases that create enormous pressures within a fraction of a second from the moment of detonation.

High explosives—dynamite is the most commonly employed—are most destructive because of this blast or pressure effect. Low explosives are less effective as "blast" agents because they have a slower rate of burning.

Heat (Flame)

Every explosion is accompanied by a flash of flame. This does not necessarily ignite a fire in the area although fire is an ever-present danger in any situation involving an explosion.

Vacuum

A vacuum is created behind the expanding gases generated by an explosion. This effect can heighten the destructive and dangerous consequences since, within a fraction of a second, pressures drop from many atmospheres (during the blast phase) to less than an atmosphere (during the ensuing vacuum phase).

Fortunately this vacuum phase is only created by large amounts of explosives, well beyond the size of the homemade bomb.

In general, then, the explosive bombs usually encountered are either the pipe bomb filled with black powder and detonated by any one of many simple devices; or several sticks of dynamite taped together and detonated by a timing device, or in some cases booby-trapped to detonate by a trip wire, pressure, or release of pressure. Bombs may also be triggered by movement, light, or the completion of an electrical circuit by opening the package.

Incendiary Bombs

The most widely used fire bomb was dubbed the Molotov cocktail during World War II. As we noted earlier, incendiary attacks occurred at a rate of about three to one over explosive bombs in 1970, and this ratio seems to continue.

Although there are many different refinements, all fire bombs of this type are essentially the same. They consist of a frangible container—usually a glass bottle—with a filler of a highly flammable substance, usually gasoline. There are various wicks which are ignited before the bomb is thrown; the bottle shatters on impact, the burning wick usually ignites the scattered gasoline which, in turn, ignites any combustible material at the point of attack.

Other fire bombs may be similarly constructed but detonated by devices such as a blasting cap on a timing device to allow the fire bomber to be well away when the fire starts. A different type of incendiary is timed, non-liquid, and can be as small as a king-sized cigarette pack.

Unfortunately, we must accept the fact that the fire bomb is here to stay. In contrast to the explosive bomb, the Molotov cocktail fire bomb is "child's play" to manufacture. The explosive bomb requires some knowledge and skill, more risk to the maker, and materials sometimes difficult to obtain. The manufacture of a fire bomb, on the other hand, requires the intellect of a three-toed sloth—and a few materials, costing practically nothing, found everywhere, and virtually impossible for authorities to trace.

We may be encouraged to remember that a fire created by an incendiary bomb can be readily controlled if the correct extinguisher is brought to bear quickly. On the other hand, an explosive bomb does its terrible damage upon detonation, with fire as a possible by-product.

Since all laymen are instructed in the most emphatic language possible not to touch anything they remotely suspect to be an explosive bomb, there is little value in describing the various techniques used in the manufacture of bombs, for leaving the bomb alone protects against all but pre-set and remote triggering.

Nor do we wish to add to the material already available on the subject. The would-be bomber has a huge bibliography from which to choose. He may select from military manuals, paperback and hardcover books, and underground newspapers. Some underground papers have gone into great and explicit detail on how to construct various bombs, where to get materials, how best to place the bomb, etc.

The would-be bomber isn't faced with any lack of information in his chosen field. Nor is he deprived of materials. The National Industrial Conference Board[3] quotes one Federal agent as observing, "Anyone who can't find explosive materials isn't really trying."

------

[3]*Op. cit.*

The Modus Operandi

The M.O. of the bomber tends to follow a pattern:

A target is chosen.

The target is "cased" to determine when, where, and how to attack the building.

A place is chosen to seat the bomb. This position will be determined by which areas are accessible and the effect the bomber wishes to create.

A test or dummy run is made against the target.

If the device is fully set in advance, one person will be all that is required to plant it. If its actuating mechanism is to be set "in place," then a minimum of two people usually make the plant, one acting as look-out while the other arms it. The decision to pre-set or arm on site is determined by the type of detonating system employed; if, for example, there is a "tilt" switch which will trigger the explosion when the device is moved, it must be armed on site. Or if the bomb were to be detonated by radio it would be armed on site, since a pre-set bomb might detonate prematurely because of unanticipated radio signals.

A telephone call is made to the target advising of the impending blast. While most bomb threats are "false alarms," the majority of actual explosive bomb attacks *are* preceded by a warning, and most are intended to explode outside of working hours.

Few, if any, offices or buildings can afford such intensive security programs as would totally exclude a bomber. This is not to say that normal security precautions will not deter or reduce the effect of such actions; they will. But if your building is the chosen target, your defense will probably not be adequate to prevent bomb placement. There are just too many ways and too many disguises by which the bomber and his device can enter the building.

As a result, the office and the building must be prepared to cope with bomb threats and the possibility of actual bombs. Many firms will feel they cannot be potential bombing targets; even if this supposition is correct, however, they must still consider that other tenants in the building may be.

The Warning Call

It is axiomatic that evacuation and locating a bomb before detonation hangs on the slender thread of the warning call. The overwhelming majority of office bombings are preceded by phone calls. On a few rare occasions warning has been given by mail, but the telephone seems virtually mandatory in the bomber's world.

Non-bombers are even more industrious in their use of the telephone. In 1970 the New York City bomb squad got over 10,000 calls announcing bomb placements. Of these bomb threats, only 128 involved actual bombs. Most estimates indicate that this ratio of actual to false alarm calls holds true throughout the country. Somewhere between 95 and 99 per cent of the bomb threats are false, whether for harassment or even as a macabre joke. Each call, however, demands some response, even if it is only a decision to do nothing.

Since we have no sure way of pre-judging the sincerity of the caller, we should act as though he is accurate and factual in his warning. This does not necessarily mean that we must evacuate all or even part of the building, but we must have a response procedure.

There are no hard and fast rules governing office conduct after receiving a bomb threat, and many different opinions exist as to the best solution to this most difficult problem. You owe it to yourself and your employees to find out as much as you can about this problem, particularly in your own community.

All of the suggestions included here are compiled from several opinions, particularly the Treasury's Alcohol, Tobacco and Firearms Division's special unit for bomb and bomb threat education.[4]

---

[4]*"Bomb Threats and Bomb Search Techniques,"* Security World, *November 1972.*

Preparation

Advance plans must be made to establish procedures and levels of authority in bomb threat response. The plan must designate a control center and at least one alternate center, in case the first location lies within the potential danger area. This control center should have facilities for widespread communication in the event of an emergency. Alternate personnel for the center should be designated in the event prime designees are absent at the time of the emergency.

It is important that all control center personnel be thoroughly familiar with their assignments and that they attend at least one meeting where the plan is reviewed, and the control sites visited. In addition, a written copy of the plan should be kept in a secure place at each control site.

Pre-planning must include both those steps that should be taken before any threat and those steps that are to be taken after the threat is received.

Evacuation

Perhaps the single most important decision to be made is whether or not to evacuate in the event of a bomb threat. Some companies have made it a rule in advance to evacuate immediately in the event of a threat, while others have established the policy that management will make the decision at the time of the threat whether or not to evacuate.

Either of these policies can be defended as the better of the two alternatives. A third point of view argues that since most bomb explosions occur in or near the building's service core, evacuation must not pass near the elevator, restrooms, equipment rooms, etc., in which the bomb may be located. In addition, if the building has a large population on many floors, how long will it take to bring personnel past the danger area, and where are these hundreds of persons to go, since glass might fall on the sidewalks around the building? This third position on bomb threat response calls for office searches, and withdrawing personnel to perimeter offices on their floor.

Evacuation is certainly the more conservative choice and—it is felt—puts the security of personnel before any other consideration. If, however, the caller is primarily interested in disrupting the company, as is often the case, he would have been successful; and if he continues to call and the company continues to evacuate, he has achieved his objective almost as effectively as if he had detonated an explosive device.

On the other hand, the percentage of actual bombs to hoaxes is extremely low, and there is no certainty as to whether a call is real or a hoax. Deferring the decision on evacuation is unlikely to give you more data on which to base a later decision. However, if the call runs true to form, and if the threat is relatively explicit, you may have time to search for the device before the decision to evacuate must be made, and this may well be enough reason to establish number two as your company policy.

It's a tough choice in any event—but it's one which management must make.

Legal Implications

While bombings have raised many legal questions as to liability and responsibility, one thing is clear—no one is sure of all the legal implications.

Considering the following possibility: The ABC Co. gets a bomb threat call, stating a bomb will explode within the hour. Management evaluates the situation and decides not to evacuate, as they have had many such calls before and nothing has happened. A bomb explodes, killing and injuring a number of employees. Survivors and families of the dead sue the ABC Co. on the grounds the company decision not to evacuate was the proximate cause. Obviously, liability must be considered in decision-making.

Procedures to be Initiated before Bomb Threat

- Determine the location of the nearest bomb disposal unit. What is the telephone number? When are they available? Will they assist in the search for the bomb or will they confine their efforts to disarming and removal?
- Establish the strictest procedures possible for the inspection of packages and materials brought into the office.
- Tighten access control systems.
- Conduct periodic physical inspections of your building or your area with police and/or fire representatives and designated staff people. This inspection will familiarize all concerned with the building and those areas where a device might most easily be concealed. (In the event you cannot get police and/or fire personnel on such an inspection tour, it is useful to get them to review a floor plan with you.)

  Pay particular attention to:
  Elevator shafts access points
  Ceiling areas
  Restrooms
  Access doors
  Accessible crawlspaces
  Unsecured points of access to plumbing or
  electrical fixtures
  Utility closets
  Stairwells
  Boiler and air conditioning rooms
  Flammable storage areas
  Main switches and valves
  Indoor trash receptacles
  Records storage areas
  Mail rooms (often accessible from corridors)
  Ceiling lights with easily removable panels
  Fire hose racks

- Review the location of, and take particular precautions to protect, classified documents, proprietary information, and records essential to the uninterrupted operation of your business.
- Train your telephone operators to handle bomb threat calls effectively, and provide a recording device at the switchboard. This usually is the most important, the most revealing part of the entire operation. The telephoned threat is your first and probably only contact with the possible bombers. The call must be handled properly; there won't be a second go at it. A typical procedure for the operator could be:

a. Keep the caller on the line as long as possible. Ask him to repeat his message. If possible, record the entire conversation.

b. Ask for the location of the bomb.

c. Tell the caller that the building is occupied and that a bomb blast could kill and injure many innocent people.

d. Take careful note of all background noise such as clinking glasses, music, dogs barking, motors running—anything that may be a clue to the location of the caller.

e. Listen closely to the voice and its characteristics. The temperament of the caller (calm, tense, excited) and his background (accent) can be important information.

f. Report this information immediately to previously designated personnel, fire and police departments, the Alcohol, Tobacco and Firearms Division of the Department of the Treasury, FBI and any other agency appropriate for your location. (The people to notify and the sequence of notification must be established in pre-planning.)

- In the pre-planning phase you will have organized and trained building personnel and office security in fast and proper search procedures. To effect speedy search routines, personnel should have floors or areas pre-assigned as their search responsibility, and be familiar with what is normally in their assigned area.

Briefly stated, when a threat is received, each area should be searched by teams of two who are familiar with the areas they are to search and who will:

- Divide the area in half and select the height up to which they will search first. This is usually from floor to hip height.
- Start back-to-back and work around the area toward each other.
- Work from the bottom up; after each round move to next height and repeat.
- After going around walls, search in narrowing circles into center of the area.

Interior offices are best searched by their occupants, who are familiar with what should be in their office area, and what is "alien."

After the Bomb Threat Call

- Alert medical personnel to standby.
- Have security and maintenance personnel begin the search.
- Direct employees to search their immediate areas.
- Have each team report completion of search to the designated warden for the floor or floors. He in turn reports to the control center.
- Mark the area on a master plan as having been carefully searched.

What to Look For

If a description of the bomb or its container has been given by the caller, then your only job is to locate it; if not, you are looking for something which is foreign to the area in which it is spotted, such as a lunch box on the public stairs, a briefcase in the washroom, a package in a plant in the reception area, or a box in a light or on top of lockers.

What to Do If a Suspicious Object Is Found

Under no circumstances should a searcher touch or disturb a strange or suspicious object or package. He should immediately report its presence and location to the person designated to receive this information. The removal and disarming of bombs *must* be left to the professionals in bomb disposal units.

Evacuate the area around the suspicious object, leaving a clear zone of at least 300 feet. It is the practice in most such cases to evacuate the floor where the object was discovered, and to evacuate the floors above and below. This evacuation should be by stairs—both fire stairs and public, where possible. Elevators, which could be jammed or severed by an explosion, should not be used. Unlike fire evacuation, public stairs should be used in addition to fire tower stairs because the time element is critical, smoke is not a factor, using all stairwells hastens evacuation and may lessen the chance of panic.

Unless the outside temperature is substantially higher or lower than the interior temperature, windows and doors on floor should be opened to allow explosion to exhaust itself. (Detonating or igniting an explosive or incendiary device may depend on changes in temperature or pressure. This also means you should instruct searchers not to turn on or off light switches or change thermostat settings.)

Assign personnel to meet and escort police, bomb disposal and fire personnel to the location of the suspicious object.

If possible without jarring, place sandbags or mattresses (nothing metal or more solid) *around* the object. Do not cover it.

Do not permit personnel to re-enter the area until the device has been removed or declared safe.

Recall Procedures

How recall after an evacuation may best be handled is a subject of some debate. There is a very real difficulty in retaining a large group outside of the building on crowded city streets. In any case, few employees are willing to stand around waiting for what may be a matter of hours.

The most practical solution appears to be to establish the policy that any employees required to evacuate the building before noon are to return after lunch. If the building or their area is still officially closed they are to return the following day. In the event of an evacuation in the afternoon, personnel will report back the following day. They may, of course, return to their offices once the building is declared safe and officially open.

Alarm Procedures

There is also much disagreement in the matter of signaling the evacuation of a building by alarms. The Alcohol, Tobacco and Firearms Division takes the view that the alarm for evacuating for a bomb threat should be the same as for a fire. They feel, in effect, that evacuation is evacuation, and that a common signal avoids unnecessary excitement and confusion. Others feel that the signal should be different since a bomb threat evacuation encourages the use of public stairs, whereas a fire does not. It is also felt that, for whatever reasons, people do not take a bomb threat as seriously as a fire and are consequently less inclined to panic, which argues for the use of a different signal.

There is no question that the best possible device is a public address system. With such a system in your office you can describe the nature of the problem and you can evacuate in an orderly and controlled manner, whereas an alarm, per se, can only order a general evacuation. A public address system can also be useful as part of the communication network during search routines. (Transceivers must not be used because of the danger that the bomb may be radio-controlled.)

Unfortunately few buildings have general alarm systems and even fewer have public address systems. In such a case it is necessary to set up a system in which pre-assigned personnel will see to the evacuation of specific areas.

In offices with telephone switchboards manned by more than one operator, the evacuation alert can be flashed throughout the company by phone. This is usually a practical method since the control center is normally in or near the switchboard. In a large multi-tenant building, however, telephone notification may be too slow.

ARSON

The fire resulting from arson can cause the most terrible damage within minutes. Irreplaceable records can be destroyed and your business brought to a complete halt until some kind of order can be restored. In the meantime —chaos.

This, of course, is true of any office fire; but arson is perhaps even more of a risk than most figures indicate. Felony crime has increased substantially over the past five years and so has the incidence of set fires to hide evidence of burglary. Incendiary bombs have been used in terrorist attacks against offices throughout the country.

Arson is defined as "the willful and malicious burning of property."

You will note the words "willful" and "malicious." Both denote intent, which is an important consideration.

Arson law varies from state to state. A review of those statutes governing arson in your own locality is advisable.

Motives

Motives for arson are numerous, but the great majority fall into one of the following:

- Financial gain: The property may be heavily insured and the owner seeks to collect.

Or, a competitor decides to burn out a fellow businessman. Normally employing a professional arsonist or "torch," the competitor hopes to increase his business or perhaps even buy out his victim, who may be forced to liquidate due to the fire. Arson is also used by "protection" racketeers.

- Arson is sometimes a handy red herring or even a cloak to hide thefts, shortages, embezzlement, tax evasion, or other crimes.
- Revenge or satisfaction of a real or imagined grudge.
- Psychotics who get gratification from watching fires. Since there is no obvious motive, these firesetters are hard to trace. When a fire is clearly incendiary and no motive can be found, a "fire bug" may be the cause.
- Political terrorism.

Setting the Fire

The arsonist must get himself or his incendiary into the building if he wants to destroy it; fires started outside solid construction are extinguished with little damage.

Since he is anxious for his fire to get a good start with as little interference as possible, he will frequently take the precaution of disabling your fire-fighting apparatus. He may shut off sprinkler valves, block fire doors open, cut fire hoses, and remove fire extinguishers. He may also open windows and doors to provide ventilation to fan the flames.

Perhaps most important to his "success" is the target area. In choosing a site he will, if possible, be very selective—although, once again, his experience may determine how wisely he chooses.

The Site

Basement: In most buildings, the maintenance department stores its paint, cleaning fluid and other flammable chemicals in the basement, making it a prime area for arson. Trash is often accumulated in or near the basement. Also, records are often stored in the basement. Finally, there is the boiler room and its fuel systems.

Stockroom: Each tenant in the building will have a room or an area where he will stock office supplies. With such combustibles concentrated in one place, it becomes an excellent target area. On the same level we could include file rooms and mailrooms.

Duplicating: This area with its supply of paper, chemicals, inks, and rags is perfect for a fire.

Utility closets: These closets with rags, cleaning fluids, mops, and unemptied trash are good fire areas.

The Roof and Upper Floor: The roof and the upper floor of an office building are not ordinarily prime target areas. Since the fire tends to rise, such a fire would be easy to control since it moves downward slowly and with difficulty. However, if the target is the firm's executive offices, the incendiary bomber will not be deterred by such a consideration.

In surveying your building or your area for possible sites in which to start a fire, you must consider what you see before you. We have touched on areas common to most offices that are probably prime areas of concern. You will undoubtedly have spaces peculiar to your building that also demand your attention. First-floor glass exposures are, of course, vulnerable to fire attack from outside the building.

Prevention

The prevention of arson starts with basic security. With effective traffic control, package checking, secured equipment rooms, and controlled access systems, security is functioning to protect the company against many kinds of attack, including the arsonist.

Prevention also requires good housekeeping, and this

is part of the overall fire prevention plan presented in Chapter 4, a plan that includes regular inspection of all office and building areas for fire violations and potential hazards. Where fire-loading is heavy, such accumulations of materials should, if at all possible, be dispersed or fire-proofed in one of the several ways suggested there.

Also in our fire plans is the distribution of adequate fire-fighting equipment as well as fire detection equipment. Smoke, heat, and flame detectors are of great value throughout, especially in areas not readily observed.

In sum, the best protection against arson is to be found in the effective operation of your total security program.

Investigation

Although it is important to investigate every crime committed against the office, this is especially true in the case of any fire.

Detailed confessions of arsonists indicate that if they fail to set a big enough fire on their first try, they often will return again and again until eventually they set a fire that suits their purpose. This is a pattern of the incendiarist, whatever his motive. Make it a rule to investigate every fire, no matter how small.

Remember that an overworked city fire department is usually unable to investigate small fires unless they are clearly the work of an arsonist. All too often the cause of fire is listed as "unknown," "cigarettes," or "faulty wiring." Certainly there are fires which, after the most thorough investigation, are unknown as to origin, and there is no doubt that cigarettes and faulty wiring are very real fire hazards and have contributed to an enormous fire loss. But these categories are also convenient catch-alls for over-worked and understaffed public authorities.

What to Look For

Obviously if the fire started in some place in the office where there were eyewitnesses—more than one—whose accounts seem to support the discernible facts of the fire, then you probably don't need to probe further the first time a fire occurs at that point. If, on the other hand, the fire started in some location where there is no evident initiating cause, then the matter should be looked into.

You should additionally be alert to various suspicious circumstances that need examination such as:

- Two or more fires occurring almost simultaneously in various locations.
- Alien flammable substances in the vicinity of the office. Those don't have to be exotic chemicals; they can be as commonplace as old rags, or trash, or flammable packing material. But should they reasonably be where you found them?
- Numerous wastebasket or trash bin fires.
- Windows, doors, desks, files, etc., forced open at the fire site.
- Fire equipment, alarms, sensors, and extinguishers sabotaged or missing.
- Explosion occurring where neither equipment nor materials could contribute to such a blast.
- Evidence of deep charring, or that the heat build-up was more rapid than the contents of the area would indicate. (This can only be accurately evaluated by a trained investigator.)
- Evidence of missing inventory in the area.

Remember that most fires start as tiny flames. The majority are accidental, but you cannot afford to overlook the possibility of an intentional set. If there is a wastebasket fire, ask yourself what might have been destroyed if it had spread. You might come across the explanation of the fire and take care of a dangerous situation before it gets out of hand.

Who Investigates?

The expert investigation of fires and their causes is highly specialized and requires the services of an investigator who is trained and experienced. Except in the case of infrequent wastebasket fires or other fires of that magnitude not showing a repetitive pattern, a special investigator should be called in.

Large companies with a large asset risk employ one or more trained investigators to look into fires in their premises. This is not practical nor necessary for many companies who would, however, find it worthwhile to research in advance the availability of arson investigators. Some of the major insurance companies, as well as the major insurance associations, have investigators who are available to their insureds.

Training

A professional fire investigator should also be consulted in regard to, or engaged for, training your security people in causes of fire and arson, and elementary fire investigation procedures.

Once such procedures are established, it should be normal practice to investigate and report on any fire on company property. Where you occupy space in a building with other tenants, it would be wise to assist them, if possible, in determining the cause of any fires they may have. This cooperative effort is simply a wise move to extend your lines of defense. Any fire in your building is a danger to you, and if an arsonist has selected a nearby tenant for his target, you can be as much the victim as if he had selected you.

Security and Professional Fire Investigation

In any situation where an investigator is called, security must seek to keep the fire scene undisturbed. This is easier said than done. The fire service people are taught and trained to create good public relations by immediately cleaning up the premises as much as possible. Such action destroys valuable clues, and hampers or eliminates the possibility of a thorough and accurate investigation. Everything at the fire scene is evidence. If anything must be moved, careful photographs should be taken before clearing begins, and the debris moved should be handled with care and secured in a safe place.

The Security Officer should also gather as much data as possible, so that he can assist the investigator, and for file and future reference.

This information should include:

- Date, time and location of fire.
- How the fire was discovered, by whom, and who turned in the alarm.
- Nature of the fire, and cause, if known.
- Description of area, including materials used or stored therein.
- Names, departments, addresses and statements of witnesses.
- List of personnel who worked in or had access to fire site.
- Dates and occasion of previous fires in that area.
- Names of any employees having access who were under notice at the time.
- Estimate of loss.
- Details of insurance coverage.

Not necessarily incorporated into the report, but readily available for reference should be

- List of employees discharged for cause in past year.
- Access control records.

Retain all material relevant to the fire under lock and key.

It is important to the community as a whole, and valuable to you as a company, to maintain open lines of communication with your local fire department. They can be of help to you in giving timely warning of new developments which could concern you and, as you feed information back to them, they can sharpen their insights into the growing problem of arson.

DEMONSTRATIONS

In the past decade we have seen an enormous increase in the use of demonstrations, sit-ins, and acts of civil disobedience against private companies. Basically demonstrations are a constitutionally-protected right to petition and "to peacefully assemble." But while many demonstrators are making a genuine protest, some demonstrations are staged as publicity devices and have neither merit nor rationality.

Management must know the general pattern of operation of such groups in order to protect itself in the face of these "confrontations."

Tactics

A demonstration begins long before "D" day arrives. Under the direction of its leaders, the group scouts the target. From the intelligence reports the committee plans its attack. Other members of the group concentrate on getting press and TV attention for the protest at every stage.

Within the planning strategy is often the seed of escalation, which can transform an otherwise peaceful and perhaps reasonable confrontation into a violent struggle that will project the cause into national prominence through newspaper and TV coverage. Counter-demonstration groups frequently contribute to this end and often unwittingly perform a great service for the very group they oppose. Frequently demonstrators use obscene, abusive and provocative language in order to incite a reaction from police or security personnel. The goals of such demonstrations are usually purely negative and have as their sole aim disruption, riot, and violence.

Before the actual confrontation, however, the group—particularly if the cause is a genuine one—will submit its demands to the organization selected as the demonstration target. If the demands are met at this point the demonstration may well disintegrate. In many situations, though, the group's leaders may be more interested in keeping the issue before the public, and may therefore escalate demands to avoid arriving at a solution.

It is rare that demands are agreed to at this stage by either side. The company may even refuse to recognize the group, and therefore refuse to deal officially with its demands. If this is done, or when negotiations break down, the demonstrators will adopt direct action to create further incident. They may picket, blockade or sit-in.

In the meantime, the demonstration group makes every effort to maintain the level of enthusiasm of the demonstrators and to recruit new followers. Mass meetings and rallies are held to air grievances and to pep up the demonstrators, and press releases are made.

All of this activity is designed to focus attention on their campaign. Their aim is to create wide public attention for their position and thus set the stage for legislation or voluntary concurrence in their views.

Fortunately, deliberately disruptive demonstrations are in the minority. Most demonstrations are constructive and sincere (whether misguided or not) and seek some common benefit. But distinguishing one from the other is an important objective in planning for dealing with demonstrations.

Publicity

This area of publicity has always been difficult and debatable, one which has frequently caused hard feelings between the media and law enforcement agencies and target companies. Wide publicity given to demonstrators' plans has frequently resulted in larger and less-disciplined crowds, which results in more publicity, which results in more crowds, and so forth. The three major television networks, recognizing this danger, have developed explicit guidelines designed to lower the profile of the news-gathering process, and thus minimize the ever-present danger of demonstrators going to excesses as a "performance" for the media.

Company Reaction

The question is, of course, how do you deal with this situation? I think we can all benefit from the basic approach presented by Carl A. Gerstacker, Chairman of the Board of that most beleaguered of all U.S. companies, Dow Chemical. Mr. Gerstacker speaks from more experience than most of us ever want to have—221 major anti-Dow demonstrations on American campuses, and vandalism attacks on computer records and on the company's Washington offices, let alone the dozens of demonstrations in Dow plants and offices both in the U.S. and abroad.

Here are Mr. Gerstacker's five points.

"First and most important, stay calm. Keep your cool. Don't overreact. Those who confront you are hoping you'll make mistakes. They will try to get you to make mistakes under the law; they will try to get you to make mistakes in the facts that you state; they will try to get you to make mistakes in your physical handling of them and of the situation. If you stay calm, you are more likely not to make such mistakes. They know this. So they will try their best in the real showdowns to shake your poise, by outrageous dress, perhaps by outrageous physical gestures and conduct. You may be outraged, and much of the time you should be, by such behavior; but the first and most important thing of all is to keep your cool, in spite of their efforts.

"Second, be prepared. You must surely be better prepared than you ever were as a Boy Scout. You must anticipate the questions and you must know the answers. You must know your rights and you must know their rights, precisely and in detail. Don't ever be afraid to over-prepare for a confrontation situation.

"Third, be confident. You should be so well prepared for any contingency that you feel as though you are dealing from overwhelming strength, mentally and physically. You must respect differences of opinion, but you must also demand respect for your own opinion and for yourself as a person, just as you respect their opinions and their persons.

"Fourth, be balanced. You should neither run away from trouble—you won't get away with it—nor should you go to the other extreme and eagerly seek out confrontation. Try to strike a happy balance between these positions. Over-permissiveness will bring on even more bizarre actions than you have experienced previously; and over-authoritativeness will merely serve as a challenge and a dare to your confronters.

"And fifth, remember the Golden Rule, which has its paraphrase in all the world's great religions. You should insist on your rights under the law, but don't yield to the temptation to overlaw it; do whatever is the proper, normal, legal thing to do. Do unto them as you would like to be done unto—and not as you may be tempted to do."[5]

Intelligence

In order to be prepared, in one sense, and to better assess the nature of the demonstration, you must go out and meet the demonstrators. The leaders of the demonstrating group scouted you and you must return the curiosity. If possible, send people to their meetings. Since they will be in the public spotlight, they cannot bar your people from their open meetings, if they wish to retain some measure of public support. From such immediate observations you can sift out a lot of the rhetoric and get closer to the heart of their demands. You should be able, at this point, to evaluate the sincerity of their appeal and prepare to respond accordingly.

In addition to attending their meetings, all printed matter distributed by them should be studied and evaluated. Also, available pictures and information identifying the leaders of the demonstrations can be useful in negotiating during the demonstration, as well as in observing the probable course of a demonstration in progress.

---

[5]*Carl A. Gerstacker, "Living with Confrontation,"* Security World, *September 1970.*

Direct Contact

Every effort should be made to establish informal contact with the leaders of the demonstration. Through this contact vital two-way communication can be established to prevent the spread of rumor or misunderstanding. And "ground rules" may be established governing the conduct of both sides during the demonstration.

It should be emphasized here that this informal contact does not constitute an official meeting to discuss the substantive elements of the demonstrators' demands; that is a totally different matter. The informal contact is established in the interests of order and safety.

It is also desirable to inform the leaders of the demonstration that any demonstrators who commit illegal acts will be dealt with to the extent of the law. This position must be publicized to avoid misunderstanding in the event the organizers don't wish to pass it on to the rank and file. Many demonstrators are young and idealistic and feel that they have right on their side—this frequently leads to dangerous excesses. The rank and file demonstrators must be advised of the consequences of any illegal acts they may commit.

Legal Action

In the event that, in spite of warnings, demonstrators do commit illegal acts, prosecution must follow. Any other course of action will only tend to invite further demonstrations. Ordinarily charges are brought by the police, but if the acts occurred within private property the company may need to file the complaints.

Business must always maintain a "two-way street" attitude toward demonstrations. It must recognize that demonstrations are basically legal, and that participants are to be protected by law if necessary. On the other hand, the company must protect rights, personnel, and property.

RIOTS

The riots in Watts, California in 1965 and in Newark, New Jersey in 1967 revealed to both public and private security officials that, in the event of a riot, the protection of a business or building is the responsibility of the proprietor. At such times public authorities are heavily involved in trying to quell the storm of mob violence by containing it within boundaries and protecting fire-fighting activities. Law enforcement manpower is spread thin and available only to protect life.

Riots and the Office

While there is very little relationship between a high-rise office building and a store, both have entrances and glass exposures at street level. It is there that both are most vulnerable. In formulating a riot plan, that point is very important. Access control is the name of the game.

A Riot Plan

In the event of a riot, an office building known to be within the affected area should be closed and all personnel sent home in as safe a manner as possible.

The building should be secured by security personnel and necessary building maintenance staff who will remain in the building for the duration of the emergency or until forced out. Pre-planning should include emergency exit procedures.

Alert

Upon notification that a riot is in progress within your area, previously designated company officials must be notified immediately.

The top operating executive in his office or able to come to the building becomes the leader in the situation. His office (or an office more appropriate) becomes central control, and all available information regarding the situation should be funneled to him. From that information he may ultimately be called upon to decide whether to send employees home, and—even more important—when and how. It is imperative that he know as much as possible.

A radio and, if possible, at least one TV set should be brought to his office. Security may have a "scanning" police radio receiver set for the frequencies of the nearest police division and the police department's special squads; this can be invaluable. Communications with public authorities should be maintained by telephone, though this may not be possible.

Simultaneously with setting up Central Control, key operations should be double guarded, locked, or closed down. These would include central files, microfilm, EDP tape storage, computer operations, and other critical areas.

Cash or negotiables should be locked in safes. Accounting files should be locked. Supply rooms, storage rooms and duplicating departments should be locked and freight entrances sealed off. Traffic into the building should be stopped and only emergency personnel allowed to enter. Only main entrances should be kept open. All others should be locked.

Manpower

All off-duty personnel should be placed on standby alert, ready to come to the office on call. Supplemental security forces (contract guard service) should be notified of the need for additional manpower in accordance with previous arrangements. (Without an existing contract or retainer, guards cannot be obtained in such widespread emergencies.)

Equipment

Fire extinguishers should be placed in ready-to-use, high risk locations. All building maintenance and security employees should carry flashlights in the event of power disruptions.

Evacuation

Based upon information available to Central Control, a decision to evacuate the office may be made. If so, personnel must be instructed in the best ways to leave the riot area. If necessary and possible, transportation should be provided to move the employees to a safe distance.

Only small groups should leave the building at one time if disorder is occurring in the area.

When conditions are particularly bad, a floor-by-floor evacuation would be best in a larger building. If the main body of the rioters is far enough away from your building, then a total and immediate evacuation is preferable. To accomplish this, all exits must be opened and manned by security personnel who are instructed to keep traffic flowing out with no one allowed to enter. Once the majority of personnel have left the building, then all secondary entrances should be closed and any remaining personnel directed to exit by the main entrance.

Securing the Building

After an evacuation all elevators should be shut down and taken off automatic systems. One can be key-operated by security or building personnel manning the building. All doors including public stairs, if possible, should be locked.

Lobby entrances should remain completely lighted as experience shows that rioters, like burglars, prefer to perform in the dark. The visibility of personnel within the lobby has also proved to have deterrent effects.

After evacuation, the Central Control post should be moved to the basement, the security control center, or an unexposed office near the street floor. From this control center security will direct the protection of the building, which consists almost entirely of preventing anyone from entering. If that fails, a secondary plan would be to secure the remaining elevator, thus cutting off elevator access to office areas. Additionally, security should call for police to remove the invaders. A last step, if all else fails, is for security and maintenance personnel to escape by pre-planned routes. If cars can be kept within locked freight receiving bays, this may be the safest method of escape.

In all security discussions, the protection of the computer and of company records is stressed, since the destruction of either or both can have dire consequences to a firm. A system of duplicate records and storage, and mutual assistance arrangements, are a basic in computer and fire security.

STRIKES

Before the first world war, unionized workers numbered about 2,500,000. That number, with a few ups and downs along the way, has increased to the point where as of 1968 (the current report from the Bureau of Labor Statistics) the figure is just short of 19 million, or 23 percent of the total labor force. Of these union members, slightly more than 3 million or 15.7 percent are white-collar workers. It is almost axiomatic that in the years ahead we will see more and more efforts made to unionize white-collar workers. And that most of these efforts will be crowned with success seems fairly certain. A 1967 study conducted by Yale University's Research Center showed that in 379 union elections, 74 percent were won by the union.

Reasons why a white-collar worker should join a union seem to go beyond general motivations such as salary protection and job security. Some of these attractions might be:

- Estimates indicate that unionized white-collar workers earn 7.5 percent more than non-union workers. In dollars an average figure is $1,000 per year.
- White-collar workers fear mergers and attendant lay-offs.
- Unions are now more acceptable to white-collar

workers, who see teachers, firemen and policemen bargaining through unions.

- Recent recessions and loss of jobs have highlighted insecurity of non-union work, where lay-off can be an arbitrary management decision.
- White-collar workers believe unionization can stamp out nepotism and cut down on office politicking.
- White-collar workers are being approached by more sophisticated organizers.

There is little doubt that you can look forward to attempts to unionize your office if it hasn't already happened. This is not necessarily a source of trepidation—especially if you have done your homework.

Unionization and the Law

Laws governing union activities have evolved over the years and are designed to curb excesses by both unions and management and to protect the rights of the individual worker. They also establish ground rules for that difficult and delicate time when a union is attempting to organize an office.

Legally, a company cannot:

- Intimidate, coerce, or punish personnel in their attempt to unionize.
- Spy on personnel for the purpose of determining who is actively engaged in unionization.
- Discriminate against employees who are engaged in unionization.
- Change company policy to terminate a union employee.
- Change working environment to eliminate unified groups from expanding the union concept.
- Ask potential employees about their position on unions.
- Imply the closing of operations or the reduction of current benefits because of unionization.
- Stop union personnel from soliciting members

outside of business hours.
- Give preferential treatment to employees opposing unionization.
- Go to the homes of employees to solicit their opposition to the union.
- Create a petition against the union.

On the other hand, you may take certain steps to prevent unionization of your office.

Legally, you can:
- Prevent the soliciting of membership during working hours.
- Campaign against unionization by stating your position.
- Air opinions, even derogatory ones, concerning unions and union officials.
- Apply all company rules regardless of the employee's position on unionization.
- Defend company policy under union attack.
- Prevent unauthorized intrusion into company space by union organizers.
- Allow your employees to talk to you about the unions.

Strikes

The union's ultimate weapon in any dispute with management is the strike. This can take many forms, but is usually the final response to a stalemate in contract negotiations.

Strikes are unpleasant situations in any case. Even where there is no violence and a satisfactory solution to the differences between the two parties is found, there is an aftermath of bitterness, of lost wages, and of a real sense of division within the company. Obviously strikes are better avoided, but when a strike cannot be avoided, the conduct of management—and security as representatives of management—plays an important role in reconciliation after the strike is over.

Picketing

Picketing is both legal and permissible as long as it is not violent, and those wishing to cross the picket line are allowed to do so. The number of pickets can be limited by a court injunction to prevent mass picketing or to reduce risk of violence where the dispute involved is a bitter one.

The real danger in picketing, or in demonstrating in a strike situation, is the very real possibility of a flare-up which could lead to general violence.

Security's Role

Because any strike situation is potentially explosive, it is important that management develop contingency plans for the handling of strikes and other labor-management confrontations. Basic to policy must be a diplomatic and restrained approach.

Overall, the role of security should be a firm neutrality which does not hinder lawful union efforts to picket or to unionize. Security's main function is to anticipate and prevent problems, and to protect the premises, the personnel and the assets of the company. Beyond these responsibilities security must not take or even imply a position in any labor-management matter.

Contingency planning for strike situations includes:

- A routine for closing affected operations. These include:
- Checking unoccupied areas thoroughly to see that all is in order, such as machines turned off, water and electricity secured, chemicals and glues properly stored, doors and windows locked.
- Removing all strikers from payroll.
- Notification to vendors and customers.
- Adjusting security routines to the situation.
- Employment of private contract security personnel where the possibility of sabotage exists. These supplementary guards should take over posts and patrols not seen by strikers, if possible.[6]

- Pre-strike steps.
- Determining what operations will remain active during the strike.
- Preparing a statement to the newspapers for release when the strike is called.
- Issuing a statement of position to employees.
- Advance notification to authorities of probable picketing, and determining what standby help will be available in the event of trouble.
- Evaluation of key control. Are key-holding employees among the strikers?[7]
- Have photographic equipment available in case of mass picketing or violence, for use in seeking injunctive relief. Visible cameras can help to cool a situation or they can provoke violence, depending on the temper of the pickets. A remote television camera with a telephoto lens and video tape recorder is probably the best answer.
- Establish a schedule of designated company spokesmen who can be reached or will be on hand to provide constructive replies to the press, and to be on the premises in the event of trouble.
- Before, during, and after, all non-striking personnel must be reminded that the strikers are fellow employees having a dispute with company management which will be resolved shortly, and that today's strikers are yesterday's and tomorrow's co-workers.

---

[6]Unions have cited the hiring of "outside" guards as a "provocation" by management. At least one major and several smaller guard companies will not provide guards in strike situations, so such arrangements must be concluded in contingency pre-planning, perhaps by means of an annual retainer.

[7]Firms having key-holding union employees often use removable-core cylinders, as these can be changed to new keys in a matter of minutes by security personnel.

CONSISTENT STEPS

Security planning against bomb threats, bombing, arson, demonstrations, riots and strikes have many similarities. And at the top of the list in each category is the ability to establish firm and efficient access control. Knowing and controlling who goes in and out is a basic for defense.

Just remember: "The majority of office security problems come through the front door."

Chapter 6

TRADE SECRETS AND INDUSTRIAL SPIES

If your company has a captive market all to itself, you're not actually concerned with this chapter. Pass on, friend—unless you think you may have a competitor or two tomorrow. In that case, join the club. Because as long as you have competition—or possible competitors—someone will be watching you.

This discussion of the need for well-defined areas of confidentiality in the conduct of your affairs assumes that you are in a business whose success—or even survival—depends on developing and keeping a reasonable share of the potential market in the face of pressures created by others. This definition fits virtually every business in the free world.

Every competitive situation starts with the gathering of information, from two little boys circling each other in a school yard, each trying to decide if the other one is tougher and stronger, to the high-powered sports organizations that gather, screen and evaluate the films of opposing football teams to give their own team a competitive edge. Most information-gathering is legal and ethical—part of the business of business. But some of it—and from all indications a growing part of it—is straight cloak-and-dagger.

It is important for every business to reduce the vulnerability of its confidential information to discovery by either legal *or* illegal means. Think—and I mean right now—of the planning advantage you would have if you had before you a schedule of the new product plans of your closest competitor. Or if you had the minutes of the last meeting of their Executive Committee, or reliable advance information on their new advertising campaigns. Curiously enough, a very high percentage of this information is available—too late to be of benefit to others. After all, you certainly don't care if the competition gets hold of your new pricing structure, or your new packaging plans, or the fact that you're test marketing in Chillicothe, Ohio—after it's well-launched. After all, you couldn't keep them from knowing —eventually. But what you need and must have is "lead time," *your* jump on the market.

Time Is Essential

So what confidentiality buys is *time*. It's vital that your plans or bids remain confidential until the last possible minute, to avoid being topped, underbid, or neutralized by the competition.

We can all learn from a shrewd sales promotion firm who had almost sold a campaign to a very big and very important client—Company A. Company A wanted the campaign but they were very worried about their equally big competitor, Company B. Company A knew Company B was planning a major sales promotion campaign. There had been enough loose talk around for them to be confident of that. What they didn't know was when Company B's campaign would start. This was vital information that would affect Company A's decision on whether or not to go ahead with the campaign proposed to them.

Agony! With millions at stake, an intrepid sales promotion consultant—with visions of a markedly improved life-style dancing in his head—came up with a notion. He flew to the city where Company B was headquartered. He nosed about until he found a warm and friendly bar where Company B executives were said to have their cocktails before taking off for home and hearth. He made himself comfortable until the bar was deserted. He then called the bartender over and, without a great deal of preamble, tore a hundred dollar bill in two and put half in the bartender's shirt pocket along with a business card. The sales promotion consultant told the bartender what he wanted to know and asked him to call any time—day or night—if he got the information. The other half of the bill would be his on that happy day.

Having set his plan in motion, he returned home. Some two weeks later, his telephone rang in the small hours of the morning. It was the bartender—with the information. Accurate information.

So the campaign was sold; Company A got a substantial jump on its competition; the bartender got a hundred dollars; and the innocent—but careless—executive of Company B may never know the role he played in altering the ever-changing balance in the mercantile world. A happy ending? Certainly not for Company B. They'd been betrayed—not by sophisticated espionage, not even by a paid informant—but by a talkative employee.

Carelessness Greatest Threat

It is this man (or woman)—the talkative employee with "inside" information—who represents the greatest threat to the security of confidential matters. And the bar favored by employees is often the hub of the information center. It's here that co-workers meet for lunch and/or for a drink or two before going home, and it's here they will "talk shop." The surroundings are familiar and reassuring. In no time at all habitues feel that it's not a public place, but a club— practically an extension of their offices. In thousands of such spas and watering holes across the country, company business is discussed in intricate and revealing detail, and usually with no noticeable caution.

To the right (or the wrong) ears, such cocktail seminars are a treasure trove of information. It requires a little patience to sit through the account of an indignant assistant manager explaining his obvious superiority to his boss's assistant, but give him time—he'll get around to some information that may prove useful, if his discontent isn't.

There are hundreds of ways in which a talkative employee can break down the discreet walls of confidentiality—everything from carelessness with his notes of meetings or plans, to losing a folder (or briefcase) of restricted documents, to boasting of his importance in new company developments. And if his information comes to the attention of competitive firms, it is not likely that they will hesitate to make use of it.

The Intelligence Operation

It is vital to remember that every competitive business in the country—however ethical—must be as alert to the conduct of the competition as to its own objectives. As in chess, the winner will be the player who is able to successfully balance the needs of his attack *and* his defense. Many players are famous for a slashing, bold attack; but unless they also present a reasonable defense, they will surely lose. So it is with business, and information is an essential of both attack and defense. Some businesses have large departments that do little else but gather, evaluate, and digest information pertinent to their company's market and competition. The information is produced in floods on virtually any topic, and constantly updated. Actually, there is more information available from non-secret sources than anyone would usually need to generally predict or plot an action, reaction or plan, be it their own or someone else's:

There are reports on labor, statistics, business, agriculture, electronics and government, to name a few. There are reports to guide you to reports. There are guides to lead you to guides. There are special industry publications and reports. There are marketing organizations who will do the same. There is the Library of Congress and the wonderful New York Public Library, if you can get to either.

And, of course, you must not overlook the obvious:

- Major metropolitan newspapers.
- Magazines—especially general business magazines or trade journals in your specific field.
- Government publications—largely from the Department of Commerce. (A list of subjects and titles that would probably circle the earth—or at least Chicago's Loop.)
- Annual reports—required for publicly-held companies.
- House organs.
- Business letters and bulletins.
- Business and professional associations' publications.

It has been said that during the Second World War foreign agents were able to plot the production of our war materials by simply reading published reference material. Our own OSS in that same period did most of its work by carefully digging through tons of data on everything from weather to observed movement of coal cars. The cloak-and-dagger operators—the operatives dropped behind enemy lines—were the glamor; but the heart of the operation was the digging through mountains of data, *almost all of which was readily available*. This method of intelligence-gathering has only grown with the years; in security circles a famous trade magazine is still known as *Aviation Leak*.

The Shortest Distance between Two Points

It is a common error to believe that complicated and round-about means must be used to achieve an end. This is perhaps typified by the advertising agency producer who was anxious to persuade a certain star to appear in a series of commercials. The producer and his assistant spent three days in the most devious machinations, trying to get in touch with the actor to discuss the project. They set up a luncheon date with someone who knew his agent's sister-in-law; they called the cousin of the director of his last show; and so on. Nothing. Finally, when things looked their bleakest and the client was adopting an ominous tone, their secretary suggested, "Why don't you try the phone book?" Amused by her naivete, they did. There he was, listed in the book just like common folk. They called him up and made the deal. You must not overlook the obvious.

What's the Problem?

All of the methods of gathering business information are not, however, as harmless as those we have discussed. While data gathered from published sources, rumor, industry gossip, common vendors, loose talk, and legally observable activity represent the bulk of the competitive intelligence amassed, the business community today is also faced with the very real problem of the professional (or "semi-pro") espionage agent.

The industrial spy is a most difficult and elusive adversary. First, in the absence of any figures establishing the extent of this activity, it is difficult to objectively define the nature and scope of the problem. This is further complicated by the wide diversity of viewpoints held on the subject.

- Congressman Wayne Hays (D-Ohio), Chairman of the Committee on House Administration, has stated that he takes for granted that every member of Congress has his telephone tapped. On the other hand, genuinely expert "sweeps" of several Congressional offices have found none.
- Security organizations, when interviewed, state that they never engage in wiretapping, bugging, or even illegal methods of industrial espionage. On the other hand, several have been caught at it.
- Business executives interviewed feel the problem is minimal, nonexistent, or confined to a few businesses.

- Small private operators would prefer that you believe the worst, especially if they're in the "de-bugging" business. On the other hand, qualified professionals *have* found bugs in phones, walls, office audio systems, and electrical outlets, just to name a few.
- Any electronically-minded teenager, radio engineer, or telephone serviceman can "bug," adapting readily available equipment.

Thus it would seem impossible to sketch in the true parameters of the problem of electronic espionage.

Bugging

The use of electronic surveillance equipment by private investigators and others, including government, became a matter of increasing concern to lawmakers, culminating in the passage of the Omnibus Crime Control and Safe Streets Act of 1968. One of the sections of this act established federal penalties for the use, possession, sale, advertisement, or transportation of eavesdropping equipment interstate, and such equipment is no longer advertised. Many states have also established their own strong penalties for the manufacture, sale, possession and use of eavesdropping equipment.[1] It is difficult to evaluate the deterrent effect of such legislation, however, as there are no reliable records—former or present—on the number of listening devices found.

Many persons or firms who have been bugged are reluctant to reveal the fact, particularly since the "culprit" is usually unknown and unidentifiable. Though it is difficult to estimate with accuracy, it is safe to assume that many violations do occur, that most of these are either undetected or unreported, and that virtually all go unpunished.

---

[1] *For example, federal law permits recording by, or with the permission of, a party to a conversation; California law forbids recording without permission from all parties to the conversation.*

Availability of Equipment

When consideration is broadened to include highly sophisticated equipment in the hands of government agencies, it must be said that the equipment available today makes virtually *total* surveillance possible. These devices can pierce the privacy of the home, office or a moving vehicle. They can, of course, monitor all normal lines of communication such as telephone, radio, television, even telegraph and data lines. No regular line of communication is secure. Conversations can be heard in public places, and despite noisy surroundings.

The kind of surveillance being used for illicit, unethical, and illegal penetration of rival business communications is not so sophisticated. It does not need to be. Effective hardware for simple eavesdropping is inexpensive to create, easily installed, and the necessary components are readily available to the general public, even though the sophisticated equipment is not.

And the do-it-yourself bugging devices are far cheaper, more available, and more effective than the anti-bugging equipment available. Effective electronic countermeasures equipment is very expensive (in excess of $10,000), requires expert personnel to operate, and is not generally available to private security agencies, let alone the public.

Where Do You Stand?

Naturally, if you are in a highly volatile business that depends to a great degree on new products regularly introduced, or unusual hard-hitting merchandising gimmicks, you already know the danger of leaking information. But if you have felt that espionage is someone else's problem and not yours, perhaps you owe yourself a question or two.

Most managers feel they have so little information of interest to a spy that they can't have an espionage problem. If you fall into this group, try this test: Ask yourself what information *you* would like to have about your competitors. What value would drawings, plans, market research, future products information, trade secrets, and fiscal matters of your closest competitor have for you? It is a rare company that can honestly say "None."

But most firms do have secrets—or information that should be secret. So your first defensive step is to identify those secrets, the confidential material that might be actively sought by a less-than-scrupulous competitor. Who would pay to get your computer payroll printout? A competitor seeking to "raid" you of your key engineering personnel. Or to collect your trash? Anyone seeking bid carbons, computer information, materiel sources, or discarded drafts of key proposals.

Identifying Your Secrets

To establish what information in your company should *remain* in your company, you must identify key information throughout the company, as well as how valuable each type of information would be to others. This applies to all aspects of your business—whether it's machines, processes, systems, or procedures; pricing, planning, new products or financial information.

And, as you identify this information, ask yourself how available the same information may be from other sources. There are more cases than you might imagine where companies go to considerable lengths to protect information that has been the subject of a press release, or a professional paper, and is actually available in publications or, at the least, is in non-restricted distribution.

If you find areas that you consider valuable to you, potentially valuable to others, and not otherwise available —you should then break down the package into component parts such as:

- Plans—physical layout or activities, new products planning, research problems and successes, etc.
- Prices—unit, bulk, favored-customer discounts, profit margin, marketing breakdown, etc.

- Performance—up and down time of equipment, the capability of a machine, a system, a method, special processes, etc.
- Problems—limitations of equipment, capitalization, cost overruns, systems, production difficulties, transportation, acceptance, sales, etc.
- Personnel—who knows, what does he know, what key executive is discontented and why, pay scales, etc.

Obviously many segments of the total information picture, such as announced prices, will be known outside the company, but the more of these elements that remain confidential, the safer you are.

Remember that, even without any effort at espionage, a good analyst can develop an astonishingly accurate picture by putting together scraps of information. The fewer scraps you give him, directly or through industry "gossip," the more difficult his job becomes, and the more likely he is to come up with a wrong guess.

Identify Current Problems

The moment you have identified a secret, you can see a problem. But ask yourself, what has been happening before? If you have never before exercised any control over company secrets, you may have experienced some of the following:

- Competitors constantly ahead of you or on the market at the same time you introduce a product or price.
- You are losing more than your share of big bids (particularly by very narrow margins) and are barely picking up small or medium ones.
- Marketing programs seem to go sour from the start.
- Your business negotiations seem known, and your decisions anticipated.
- Competition is hiring away your key executives, often just when they are most needed.

- The mail room knows your secrets before your secretary—and your secretary likes to talk.
- Your proposals and presentations seem to appear in part in competitors' proposals.

Plug Leaks

The average office is not capable of dealing with a determined professional spy, but, in most cases, simple precautions can prevent most of your potential or present problems.

If something is secret, handle it that way. An overall company policy should be formulated. Such a policy should emphasize the basic security practices that prevent careless loss of information, rather than the sophisticated countermeasures necessary to thwart the professional spy. Where you feel that professionals may be at work, you must resort to more elaborate policies and measures.

A basic security policy should define areas, actual work, statistics, and documents that should be classified as secret or, more commonly, "company confidential." Decisions should be based on business and industry conditions that exist under normal circumstances. For example, in the chemical industry many things may be secret—the name of a project, areas of work, papers, formulas, plans, etc. On the other hand, the management of a retail food store chain may only need to keep secret store grosses, the location of the next store, or the prices in next week's ad. (The latter information actually was once the subject of espionage; spies photographed it from drawing boards in an art department.)

In any event, once confidential information is identified, employees should have company procedure to follow in handling it.

Documents

Any document classified secret or "company confidential" should be marked as such. Inexpensive rubber stamps, and stamp pads in a conspicuous color, can be purchased from local stationers for this purpose.

Storage of Proprietary Information

Documents considered secret are about as safe from examination in an ordinary filing cabinet with a lock as they would be in a desk drawer. Special filing cabinets[2] are needed or vaults should be used.

Numbering and Logging

Classified documents should be numbered (as "Copy 4 of 7") and only allowed out of central files on a sign-out basis. Each item taken from the file should be described in an appropriate log and signed for by an authorized recipient. When documents are returned, the clerk should sign the log to indicate the return of the copy, and by whom it was returned. Obviously this does not protect you against the documents being photocopied, but it narrows responsibility to trusted persons.

Distribution

Access to, and distribution of, confidential and critical information should be strictly limited on a "need to know" basis. Some persons will need to see some confidential material, but not others. For this reason you will want to limit the number of copies generated, to indicate—on the document—its distribution, and to require accountability from each recipient.[3]

---

[2]*While filing cabinets which resist undetected entry are made, they are not available for purchase except by defense contractors and government agencies. Unless you are able to purchase one or more of these GSA Class 5 filing cabinets secondhand, confidential papers should be kept in fire safes or records vaults.*

[3]*We are all familiar with the "overgrown" distribution list by which confidential reports are sent to persons who no longer need or use them. The classic method of identifying overgrown distribution is to insert a sheet stating "Unless (the department of origin) is advised to the contrary, this copy of this report will be stopped effective with this issue." A similar technique is used to reduce the number of copies of computer printouts.*

Public Communications

All press releases should be examined for the possible accidental inclusion of confidential information. If the release (or annual report, or prospectus) relates to a subject area in which there is confidential information, the text should be cleared by a designated executive knowledgeable about that area.

Employees must be cautioned against discussing confidential subjects and information with non-employees, including their families, and even with fellow employees who do not have a "need to know" such classified information. You cannot stress this precaution too much, for getting an employee to talk to a person they trust has been successfully used time and time again.

Employment Practices

Applicants for jobs involving or near confidential information should be backgrounded, to detect "plants." New employees should sign a pledge (prepared by company attorneys) not to reveal company secrets. At termination interviews, this position must be restated and an "exit agreement" signed confirming the employee's obligation to withhold company secrets for an agreed-upon period of time. Without this signed agreement, your company's legal position will be most difficult if the ex-employee "sells you out" to your competitor.

While it is common to suggest that new employees be assigned to non-classified work, if possible, experience shows that "plants"—employees planted on the company for the purpose of getting the protected information—tend to be hard-working able employees who are rapidly promoted to the positions they need to reach confidential information.

Home Work

Confidential documents should neither be worked on at home, nor on vehicles of public transportation. Ideally, highly confidential material should be transported only when absolutely necessary, preferably in private vehicles, and never unaccompanied.

Meetings

Business meetings and conferences concerned with highly sensitive information should be held in the company conference room only when it is unavoidable. A better practice is to take all members of the meeting—without briefcases—to an unexpected place reserved in the name of an unrelated company or association. This practice is the most effective in preventing "bugging" or surreptitious recording of the meeting.

Paper Shredders

Paper shredders should be available and used in all areas where classified documents are originated or retained.[4] Confidential documents and tab runs should always be shredded, pulped, or burned—never discarded in wastebaskets.

Access Control

As in all company security, access control is of prime importance. Strict control must be maintained over traffic into classified areas or where classified material may be exposed on desks. Authorizations for entry into such areas should be pruned to the smallest practical number, and the list regularly re-evaluated and revised. Badges with distinctive colors are used where traffic in and out is high. You must make it clear that it is the responsibility of employees to challenge apparently unauthorized "visitors" in their area, even if they too are employees.

Eavesdropping

Bugging or eavesdropping in some form (commonly, wiretapping) can be remarkably sophisticated and its

---

[4]Paper shredders do not meet the requirements for classified defense information, which must be burned or pulped. Shredded papers can be reconstructed, given sufficient time and determination.

frequency will probably increase in the future. It is difficult to keep up with developments in this field; your best defense will always be eliminating the opportunity the "bugger" needs.

Privacy in Meeting Rooms

When important meetings must be held on company premises, the conference room should be "screened." By that we mean the walls should be interior walls, none of which are common to alien space; and they should be acoustically and electrically protected so that sounds within the room cannot be heard beyond the room by means such as an electronic stethoscope pressed against the exterior wall of the room, or from a transmitter within the room.

It might be worth considering building such a room as part of new building or remodeling plans.

In cases of very top secret meetings it is often wise, as suggested, to meet in the company conference room and from there go to another, unannounced location. This will eliminate the chance of pre-bugging. At such meetings, briefcases should be banned, and telephones removed from the room, since either can be rigged to act as eavesdropping devices. If the matters to be discussed are of a particularly sensitive nature, and you have reason to suppose that the room may have been bugged despite all your precautions, you can provide some protection by playing a radio or record player at normal volume. Unfortunately, the "pros" of eavesdropping can filter out all sounds above or below voice frequencies.

Telephone Privacy

If the discussion of extremely confidential information by telephone is unavoidable—there are no possible alternatives—then it should be done through busy switchboards and on extensions other than easily-identified private lines. Perhaps calling from an extension in another office within the building would be your safest bet. Private lines are straight-line invitations to wiretapping and should be avoided in confidential telephone talks.

As pointed out in Chapter 2, all telephone servicemen must identify themselves, and their assignment verified by a call to the telephone company.[5] All too often this is the disguise of the electronic eavesdropper.

De-Bugging

The average de-bugger under normal circumstances will discover only the most unsophisticated and "findable" devices—even when employing electronic "detectors." On the other hand, even with highly sophisticated electronic sweeps, you can never be *totally* certain that a room is "clean." As a result, part of your protective system is breached whenever you announce classified meetings and particularly when the time, place, and subject are announced well in advance.

Declassifying

When information is no longer confidential, it should be removed from protective procedures. Ideally, all papers should be stamped with the termination date of their particular classifications (unless this information, too, would be useful) and should be refiled or shredded at that time. It is most important to avoid cluttering classified files with harmless documents.

Where secret information has only one-time value, it should be destroyed by shredders after use. For example, a memo may request the presence of John Doe at a confidential meeting. It may further request that he bring

---

[5]*No one is better equipped to tap or hot-wire a telephone than telephone service personnel. It is to the credit of telephone companies that so little wiretapping has disclosed "renegade" telephone employees. Nevertheless, a court decision has held that the telephone company was not responsible for wiretapping by a company serviceman working on company time, on the grounds the serviceman had no instructions from the telephone company to do so. Hence, you should always verify the serviceman's assignment with his company, and with the person in your company who requested his call.*

certain confidential information with him. Such a document should be read and destroyed at once.

General Vigilance

Office security should act as a constant watchdog for all classified systems to insure the integrity of proprietary information. In these, as in all security systems, constant vigilance is required. It is vital that the systems themselves be supervised and regularly evaluated for continued effectiveness. No system will continue to operate on its initial momentum alone.

In this respect, classified papers should be checked for accurate stamping, paper shredders must be in operation and used as prescribed, and wastebaskets checked. Classified files must be properly secured. Classified materials, wherever held, should be audited periodically, and any misuse noted should be reported. Management should be kept constantly updated on violations, violators, and potential leaks of classified information.

If you employ these basics, the amateur spy, the random information peddler, and the disgruntled employee should no longer have you at a disadvantage; you will have neutralized much of their effectiveness.

Professionals

Although there is every reason to believe business spying is on the increase, the use of professionals is limited to exceptional companies and exceptional circumstances. Use of professional techniques to spy on a competitor leaves a company open to lawsuits, loss of public confidence, adverse publicity, and a host of other unpleasantnesses—as those linked to the Watergate caper can testify.

Normally, the average business only needs to protect itself from carelessness by hiring and promoting loyal, competent personnel, by denying unauthorized access to sensitive material, and by training employees. These measures require thought and a careful study of your operation, but they certainly are not difficult to achieve. But be on guard for any breakdown in your system. For example, a planted janitor asked for and received permission to take carbons in wastepaper baskets "home to his children." The basket he wanted was in the sales department where they figured bids with one-time carbons that were readable after use. A tiny oversight. The smallest flaw —in an otherwise tight operation—and the spying competitor had all the information he needed to get any bid he wanted. Worse, no law had been violated; permission had been given. In another case, where the janitor was alone in the building, he was bribed to admit a search party for a leisurely examination of desks and files.

Remember, too, little pieces of information can complete "the big picture" for your competition.

Employee Education

Few measures you take to protect your classified information will be as effective as the concern of your employees. If interested people have been educated to understand and appreciate company policies regarding secrets, your problem is virtually solved. Trade shows and the meetings of professional associations are notorious (and legal) sources of information from unguarded conversations.

Establish Your Program Today

Now is the time to establish a clear policy on company secrets. If you delay, you may find you no longer have secrets —which, in many cases, can mean no future and even no company.

By the way—have you had your telephone checked recently?

SECTION II

THE ENEMY WITHIN

Chapter 7

THE THIEF YOU PAY

PART I: THE "INVISIBLE MAN"

It's closing time. Office personnel have put away their papers, locked up their desks, and gone. A few industrious folks are clearing up reports or finishing that last column of figures, but they'll be gone soon. Then Office Security will lock up the office for the night.

Alarms will be turned on, windows and doors checked to make sure they are locked, and the night security force will begin its regular routine. All doors to the building will be secured. If after-hours employees are working, the main entrance will be opened for them and re-locked by a guard, after they have signed his after-hours book. Only one elevator is operating. It's the end of a good day. No incidents have been reported, and the night is even more uneventful. Security has only routine reports to submit. And yet $1,000 was stolen from this office today.

At 9:00 the next morning, the thief returns to steal again. He waves good morning in the lobby. He chats with acquaintances on his way up in the elevator. He nods to the receptionist and moves purposefully to an interior office where he begins his day's work. Who is this bold bandit? He is an employee of yours. He is a thief you pay.

Can You Recognize Him?

Unfortunately there is no sure way by which the potentially dishonest employee can be recognized. Your employment practices can, of course, eliminate applicants with a high risk potential; tests can often tell you if they are honest *when they are hired*. But you must accept the fact that *anyone*—man or woman, new employee or veteran, accountant or clerk, salesman or engineer, janitor, secretary, or high-ranking executive—can be a thief.

It is generally accepted by bonding companies and professional security people that potential workers divide into three groups insofar as security is concerned. The first group, about 25 per cent, will be consistently honest no matter what opportunity to steal is given them. Another 25 per cent are outright thieves; in *any* environment, they will be actually looking for ways to steal. The honesty of the remaining 50 per cent is up to you. *This* group could be on either side, depending on the circumstances. If the opportunities for theft are there, then the temptation is there and given sufficient temptation—particularly the example of others—this 50 per cent will steal, too.

Obviously these percentages are at best an approximation of a difficult-to-define situation, but it should give you food for thought. Maybe even a nervous start! It should, because it means that, barring effective hiring precautions, you start with 25 per cent of your employees just biding their time until they can steal you blind, and another 50 per cent who could easily go the same way! In other words, you are faced with the possibility of having 75 per cent of the employees of your company ripping you off, unless you institute a thoughtful and vigorous program to protect the assets and the profits of your company.

Why Do They Steal?

Since we have no never-fail method of recognizing the potentially dishonest employee at sight, perhaps we can develop a technique for getting some advance warning. If we know why trusted persons steal, perhaps we can watch for specific patterns that will indicate the potential is there, and that the time may have come for him to make his play.

There is no simple answer to the question of why otherwise honest men and women begin stealing from their employers, for there seems to be no single motivating factor that triggers this attitude.

Some employees may begin to steal because of a sudden temporary financial emergency. Usually they think of their theft as "borrowing"; and tell themselves they will replace the money they've taken. Theft of goods is usually excused by such thoughts as: "I need it more than they do"; "They owe it to me"; and "Everybody else does." Curiously enough, a significant number of early thefts by non-professionals are for others; to help with a friend's hospital bill, or to give a hand to a relative who's in trouble.

Some employees steal simply because they feel like living the good life for a while, or that they "must" make an impression on someone. Some steal because they think —or, rather, tell themselves—they "have it coming to them." Some steal to avoid losing "status" when they're hit by financial problems. And, in a great many cases, they begin to steal for no other reason than that they can't resist the daily opportunities that a lax or naive management lays before them; "They'll never miss it."

Nevertheless, despite the seemingly unrelated causes of employee theft, it is possible to generalize some principal factors:

First in importance is a pattern of financial irresponsibility. This does not necessarily mean a person with expensive tastes, nor even one having a need to "show off" by spending. This is simply someone who has never been able to come to grips with his own economic realities. He is always in financial hot water, and such a person often looks to a few of your company assets to bail him out. A credit check usually identifies him for you.

Second is the "big swinger"—the high roller with the fancy car and fancier women. He may spend a lot of time at the track and make a few trips to Las Vegas every year. In between junkets his bookie, his bars, and his broads see a lot of him. He's a "natural" for theft.

The third category is the employee caught in a genuine crisis—often an extended illness, either his own or someone in his family. Or it could be a devastating judgment against him in some liability action. He is a victim of circumstances and he needs help—fast. You may find that your assets provided that help, without your knowing it.

Obviously an employee falling into one or more of these three categories should be "handled with care" and his opportunities to steal watched. You will also watch for any of the following danger signals:

- Close and regular association with someone from a vendor company.
- Gambling (beyond the office pool on the World Series).
- Borrowing from co-workers.
- "Bouncing" personal checks.
- Heavy pressure from creditors including telephoned threats, visits to the office, and garnishment of wages.
- Mis-use of personal checks, such as obtaining cash with undated or post-dated checks.
- Excessive drinking.
- Obvious spending in excess of his known income.
- Refusing to relinquish custody of records during the day or to assign them to others.
- Consistently passing up vacations and (more rarely) refusing promotion.

What Is Stolen

The temptation exists to say that anything that "isn't nailed down" could be—and its counterpart elsewhere probably *has* been—stolen. Unfortunately, even if it *is* nailed down, it's still fair game for the determined or desperate thief.

It is common for employees to conduct their "sideline"

on the spot—no overhead for them! Buying and selling to or through contacts made in the course of legitimate business and delivering by company truck, as well as using company telephones, postage meters, files and even computers, is amazingly common.

One company executive made an unexpected visit to his office on a weekend and discovered his computer room in full operation. It seems a computer operator who had been with the company for twelve years had "gone into business for himself," and had set up a thriving data processing service bureau using company equipment. The executive was astonished to learn that he had a partner—unknown and greedy, but having a partner's share all the same!

We know from experience that anything may be stolen. The following list of attractive items for theft is made up of most of the elements of your office:

Cash

Stolen through padded expense accounts, by kickbacks, or from cash storage accessed through unauthorized keys, combinations, or carelessness. Cash is also attacked indirectly, through counterfeit or stolen forms (blank checks, vouchers, invoices, etc.), or through collusion with vendors or customers—paying for goods not received, failing to show short counts, over-loading, tipping hijackers, approving altered invoices.

Equipment

Typewriters, calculators, adding machines, dictating machines, projectors, tape recorders, etc., all find a ready market. One enterprising executive sold his company's manufacturing equipment—with delivery on Saturdays, of course.

Furniture

Desks, chairs, tables, lamps, file cabinets, clocks, rugs, stereo speakers, paintings, etc. (One office lost the speakers to a stereo system, and then lost the speakers with which the insurance company replaced them.)

Supplies

In addition to petty attrition, supplies may be stolen in gross lots—pens, pencils, pads, paper clips, etc.

Proprietary Information

Computer programs, mailing lists, accounts, customer lists, bid estimates, research data, preferential discount schedules, sales plans, advertising, promotional and merchandising programs, etc.

Miscellaneous

Personal use of postage stamps or postage meter, company equipment, lighting equipment, tools, company time and material.

Misuse of Assets

Even the misuse of the smallest item can cause a criticial erosion of profits. A study made in the late 1950s estimated that an average office employee took $75 in office supplies from his firm annually.

Very few employees—and not many employers—consider a pencil here, a pad of paper there, as theft. But it certainly is misuse of company assets, and in an office of 100 employees represents $7,500 in a year, based on the 1950's estimate—and the 1950's dollar! Compute for yourself the gross income required to make up for that net loss of $75 per employee.

In addition to the theft of company property, let us not overlook personal property theft in the office, a regular occurrence in many places. We have discussed the sharpshooters from the outside who prey on purses left on desk tops and on wallets in jackets hung on office doors or coat racks, but it is a melancholy fact that a significant number of these thefts of personal property may be by fellow workers.

Unfortunately, personal property is difficult to protect and security cannot be directly committed to safeguarding such items. Essentially, anyone who keeps personal property within the office is risking its loss. Until the rate of crime in the office declines, each employee can best protect his personal property by bringing as little as possible to the office. Wallets and purses can be placed in locked drawers (the petty thief is not familiar with these simple locks), kept on the person, or put out of sight in occupied or locked offices.

It is important that employees be made aware of this risk to their personal property. It is equally important that they recognize the plain fact that, while security will institute every possible safeguard, the security responsibility is for their safety and for the security of company property and operations; security cannot assume responsibility for personal property brought to the office, about which they do not know and whose handling they cannot control.

Collusion—The Concerted Effort

While the dishonest employee working alone can do enormous damage to his employer over a period of time, he is even more formidable a problem when working in collusion with others. His confederates may be co-workers, or they may be vendors' or customer personnel, messengers, truck drivers, or servicemen, all on different payrolls. The most costly combination generally is a group of your employees working with a group of these outsiders.

Security people agree that employee theft involving more than one person is far more serious than the "lone wolf" operation. Detection is more difficult since, with two or more working on the caper, there are better opportunities for cover-up. Key members of the ring will be those employees whose job it is to enforce and oversee security procedures. The combination is so effective in many cases that the only way the ring can be exposed is by placing an undercover man in the company within or near the suspected group.

"Inner Office" Special Danger

In terms of dollars and financial damage, the office is the "Achilles' heel" of most business operations. This is the sensitive nerve center of the entire function. This is where approvals and authorizations originate. This is where receipts and invoices are handled. The thief in the office, working alone or with confederates, indeed has the fate of the company in his hands.

And his hands are none too gentle. Fidelity underwriters, who bond the nation's employees and are in the best position to know, put employee theft at *twice* our national fire loss. This estimate would put the annual tab for employee dishonesty at $5 billion.

And when we consider that it is conservatively estimated that 7 per cent of business failures are the result of employee dishonesty, we shouldn't have to "sell" the need for internal business security.

How They Do It

In reviewing theft in the office, we find that its forms are limited only by the ingenuity of your staff. Remember that you've gone to a lot of trouble to train your staff in the systems they help to operate. And the better they know the system, the better they know how to use or evade it.

Look over these examples to see how many could apply to your operation:

- Receiving clerks and truck drivers getting together to falsify counts. Uncounted items are resold, or (in a "long count") a cash kickback is made.
- Payroll and personnel employees creating false "hires" or retaining resigned employees on the payroll, thus producing authentic checks made out to nonexistent employees.[1] (These false checks are

---

[1] *One classic case of this method was disclosed only because the company cashier cashed paychecks for nonexistent employees through an employee who was an ardent union member. The company learned of the "shadow" employees because their union contract called for all new hires to join the union. "Where are our new members?" was the union's demand.*

frequently cashed by confederates, to protect the perpetrators.)

- Computer programmers and operators working in collusion, or programmers working under insufficient supervision and/or having direct access to the computer. Increasing business dependence upon computerization makes many companies extremely vulnerable to this type of virtually undetectable attack. (*This specialized problem is discussed in greater detail in Chapter 8.*)
- Maintenance personnel and outside servicemen who cooperate to steal office machines for resale. With the introduction of "desktop" computers costing in the thousands, this type of theft will become even more serious.
- Purchasing agents or accounting personnel working in conjunction with vendors to produce false accounts payable records. Payments are split. The accounts payable clerk or supervisor falsifies shipment receipt and issues voucher on vendor's invoice for goods not shipped. Vendor-purchasing agent collusion may also involve approving purchase of merchandise at an inflated price. (Vendor kicks back extra profit to purchasing agent.)
- Mailroom and supply clerks combine to pack and mail merchandise to themselves for resale or personal use.
- Mailroom supervisor and accounting clerk produce false figures that exceed amount of money placed in company postage meter; excess cash goes into their pockets.
- Stockroom clerk and janitor (or janitor alone or in combination with trash pick-up personnel) remove office equipment and supplies in trash.
- Issuing checks in payment of bills from fictitious suppliers and depositing them by means of false endorsements to accounts set up for that purpose.

Another version is to set up a new company bank account—without telling the company.

- Raising the amounts of checks after voucher approval.
- Taking incoming cash and not crediting customer accounts.
- Forging checks, destroying the cancelled checks when they have cleared the bank, then concealing the transactions by altering bank statements and forcing footings in the cash books.
- Padding payrolls as to overtime, rates, etc. Employees "kick back" to the authorizing supervisor. One plant of one firm discovered it was paying $40,000 per month for unworked overtime.
- Paying creditors' invoices twice and appropriating the second check.
- Pocketing unclaimed wages.
- "Lapping"—pocketing small amounts from incoming payments and applying later payments on other accounts to cover shortages.
- Appropriating checks made payable to "cash" or bank which were intended for payment of notes, creditors, etc., or checks pre-signed in blank.

These are only a few of the methods of internal crime committed regularly in offices around the world. But the known cases represent only a tiny percentage of the probable crimes; it is estimated that for every thief who is caught there are thousands who "get away with it" for years until they have accumulated enough to retire in comfort—at your expense.

PART II: INTERNAL SECURITY

Clearly, the problem of internal theft is an enormous one. The yearly dollar cost to American business staggers the imagination—and the figure continues to climb.

We all have some idea of the dramatic increase in crime generally across the country in the past decade. As shocking as those figures are, bear in mind that inside, or employee, thieves outsteal the known criminals (like automobile thieves, burglars and armed robbers) by about five to one—and only a miniscule percentage of them are caught and prosecuted. The next time you find yourself shaking your head over the crime rate—which almost wholly represents external crime—remember the rest of the iceberg, the five-times-more you are the victim of.

Fortunately you *can* do something about internal theft. You can reduce losses by dishonest employees to relatively unimportant amounts—if you set up a continuing program of prevention, education, and control.

The first step—the first essential—is to accept the possibility that some of your employees *might*, under the proper (or improper) circumstances, steal from you. You must leave that astonishingly large group of employers who close their eyes to the possibility of dishonesty among their employees.

Security professionals report case after case where the employer was willing to believe that employees of competitive firms stole from *their* employers, but the same employer refused to believe that any of "his people" would steal from him. Management, they report, is always aghast —the first time—to find how actively some of the most trusted employees have been lining their pockets at company expense.

You need not believe all the figures cited here in order to establish effective defensive programs. What is important is for you to recognize the potential of internal theft, the crippling losses you could suffer—and may be suffering—at the hands of one or two or several dishonest employees.

With that threat in mind you will be better able to establish a program of countermeasures to secure your operation against the thief on your payroll.

Loss Can (and Must) Be Cut

The first step in instituting a program of countermeasures against internal theft is a matter of attitude. It is outrageous—and immoral—to accept employee dishonesty as part of the "cost of doing business." It is probably true that there will always be petty pilferage, some loss to dishonest employees—no system of internal control can absolutely prevent every kind of theft, and a continuing effort is essential if such a system is to be even as effective as possible. No percentage of loss to embezzlement or pilferage is acceptable; theft is "contagious," and today's pilferage is tomorrow's theft ring. Whatever the figure at which theft begins, sincere effort must constantly be made to reduce it.

Every business necessarily makes an effort to reduce costs and enlarge profits. In highly competitive fields this effort is truly a matter of life or death. If a company in such a competitive situation finds its overhead is higher than industry standards, it must cut these costs to an acceptable level simply to stay in business. It's good business sense, whatever the competition, to regularly examine and reduce costs wherever possible. Certainly internal theft is an important—and totally useless—area of operating cost.

As Raymond Farber, publisher of *Security World* magazine, pointed out, "Profit is the margin between cost and sales, a margin always under severe pressure from the normal costs of business operation and competition. No 'cost' of business operation is more beneficial than reduction of the cost of losses due to theft."

A good way to examine how beneficial such a reduction can be is to examine the alternatives.

A case in point was a savings and loan association in Northern California. The cashier was a motherly widow in her middle fifties whose three children were married and living away from home. She wanted to help other people and she did—at her employer's expense. She provided food, mortgage payments, tuition payments, clothes and even a car, to grateful and unsuspecting friends and acquaintances. By the time her activities were uncovered by her employer, this lady had "helped" to the tune of slightly less than $120,000 in only three and a half years. Her explanation was that she "wanted to be useful to people" and "it was so easy" and "no one (at her office) seemed to be interested in what I was doing."

What would that kind of loss mean to your company? Think how you and your people work to increase your business by just a few thousand dollars a year. If your profit margin is 5 per cent, a loss like that would wipe out the profit from almost $2,500,000 in sales. Just think: $2,500,000 in hard-won sales wasted—because of one employee!

With proper controls this loss could have been either totally prevented, or detected and stopped much earlier. You owe it to yourself *and* to your employees to institute controls.

As we have noted, there are two elements that exist in the crime of embezzlement—desire and opportunity. If management permits the opportunities for theft to present themselves regularly, the day will inevitably arrive when a need or the desire for more money combines with the opportunity, a temptation too strong to resist.

Management has a very real moral obligation to protect the integrity of its employees by taking every possible step to avoid presenting those opportunities for theft that will tempt otherwise honest people to take advantage of the trust placed in them. This is not to suggest that employers must bear the responsibility for thefts by their employees, but that it is their obligation to remove the opportunities, and hence the temptation, and to make such theft "unthinkable" by all but the most determined employee-thief.

Begin at the Top

A plan for internal security, like any plan involving policy, must begin at the top.

Here, at the management level, more than at any other point or in any other area of the office, is enthusiasm and total commitment an absolute necessity. Even if the larger percentage of your staff probably is never in a position of handling cash, or merchandise, or even papers by which they could divert assets to themselves, still they too are part—an important part—of the "climate of honesty" in your office. Management's vital involvement must be on a continuing basis and clearly supported from the highest level. Without this support, security cannot be effective.

It may be necessary to overcome objections to the institution of internal security procedures; we all know there are people who instinctively resist anything new. These people must be sold by the tact and firmness that you would use in instituting any other new procedure. However, once you have proved that it is both necessary and beneficial, you will find that most employees are glad to cooperate.

Initiating a Plan for Internal Security

Screen Applicants

Certainly the key to any system of internal security is the basic honesty of the employees. If all the employees are honest, the system will be fool-proof. If a high percentage of them are thieves, the system may be tested to the breaking point.

The best place to screen out bad risks is in the personnel office, *before* they're put on the payroll. A careful, selective employment policy may take more time and cost a few more dollars, but it will pay for itself many times over. The savings in reduced staff turnover, employee training, and greater efficiency can repay the cost—let alone the savings in our area of concentration, the reduction of internal losses.

It is important that you use an application form which, among other things, asks for a chronological listing of all previous employers. This provides a reference source; but it can also show a gap, where the applicant didn't wish to list a previous employer, such as the County Jail. These dates of employment are facts previous employers usually have no objection to verifying—or contradicting.

Check References Properly

You will, of course, ask for business and personal references—these *must* be checked. In checking with these references, however, remember that the applicant has selected them. He obviously hasn't selected someone who will give him a bad report. It is important that you check another contact at each previous employer—and that you check by telephone, if not in person.

Why check by telephone? Because people tend to be considerably more candid on the telephone than in a letter. In addition, you have an opportunity to hear the inflections with which they respond. If a former employer says, "Oh, yes, Smith was a good worker," the manner in which he says it has real significance. There are enough different inflections in such a line to keep an actor, much less a former employer, busy for quite a while. But a form asking the same question comes back with only a "yes" or a "no." It can't give you any shadings; you get no additional insight into Smith as a potential employee. Another vital question for previous employers is "Is he eligible for re-hire; would you re-hire him?"

Applicants for supervisory jobs, including those promoted to these positions, should of course be checked more thoroughly than is possible simply by following up an application.

Consider Professional Backgrounding

Professional backgrounding involves extra expense, but is paid for many times over each time backgrounding turns up the fact that an apparently acceptable candidate has an unacceptable past he conveniently forgot to mention to you. This backgrounding involves a discreet investigation into the past and present of a potential employee, and can uncover serious problems that you should know about—in character, in work habits, in past performance—but could never effectively uncover by your own efforts.

It is conservatively estimated that 93 per cent of all employees *known to have stolen* from their employers are not prosecuted; mostly they are fired without charges being brought. These workers are, in fact, unknown as thieves except by a few persons where they formerly worked. They are not known even to the police. One of this 93 per cent could be applying for employment in your firm now.

A professional investigator could find this background —at some expense, granted—but when we think of the potential losses just one dishonest employee can cause, we know the worth of this information if the position under consideration is in any way sensitive. Personnel and security experts alike agree that less than 20 per cent of the work force is responsible for 80 per cent of personnel problems of all kinds. Any measures that can "weed out" that 20 per cent save time, money, morale and administrative headaches. And backgrounding is legal, discreet, and the results are confidential.

It can be very useful to announce on the original employment application that employees must be bonded if hired. This announcement will instantly dampen the enthusiasm of the professional thief; he knows bonding entails his being fingerprinted and giving permission for access to criminal records. Knowing he will almost surely be exposed by a bonding investigation, he will withdraw his application and move on to a company with less stringent requirements.

Investigate Before Promotion

It can also be important to background any employee who is being considered for promotion or transfer to a more responsible or more sensitive position. Remember that without opportunity there is no temptation. But an employee suddenly thrust into a new situation, where he is regularly tempted to steal and has opportunity to do so, is placed in a most wrenching position—especially if his personal circumstances place him under financial pressure.

The model citizen of ten years ago may be having an extramarital affair today that is squeezing him for his last penny. The young man with a modest interest in stocks and bonds when he was originally hired may now be the local wolf of Wall Street under heavy pressure in a declining market. By determining his real situation, you are in a position to help the employee work his way out of his family or financial problems before he moves on to new responsibilities and temptations. This kind of interest on your part in employees' personal problems not only builds company morale, but also results in a reduction in losses from theft.

Polygraph Examination for Certain Jobs

In some cases where the position under consideration is highly sensitive, it could be valuable to screen prospective employees or candidates for promotion by the use of a polygraph test, if this is legal in your state. While this procedure is a matter of some controversy, veteran security men are generally agreed that the so-called "lie detector" can, in the hands of competent and ethical professionals, play a most constructive role. A polygraph test can quickly establish the validity of the truthful applicant's statements of background. This can be particularly valuable where the applicant has claimed experience or training in areas difficult, time-consuming, or expensive to check out.

In the words of G. H. Lawrence, M.D., a practicing neurologist and psychiatrist as well as Assistant Professor in those fields at St. Louis University School of Medicine, "the polygraph obtains information that cannot be obtained from any other source such as the application, background investigation, psychiatric testing, or psychiatric examination."[2]

[2] "The Psychiatrist, The Polygraph, and Police Selection," Security World, March 1966, page 23.

It is of course important for you to check the legal status of the polygraph in your state before you consider its use. Several states forbid its use as a requirement for employment, but permit it to be used on a voluntary basis; one state, as of this writing, prohibits its use for any reason, even at the request of the accused.

Many firms do, however, use the polygraph in their hiring practices, as well as in investigations, and those that do so report such use as beneficial.

You must make your own decision as to whether polygraph use is indicated. A test may cost anywhere from $50 to $100—or more—depending on the length of the test. Ask yourself whether the risk involved doesn't warrant that kind of expense. Is the exposure such or the job so sensitive that it's worth this extra cost? While one might say many jobs would not justify the money, polygraph examinations are used by some "fast food" franchisers, where profit margins are so narrow theft is intolerable. Only you can make the final decision, but you might be well advised to contact some polygraph examiners who are members of the American Polygraph Association and learn more about your state laws and the methods used by ethical examiners, before the need arises.

Conclusion

If you make every effort to avoid hiring both potentially dishonest and troublesome employees, you will have taken a most important first step toward reducing internal loss. Any program that weeds out undesirables before they are employed is bound to cut down on "shortages," that catch-all term which conceals so much theft. The more conscientiously you check, test, and background each prospective employee, the more successful "protective hiring" will be.

But to avoid later problems with *all* applicants—some of whom may be cleverly deceptive—you must set up a program which covers the points discussed:

- Design a form asking for a chronological listing of all prior jobs and employers and examine it for gaps.
- When in doubt (or when hiring for, or promoting into, a key post)—background professionally.
- Check all previous employers—preferably in person. Failing that—check by phone.
- Consider use of polygraph for all management or for particularly sensitive positions.

It should be noted at this time that, beyond your search for competent personnel of a certain level of training and experience, you also are seeking to uncover forgers, thieves, and embezzlers who have covered their past when filling out your application form. By eliminating them you are helping to build strong defenses against loss. It would be unjust and irresponsible, of course, to apply the same standard to ex-convicts or parolees who openly acknowledge their past records. Experience has shown that these men, knowingly hired in the right position and properly supervised, are not only acceptable but frequently highly responsible and trustworthy. These men should be given the opportunity under discreetly controlled circumstances to "make it" as a member of the "straight" society.

PART III: REDUCING OPPORTUNITY

As we have noted, it is estimated that 50 per cent of your employees can go either way; given ample and repeated opportunity to steal, or the example of others stealing, they will steal—but if these opportunities are eliminated, they won't seek out opportunities for theft.

If 25 per cent will steal no matter what you do (although we hope that a thoughtful and vigorous screening in the hiring process has sharply reduced this figure), and 25 per cent will never steal, we must be prepared to catch the one group, and can safely overlook the other. It's that changeable 50 per cent with whom we must be particularly concerned. We must be concerned with the climate in which they operate, as well as with the physical and procedural weaknesses which might invite them to steal, whether alone or in collusion with others.

Security professionals find themselves almost constantly in the position of persuading management that dishonesty is even *possible*. In many offices, management acknowledges that the problem exists elsewhere but vehemently denies the possibility of its existence in their own organization. As a result, these well-meaning executives overlook the many opportunities to steal they have provided to tempt otherwise well-intentioned employees.

If we recognize that we are all subject to temptation and take steps to eliminate that temptation and the causative opportunity, we will have gone a long way toward discharging a moral obligation to our employees—as well as substantially reducing what can be a crippling—indeed, a business-killing—"cost."

Improve Morale

It is important that each member of your organization feel that he is a fellow human with a significant function to perform. Or—to put it the other way around—that he *not* feel simply a statistic on some efficiency expert's chart.

This sense of interacting dynamic involvement is vital to the ultimate success of any operation. And before you pat yourself on the back and mutter something about your office being one big, happy family, take another look. It's not always easy to see the problems, especially from above.

Some years ago a gentleman we'll call Mr. A, a labor negotiator esteemed for his ability to get to the heart of labor difficulties, was called in on a seemingly unresolvable case. A major manufacturing firm, which had long enjoyed a trouble-free labor-management relationship, was in the third month of a bitter contract negotiation with an ugly strike imminent. Mr. A was puzzled. The pay scale was higher than industry standards; benefits were generous and imaginative; vacations and sick leave privileges were liberal; union members sat in with management on many policy-making matters, and on all matters having a direct effect on employees. Mr. A could find no serpent in this industrial Eden.

The workers' demands were routine—higher pay, shorter hours, more retirement benefits—all common demands. Somehow Mr. A didn't feel that these were the issues. He kept on looking. He took one more tour of the handsome plant. He'd been through it dozens of times, but he felt that somehow he might stumble on a clue if he went through one more time. It was a hot July afternoon— but then almost 90 per cent of the plant was comfortably air-conditioned. The plant was freshly and tastefully painted, and immaculate. The recreation rooms were well-equipped and well cared for, the vending machines supplied all manner of food and conveniences, the bulletin board held a number of—wait a minute—the bulletin board! That was it! Here was the symbol of the problem.

Over the board was a long, faded streamer. It read, "The Management of the X Corporation wishes all its Employees a Very Merry Christmas and a Happy New Year." Christmas in July! A clear statement that on the one hand there was "management," on the other "employees." Mr. A arranged for the sign to be immediately removed and statements made to counteract the stated division within the company.

Negotiations proceeded and matters were resolved. Because of a sign being removed? Of course not. But the sign's removal was a beginning, and an understanding of *why* it should be removed helped in re-establishing a rapport that had been lost. In this increasingly impersonal world, the suspicion that management's "best wishes" were simply a mechanical reflex was being confirmed with every passing day; the banner was a daily reminder of the gulf between "them" and "us." And the message hung above the bulletin board every employee in the plant had to pass every day.

Little wonder that a nameless antagonism grew up in the firm. This is inevitably the case when people feel they are merely statistics. And with antagonism comes, among other things, theft. So look at your employee relations program and give thought to ways in which it might be improved. You might want to pay particular attention to the following:

- Are the physical surroundings—decor, cleanliness, sound control, temperature control, general housekeeping—at a high level?
- Are wages and wage policy regularly reviewed and updated to assure equitable wage levels?
- Are company policies clearly stated and consistently and justly carried out?
- Are two-way avenues of communication developed and kept open?
- Is there some kind of useful house organ, newsletter, or constantly-changed bulletin board?
- Are there procedures facilitating the airing of grievances or personal problems with supervisors?
- Is there a training program to improve job skills, and to provide for advancement?

Establish Specific Controls

If you have exercised good judgment in the selection and promotion of your employees, and if you have shown sufficient concern for the internal theft potential by reducing the rationalizations for stealing, as well as taking pains to keep company morale as high as possible, you should have the problem of employee dishonesty fairly well under control.

But not entirely. And certainly not enough to justify feeling secure from attack by a determined thief who has managed to penetrate your hiring defenses, or from an employee who is under heavy financial pressure of some kind. For them, particularly, you must establish a system of controls—an internal crime prevention program.

Set Up a Survey Program

The first essential for a program of controlling internal theft is to survey each department in your company to determine what and where your risks are. This survey should also identify, and confirm the use of, existing control systems and review their effectiveness. You can be confident that if such a survey is energetically and competently carried out, and if it produces specific recommendations acted upon with intelligence and vigor, losses from internal dishonesty will be even further reduced.

The first step is deciding who will make the survey. In a small business, the owner or manager would be the logical but perhaps not the best choice, as he may be "too close to the forest." In a larger business such a survey would be handled by the security department, while the smaller company, or the troubled larger company, should consult with a firm of security consultants with proven expertise in security surveys. An independent survey of accounting practices could properly be assigned to a specialist in operational audits from a firm of outside auditors. Such auditors would probably be from the same firm that handles the company's annual audit, although it is important that the survey be totally separate from the regular audit.

In any event, whoever conducts the survey must be familiar, or must familiarize themselves, with all the various operations of the business. And this familiarity should be as specific as possible. The pressures and tensions of a business are important in putting together a survey of this sort. Also, an awareness of the formal and the informal organization in the firm is invaluable in identifying working arrangements offering a potential for collusion.

The survey must proceed on a department-by-department basis, with the question, "What is the loss potential here" always in mind. At every stage you and/or your surveyors must put yourselves in the position of a thief seeking opportunities to steal. You must extend your imagination to every corner of each department in your effort to identify every "weak link." You must examine each *possible* exposure to theft, rather than trying to limit your observations to what seems (to you) to be "probable."

The survey must include "the whole ball of wax." It must start with a review of hiring and promotion practices, and progress through a close look at the handling of receipts and disbursements, accounts receivable and accounts payable, customer accounts, credits and rebates, petty cash funds, payroll, bank deposits, methods of safeguarding cash and negotiables on the premises, inventories, data processing, purchasing, supplies, receiving, shipping, customer deposits, and any other area where opportunity for dishonesty exists. *Cover the entire operation.*

Establishing and Supervising a Control System

Upon completion of the study, the resulting data must be used to develop controls wherever they appear needed to protect against *possible* breaches of trust. These controls will, of course, require cooperation at every level. Managers, supervisors, and non-management employees alike must be made aware of the need for accountability controls and for adhering to them.

In this, as in other areas involving the reshaping of policy, your executive skills will be needed. Controls of this nature frequently must cut across departmental lines— and they frequently appear to personnel to be altering spheres of authority and responsiblity. It's an age-old problem. But for the program to be effective the absolute essential is its being firmly established as having highest priority from top management. The slightest perceptible hesitation or equivocation by management will doom the program before it is fairly started.

Generally, top management meets with supervisory personnel, and supervisory personnel meets with employees. Such meetings explain the need for controls, including the destructive potential of theft to jobs, benefits, profit-sharing, etc. Such meetings additionally serve notice that management will not tolerate dishonesty. It is often surprising to managers who undertake such a program to find how enthusiastic employees become. The policies often serve to clear the air, to put the company "on the record" in the matter of internal dishonesty, and they reassure that majority of the office force which has been apprehensive or uncomfortable about those employees who are stealing—and about the company's seemingly wishy-washy attitude about theft. A clear, uncompromising policy is usually felt as healthful and welcome.

Maintaining the System

All procedures are subject to erosion and modification over a period of time. With a national turnover average among white-collar workers of 50 per cent, it won't be long before new employees are doing things in a new way, or doing the right things for no reason they can see.

New ideas may, in fact, create better systems. It is, however, most unlikely that new employees will suggest more stringent controls. On the contrary—they are likely to become impatient with what they consider to be senseless restrictions and seek to create an easier, quicker, "more efficient" way. The quicker way bypasses key security controls.

We know that some controls can be time-consuming, but they are necessary. Don't, however, get the notion that controls *per se* represent time-consuming red tape; many of them are as fast as, and frequently more efficient than, non-control techniques toward the same end. This is not to say that controls should not be changed as operating systems alter; when that occurs, security controls should be re-evaluated and, if necessary, new ones developed to secure the new operational procedures.

What must not be allowed is the arbitrary elimination of security controls by employees. To protect against this possibility, security systems and procedures should be policed by supervisors and by management to insure their continuance. A good method is to have spot checks made at random by management.[3] Follow-up checks should be made by the external company that made the initial survey and report. Internal auditors, if any, and office security personnel, should regularly check on all phases of the internal control system.

Violations should be dealt with quickly and firmly. A laxness toward security procedures is contagious and, if offenders are not corrected promptly, this attitude will quickly spread to other employees. It is also important to note that, while compromise of the control procedure is generally the result of laziness or indifference on the part of the offender, a significant number of such instances are the result of an employee consciously sabotaging the system in order to achieve a dishonest end.

Important Areas to Control

The controls and safeguards dealt with here cannot represent a complete, or even an ideal, profit-protection program. They are, however, indicative of the fundamentals of such a program and should be useful to any company interested in establishing anti-theft controls. Every company has some areas unique to it or its type of business. Those areas will have to be controlled in the spirit of the program elements common to any office and with which we will treat in this section.

Periodic Audits

Periodic audits by certified public accountants are absolutely essential for every business concern. Firms employing internal auditors should augment periodic external

---

[3]*Saul Astor, "The Security Survey,"* Security World *Magazine, February 1968*

audits by a continuing internal audit of all company operations. The outside audit should be made at least once a year, and should cover an examination of inventory schedules as to count, prices, extensions, footings, and any other tests that seem indicated. This audit should also verify company assets (by physical inventory sampling), liabilities, net worth, income and expense accounts. One or more surprise audits per year are also valuable in protection of assets—and peace of mind.

Cash—Receipts and Petty

The most obviously sensitive operation in any company is the handling of cash. If yours is a business in which only minimal amounts of cash pass through your office, you are indeed fortunate; you are spared the headaches of formal cash control.

If cash is embezzled before it is recorded as received, the theft will be difficult to spot. Very special attention should be paid to controls established to supervise these receipts. Where cash is received by mail, the receiving and subsequent handling should always be supervised by a responsible administrator. This official should not be responsible for other handling of cash, for verification of cash payments, or for any bookkeeping functions. This person should see that all receipts are listed, giving the amount, from whom received, etc. This list should be made in duplicate on sequentially numbered forms, both copies being signed by the person opening the mail and by the cashier who receives it. The cashier holds one copy while the other goes to accounting for file; both verify the numbering sequence.

Cash book entries must be checked daily against cash receipts. Spot checks before the end of the day are useful.

Cash book footings must be verified at least once a week to check for underfootings.

All cash receipts should be deposited in the bank intact and each day's receipts balanced with the daily deposit. If petty cash is needed, it should be drawn by check.

Bank deposits should be accompanied by three deposit slips, one of which is stamped by the bank and returned to the cashier. The second is mailed to the office auditing or accounting department, while the third is retained by the bank.

Each day's deposit slips should be balanced with the day's list of remittances and cash receipts.

Bank statements must be received and reconciled by someone other than persons empowered to make deposits or withdrawals, or who account for receipts and disbursements. Cancelled checks should be checked against vouchers for any alterations and for proper endorsements by the payee. If the bank statement itself appears to have been erased or otherwise tampered with, the bank should be asked to issue a new statement for that period.

A specific petty cash fund adequate for daily business should be established. Funds from petty cash should *never* be mingled with, nor petty cash drawn from, cash receipts. No disbursements should be made from petty cash without an authorized voucher signed by the employee receiving the cash and countersigned by an authorized person. The receipts must of course be typed or written in ink, and signed in ink.

If possible, vendor receipts supporting petty cash vouchers should be attached to the voucher they substantiate.

The fund should be replenished as necessary by a check drawn for the amount of paid vouchers submitted. These vouchers should be verified by an employee other than the one in charge of the fund. *All* vouchers and invoices paid should be cancelled by rubber stamp, tearing a corner, perforation, etc., to avoid re-submission.

The petty cash fund should be balanced from time to time by management and spot-checked for altered vouchers or any other irregularities.

Separation of Responsibility and Authority

The jobs of persons engaged in any aspect of the finances of the company should be divided. You invite embezzlement whenever one person is wholly responsible for a given operation. In effect, you are making him his own auditor. This opportunity can put him under considerable pressure—so much pressure, in fact, that if he finds himself in some personal financial difficulty he may be unable to withstand the temptation. He may solve his problem at your expense, when the thought might never have occurred to him if he hadn't been, in effect, the sole arbiter of that portion of the cash flow.

It is vital that the duties of cashier and bookkeeper be handled by different people working separately. If this is not possible, as in very small businesses, a careful system of countersignatures and approvals must be set up involving a member of management. The separation of function, with access to the other's records denied, is more desirable, of course. Such separation is important throughout your operation. For example, since payroll prepares checks, they should be distributed by personnel, with surplus checks returned to a third party, perhaps the controller or treasurer.

Promotion and Rotation of Personnel

The movement of employees upward or (and perhaps especially) laterally is good management as well as an extra protection against theft. One of the characteristics of successful embezzlement is an employee who is thoroughly familiar with a system, both with his own operation and its related check. Shifting employees is not only a morale builder but reduces the risk of overfamiliarity.

A regular re-evaluation of all systems is important, since it is beneficial to up-date them from time to time. Every time parts of a system are changed, or the authority and responsibility for it are reassigned, any existing pattern of embezzlement—if it has existed—is at least threatened, and may be invalidated. Upward promotion without procedural changes, for example, could simply broaden the opportunity for theft.

Vacations

Historically, embezzlers refuse vacations; they're always "too busy" at their job. Their attitude is frequently applauded as self-sacrificing, or seen as in the best interests of the company.

Don't be deceived; vacation policies are established in the best interests of everyone, and benefit company and employee alike. Many people return from their vacations totally exhausted from the pace they have set for themselves, but they are nonetheless refreshed emotionally and even intellectually by the change of scene and pace. An employee who passes up his annual holiday does a favor to no one. If he has financial responsibilities in your office, take a closer look. Just as you promote and rotate key positions, insist that all employees take regular vacations.

Forms

All too often overlooked in the office security picture is the proper handling and safeguarding of company forms. It is important that these forms be secured and made safe from unauthorized usage by internal as well as external thieves.

Any forms which authorize or verify transactions are fair game for forgers or embezzlers, and must be accounted for and kept out of the hands of all but authorized employees. Blank checks, order forms, payment authorizations, vouchers, receivers, etc., all can be used illegally.

Since every office is unique in its need for and use of forms, a full scope of countermeasures cannot be prescribed. We can, though, point out your need to be alert to the problem generally and to the importance of establishing a system to protect you against unauthorized usage of your forms.

Two elements which apply to every office should be effective in the control of such forms.

- Number all forms, use them in numerical order, and keep a record of each one. Remember that it is just as important to file and record voided or discarded forms.
- A log should be established to record issuance of accountable blank forms. Periodic inventory of all sensitive forms balanced against this log is an important step in retaining forms control.

Access and Protection of Records

Access to valuable, important and confidential company documents must be limited to specifically designated persons. Obviously such papers should be kept in locked fire safes, or in locked sections within safes or vaults, and the keys or combinations issued only to personnel authorized to have these documents.

Departmental Controls

In this discussion on the exposure to theft by departments we must, once again, recognize that each office has its own special problems. Each office's problems require painstaking analysis based on the all-important security survey.

We will deal with those departments and those areas where experience has shown the risk to be the greatest and, though we cannot cover every eventuality, we can identify known trouble spots from which you can expand your own controls.

Purchasing

If the purchasing function is centralized under one manager and the forms used for purchasing are properly set up and controlled, you will have gone a long way toward reducing widespread purchasing theft.

Placing the purchasing responsibility in one area reduces the number of individuals who can take advantage of you, as well as eliminating the problem of a number of cost centers operating somewhat differently, and frequently at cross-purposes. Many large companies have found after making huge expenditures that different departments within their own company had been dealing independently with the same vendor, and bidding up the price against each other. A centralized purchasing function would obviously eliminate this problem.

To control the purchasing process, pre-numbered four- or five-part forms should be used to initiate any purchase. The original requisition goes to the vendor, the duplicate to unfilled orders, the triplicate to accounting, and the fourth copy to receiving. (The copy to accounting is useful in accruing accounts receivable, and as another check against order alteration.) The fifth copy should go to the originating department.

We strongly suggest that you prepare the fourth, or receiving clerk's, copy with a short carbon so that the *quantity* is left blank. Upon receipt of the order, the receiving clerk must insert the quantity he has received on his copy, which he then returns to Purchasing. This copy is checked against the vendor's invoice and against the requisition in the unfilled order file. If these are in agreement, the invoice can now be approved and forwarded for payment.

Just as the purchasing function should be centralized, so it should involve no other function; and it should be completely removed from both accounts payable and from receiving.

Competitive bids should be sought whenever possible, to avoid favoritism, kick-backs, or collusion between the purchasing agent and the vendor.

Be sure paid vendor invoices and receivers supporting vouchers are prominently stamped or cancelled "Paid." On too many occasions embezzlers have resubmitted authorizing documents for second payment.

The purchasing function should be periodically audited on the management level. Included in that audit should be a method of verifying the existence of new vendors. Documents should be checked for erasures, falsification and forgery. Incoming orders should be reviewed at random to verify Receiving's receipt and count of the merchandise. As in all spot checks and random audits, irregularity is essential; the regular habits of management are well known to employees.

Payroll

Whenever possible, employees should be paid by check rather than in cash. This measure protects both the office and the employee. To avoid possible confusion, as well as to reduce opportunity for potential fraud, payroll checks should be of a different color from those used for other purposes, and should ideally be drawn on a separate account devoted exclusively to payroll purposes.

The payroll should be prepared from personnel records by employees who will not be involved in writing and distributing the checks. Any unclaimed checks must be returned to a third party (we have previously suggested that this third party be the controller) for re-deposit in, or credit to, the payroll account. All payroll checks voided or returned as unclaimed should be mutilated to prevent unauthorized use, audited, and filed.

Time cards should also be canceled or otherwise made invulnerable to re-use.

Surprise examinations of rates of pay, and computations of amounts earned should be undertaken with some frequency. The payroll should be audited periodically on a management level. Verification of the number of names on the payroll as compared to the number of employees should be part of the audit. The accounting manager or supervisor should personally distribute a certain percentage of payroll checks on a random basis, to confirm the existence of listed employees. These measures prevent collusion between payroll administration and payroll distribution functions.

Accounts Payable

As in the case of Purchasing, where we suggested that the function be centralized, accounts payable should handle all disbursements, and all disbursements other than petty cash should be by check.

Checks should be consecutively numbered, used in series, and printed on safety paper which reveals any attempt at alteration.

The amount of checks should be written with a check writing machine, which uses permanent ink and is as identifiable to the expert as a specific typewriter is.

If a check is drawn incorrectly it should be clearly and unalterably marked "void," filed, and a new check issued. Attached to all checks prepared for signature should be billing information, payroll sheets, etc., and the payment authorization.

Periodic audits should be made to verify the existence of accounts and to inspect supporting documents for forgery or fraud, such as non-receipt, "phantom" vendors, forged requisitions, excessive requirements, etc.

Other Departments

Any departments which handle a significant volume of cash or are responsible for the disbursement of funds are certainly the most sensitive areas in the office. They constitute the most logical attractions for your staff thieves. But don't overlook other areas; for example:

The head of the mailroom in a fair-sized Eastern firm managed to pick up $100,000 in less than three years from his unquestioned authority over the postage meter.

Another mailroom employee, in collusion with a maintenance employee, got away with almost $30,000 worth of office equipment by simply mailing it to himself and to friends.

Remember that postage is cash—metered or not. Any office with a heavy mailing schedule must have a regular inspection of the mailroom operation along with periodic surprise audits. Many firms have been badly hurt by inadequate controls over what management felt was a penny ante operation.

Employees in the maintenance department have stolen hundreds of thousands of dollars worth of merchandise or office equipment simply by stacking it on the fire escape for later pick-up, or putting it into the trash for later recovery, often by a confederate. Few offices have any system for checking what besides refuse is in the bins and boxes that pile up on the service dock waiting to be trucked out. Trash compaction on the premises not only reduces trash volume and is ecologically helpful, but it is also frustrating to thieves.

In Accounts Receivable, too, responsibilities must be separated to avoid having one person serve as both the receiver and the record-keeper for transactions.

Issuance of credit memos and adjustments should be entirely separated from accounts receivable ledgers and operations.

Do not charge off an account as uncollectable before independent verification that such an account exists and is uncollectable. (Private collection efforts by enterprising accounts receivable clerks of seemingly dead accounts can add up to a fair income for some energetic entrepreneur on your payroll.)

There are undoubtedly many more sensitive areas in your office, but only you can determine where these are. The important thing is to determine where your risks *could* be and to set up a control system now to minimize them.

PART IV: OTHER CONSIDERATIONS

Insurance

All that we have discussed so far has pointed up the need for being alert to internal theft and suggested some techniques to reduce this kind of shrinkage. In theory, if your security survey is thorough and your controls vigorously administered and audited, your losses will disappear.

But they won't. No system can totally eliminate theft, since the systems are operated by the very people who may turn to theft. Hopefully it won't happen to you—but it might. And you must be prepared for it because, as we have seen, just *one* dishonest employee can put you out of business.

Insurance is your final line of defense against the employee who manages to embezzle in spite of all your precautions. Strangely enough it has been estimated that only about 20 per cent of businesses carry insurance against employee dishonesty. The other 80 per cent are gambling —but the odds are getting worse as the game goes on. You would be wise to seek reasonable coverage of honesty bond insurance, at least against large losses.

Few firms would consider opening their doors without adequate coverage against fire, burglary, liability, or personal injury; and yet only one-fifth are motivated to insure against internal theft. If you are among the uninsured, you may want to reconsider and to at least look into insuring against the second greatest danger your office faces. (Fire is usually considered to be the greatest dollar risk.) The cost of fidelity insurance is not as high as you might suppose— and the benefits can be enormous.

You must, however, be aware of some areas that call for careful study. First, what is the deductible? If you are considering such a policy, remember that you absorb all the *proven* loss up to the deductible figure, plus, of course, any loss over the limit of coverage. Remember—for recovery from any honesty bond insurance the loss must be proven and the burden is on the insured. Inventory shortages alone are irrelevant. Even a confession, or sworn affidavits of witnesses, cannot wholly establish the dishonesty loss. Confirmation of the amount of loss must be found in company records. If a thief has "covered his tracks" so that the inventory does not show the loss, you will probably have to compromise on the amount of recovery. On the other hand, inventory shortages alone are no proof of loss and no recovery can be made on these, since you must prove who, how, and how much, information no statistical shortage can supply. Admissions, like investigations, should be done by experienced security professionals, preferably aided by voluntary polygraph examinations. (You must also face the fact that, once you have incurred a significant loss from internal theft, your insurance premium and, probably, your deductible will be substantially increased come renewal time.)

It is vital that you be fully aware of all the conditions of your policy. What is the limit of liability per employee? What is the deductible? What constitutes proof of dishonesty? What constitutes proof of extent of loss? What steps can you take which would reduce premiums? It is vital that you explore all these questions before undertaking an insurance program, and keep these answers well in mind for the duration of the coverage

Undercover Agents

When firms are suffering severely from employee theft, management is hard put to know whom to trust. Those not involved hesitate to "peach" on fellow-workers. When the problem reaches this level, it is probably wise to engage the services of outside agents, whose trained personnel can quietly uncover those employees involved and the methods they are using to steal from the company.

An undercover agent can observe what would never occur in your presence. He can pick up shreds of conversations that will develop leads in his investigation. He may even be asked to join a group of employee thieves. One undercover agent, posing as a maintenance man cleaning ceiling lighting fixtures, broke up an employee group that had already stolen over $50,000 in merchandise from a department store.

Such investigators are not inexpensive, but in the proper circumstances they earn their fee many times over. The information they develop forms the basis for professional interrogations establishing the extent of the thefts.

Please be warned, however, that under no circumstances should you think of "economizing" by using other employees or amateurs. This can be dangerous; at the very least, it is usually a dismal failure. Worse, it can alert the thieves and lose you the opportunity to identify them and their methods.

Set a Consistent Policy

After you have conducted your security survey and set up your profit protection program, it will be necessary to establish and publicize a consistent policy on internal theft.

Such a policy, if it is adequately publicized within the office, will help to put employee dishonesty into the proper perspective. It will emphasize that management *does* care —that you are not indifferent to internal losses as so many employees are ready to believe.

It is important that this policy be exactly what you have announced. It must be firmly administered, *and observed by management as well as the rank and file.* You'll find your personnel will get the message very rapidly.

On the other hand, you cannot set up a dictatorship. You are, after all, dealing with human beings, most of whom are honest and all of whom will react with hostility and resentment if they are made to feel distrusted and under constant suspicious surveillance.

Each employee must be made aware that control systems and spot checks are precautions that protect him as well as the company. He and the company have many mutual interests, and anything that damages the company damages him. He must be made to feel that he shares an interest in putting a stop to employee theft—not by active participation, for nothing must give any employee the notion that he must act as an informer—but rather as a full partner with management in systems which of themselves substantially reduce internal losses.

Prosecution

The question of what to do with an employee found stealing seems to have many answers. Not even professional security people are in agreement as to the one policy to adopt.

You are faced with three alternatives: to prosecute, to discharge, or to retain the thief as an employee.

As difficult as it may be, you must establish in advance those elements that will determine your course of action. It's tough to establish those parameters; but for the sake of your company, as well as for the sake of all your employees, you have to do it. This doesn't mean that your approach to the problem has to be rigid and unbending. Quite the opposite. You will need to continually review your policy to determine whether it is still a wise course in the face of changing circumstances.

Most firms find that discharge is the simplest answer in case of employee theft. Experts estimate that 90 percent of those found with their hands in the till are simply fired—and an overwhelming percentage of these are fired on a charge such as "inefficiency" or "failure to perform duties adequately."

The reasons for such a policy are numerous, but the most common are:

- Discharge is a severe punishment and he'll learn his lesson from that.
- It's not our business who he steals from—as long as it isn't from us.
- Prosecution can be expensive and, if he gets off,

there's a real danger of a successful civil suit for slander, libel, false arrest, etc.

All of these answers are, in their own way, valid. They should be examined a little more closely, however.

As to learning a lesson from discharge, experience has shown that a high percentage of employee thieves are repeaters. In a recent study, a security organization found that 80 percent of the known employee thieves they questioned with polygraph assistance admitted to thefts from previous employers. (Of course it *might* be said that they would learn their lesson by being discharged, because most of these other thefts had never been detected; while they might not have been "virgin thieves," they were at least on a first-time-caught basis.)

You might also reflect that theft breeds more theft and that if you are indifferent to the peculations in the world around you you are, in the long run, indifferent to your own welfare. It could be argued that if you, in effect, condone criminality by turning out a thief to steal elsewhere, you will eventually "reap the whirlwind" you helped to create.

As far as the difficulties of prosecution are concerned, it is true there are many. But most of these difficulties arise when matters are handled by amateurs, or are handled without careful guidelines established in advance by company counsel.

About the expense of prosecution there can be no question. Personnel called as witnesses may lose days in court appearances. There will be time and money spent in investigating in order to establish a tight case. Money will be spent in conferring with counsel. Yes, there is certainly an expenditure of time and money in order to prosecute an employee thief, but can you afford not to make this expenditure? Certainly there are cases where the very size of the theft requires you to move against the criminal. And cases which indicate a cool professionalism demand that you take action against the veteran crook. However, any decision must depend upon the advice of your fidelity bond carrier, who may prefer restitution.[4]

On the other hand, there are many cases where the decision doesn't come easily. Most of these involve the long-time employee, the petty larcenist, or the employee who finds himself in an overwhelming, seemingly unsolvable financial squeeze. This employee pleads that he succumbed to a sudden opportunity. What about him? Many companies would continue to employ him, provided he makes restitution, and in many cases have found in him a grateful and effective employee.

Only you—after consultation with counsel and your bonding company—can decide what policy your company will pursue. Only you can determine what the mix of toughness and compassion should be, but both must be there.

---

[4]*An example of the reason for the warning against amateur interrogation is that no promises, such as the possibility of restitution, can be given if prosecution is still under consideration. Further, there must be no coercion or intimidation, and courts are liberal in their definition of these terms.*

A LITTLE BIT...
IS A LOT OF SECURITY

A COMPUTER OFTEN PRINTS OUT A
CONTINUOUS STREAM OF CONFIDENTIAL
INFORMATION. ALL SURPLUS COPIES AND
RELATED PAPERS SHOULD BE SHRED.
REMEMBER, A HARD COPY IS EASY TO
READ, BITS AND PIECES ARE NOT.

THINK, SECURITY

Chapter 8

COMPUTER SECURITY

Added to the wonder and respect that still surround today's computer is a growing sense of anxiety about its security. The more sophisticated and complex it becomes, the more functions it can and does perform for us. The more functions it performs the more dependent upon it we become. Many modern companies frankly admit they could not operate without the computer. Never mind what they did before 1944; there it is. And it's our problem.

It's a little mind-boggling just to name the evils that can befall a computer center: embezzlement, operator error, input error, programming errors, programming fraud, hardware failures, software failures, sabotage, magnetic destruction, program and memory penetration, electromagnetic monitoring, "bugging"—the list goes on almost endlessly, and still to be added are the more down-to-earth problems of fire, flood, riots, incendiary and explosive bombs, and vindictive employees.

In spite of the risk potential and business's ever-increasing reliance on the computer, many firms continue either to ignore these risks, or to put their reliance in the complexity of the computer to keep outside individuals in ignorance of effective means of compromising it. Ignorance may have been effective in the mid-nineteenth century, to protect the first electrical fire alarms, but computer programming is taught to junior high school students; there is not much "mystery" about *this* modern miracle.

Dependence upon the ignorance of the general public for "protection" is a sign of a total lack of understanding on the part of management of the computer operation and computer science. Unless they have had some meaningful indoctrination in the computer operation they may feel, as so many laymen do, that the computer is mysterious, mystical, infallible, and somehow invulnerable.

Some of this inadequacy in computer security is understandable. In the 25 years following World War II businesses and institutions of every type jumped into the computer age. Many of them tried to convert huge chunks of their accounting operation into electronic data processing (EDP) overnight. Technicians and programmers frequently worked around the clock. Establishing security controls in a chaotic period such as this would have been impossible, and the attempt discounted as absurd and unnecessary. The point was to get the program running—not to get it running in a manner which would satisfy some vague (and as yet unknown) security requirements. The day has now passed when programs need be run on a crash basis; unfortunately, many companies continue in that manner, leaving themselves wide open to catastrophic loss.

The evidence is overwhelming that this attitude is simply no longer possible. An effective security program is essential to any EDP operation and it must have the vigorous support of an informed management. It may be difficult for a security director to explain to the company's president that they have a machine that could wipe out the company, but he has to get that message across somehow.

And the more the president understands, the more he will come to see the grave consequences of damage or loss of data, whether by accident or by malicious intent. Realizing that the threat is a constant one, he will agree that a comprehensive physical and financial security program is necessary to safeguard the computer system, whether company-owned or a computer (EDP) service.

Physical Security

Physical security of computer installations has become a matter of increasing concern. Only a few years ago a computer was considered to have great public relations value, and the computer facility was displayed in a street-level, glass fishbowl for inspection by interested spectators. This is no longer the case; today most companies no longer publicize their computers and rarely if ever acknowledge their precise location. Computers are no longer on many company tours.[1] Where once computers were on display, today they are, while not exactly concealed, secured against unauthorized traffic and generally located well away from visitor traffic.

If you can determine the location of your computer, your decision will be a vital one. In many cases it is desirable to locate the EDP operation off the premises. Certainly another building is a better location than a visible or ground-level "space available" site in your own building.

Some items that must be considered in determining location are:

- Power source: Record of dependability and availability of back-up power; quality of maintenance and reputation for speedy, efficient response to failures.
- Fire Department: Speed of response, training received. (Each city has a "fire rating" based in part on effectivity of the fire force. Check with your insurer.)
- Labor force: Remote locations can make it difficult or easy to get and keep competent personnel. Locations in a high crime area might have an adverse effect on personnel retention, as well as increasing insurance premiums for the installation.
- Access: A remote or rural site is easier to isolate and

---

[1] *One company still shows its computer; favored visitors view the computer through bullet-proof glass from a room having no entry to the computer area.*

"defend," but may present personnel problems. Too, fire and police service may not equal big-city standards.

- Natural phenomena: Your choice of site should take into account the possibility of flood, earthquake, heavy snow, frequency of electrical storms, etc. and the effects each could have on your operation.
- Maintenance: How long will it take manufacturer maintenance personnel to arrive at your location?
- Space required: Your machine configuration and the amount of peripheral equipment required for your operation may take more space than your headquarters building can provide.

Controlled Environment

For protection of the computer a constant, controlled environment is essential. This requires air conditioning to the computer in addition to the air conditioning of the computer work area, extremely sensitive fire indicators, humidity monitors, fresh air intakes, sensors to detect air pollutants, filters to eliminate internal and external dust, and vibration alarms. Since high heat and humidity can destroy tapes as effectively as any vandal can, fire is the most feared enemy of the computer operation.

Some companies have enclosed the computer area in shatterproof glass, reducing the size of the area needing a heavily controlled environment while adding an extra security feature.

Electric Power

Any fluctuation in line voltage can cause inaccuracies in data transfers; this problem should be anticipated and compensated for.

While some computer operations are not greatly hampered by line fluctuations or momentary outages, the damage to other operations may be catastrophic. Where this is true, or might be true, the recommended practice is to isolate the computer from the primary power source by "floating" batteries (constantly recharged by line voltage), which in turn supply the computer through alternators. This effectively buffers the computer from the usual line voltage power problems. Standby diesel or gasoline generators are adequate for alarms, lights and safety equipment. Air conditioning should have a separate power supply (and multiple manual power cutoffs, for fire protection).[2]

Fire

> Three Air Force Statistical Division Office computers within the Pentagon were destroyed by fire. Estimated loss approximately $7,000,000. Recreating the information on 7,000 tapes could increase loss to $30,-000,000.

This item, though on a grand scale, is the basic story of serious fire in a computer facility. The loss is large because we are dealing with extremely expensive equipment but that loss may be relatively unimportant beside the loss in data which, if recoverable at all, will require incredible numbers of man-hours to recreate. And while this data base is being reconstructed, business could be at a standstill. For example, RCA concluded it would take 9.2 man-*years* and 478 computer hours to reconstruct the master files of its New York City EDP center.

Fire Causes

Stated succinctly the major causes of fire are:
1) Fire in adjacent occupancies.
2) Accumulated combustibles, usually waste paper.
3) Electrical fires.

[2]*The Fresno State College computer fire (which destroyed the only records of college credits) was made serious by the fact that the incendiary bomb thrown through a window blocked access to the console where the only air conditioning shut-off was located. Gasoline fumes were drawn through the main frame of the computer before they exploded. The air conditioning continued to operate, fanning the flames, until power to the building was cut 20 minutes later.*

Electrical fires are not a common cause of fire in EDP centers. The largest losses have occurred because of fires originating outside the center, and burning through. In most cases the EDP center had good fire protection, but little thought or effort had been expended to protect the remainder of the building. It is, an expert has said, as if they thought they would be able to climb through a charred building to an untouched computer center.

Accumulated waste paper ignited by cigarettes or matches is the second most common cause of EDP center fires; hence the importance of having hand extinguishers available to extinguish paper fires before they become general—and personnel trained to use them.

A fire in an EDP facility is worsened by damaging side effects. In many cases the fire itself—that is, heat and flames—may be minimal, while damage from smoke, dust or fumes may be enormous. While this can be true anywhere, it is especially true in EDP areas. An RCA facility in Florida is said to have suffered $4.5 million in damage from hydrochloric acid fumes created by an electrical fire. In any event, corrosion is a primary enemy of computers, and it should not be overlooked that tear gas is a corrosive. Whatever the company plans for a "last-ditch" defense, tear gas cannot be used where it could be drawn into the computer center.

Alarms

Although the human nose can detect a fire faster than many artificial sensors, we can hardly depend on it, particularly when we realize that tape begins to deteriorate at 150°; a sophisticated fire detection system is necessary to protect any computer installation.

There is no doubt that the best time to install a fire warning system and fire extinguishing system is during initial construction of the center. At that time the cost of installing detectors throughout the facility is relatively small. Doing it later may be more costly, but it must be done. Detectors should be placed on ceilings, under raised floors (if any), in suspended ceilings, within air ducts, in cable channels, and within the equipment itself.

The fire sensors most acceptable for the critical risks represented by the computer facility are ionization detectors, which sense the charged ions which are the precursors of fire, preceding smoke or flame.

Equally important is to check the fire detection system periodically to be sure it is fully operational at all times.

Fire Extinguishing Systems

Directly related to a fire detection/alarm system is a method of controlling and extinguishing fire. The detection system we have discussed can directly trigger an extinguishing system, or sound the alarm, or both.

The extinguishing system of choice for a computer installation today is one using an inert, non-lethal gas, Halon. Carbon dioxide systems have been used with success, but such a system requires immediate evacuation of personnel for life safety. Dry chemicals are effective but leave a residue on the equipment and in the air which must be very carefully cleaned and filtered out before the machines are put into use again.

Sprinkler systems—indeed water from any other source—can be more disastrous than the fire itself. It can short out electrical circuits, damage delicate components and wreak havoc with tapes. However, equally firm opinions favoring sprinklers are held by the Factory Mutual group of insurance companies. To this apparent stalemate, IBM has said "If your insurer requires sprinklers, install them. Just make very sure they never go off."

Portable Extinguishers

CO_2 extinguishers should be placed throughout the facility including the tape library, usually a fire vault. Hand extinguishers cannot replace a total extinguishing system, but are invaluable in bringing small fires under quick control, avoiding the expensive discharge of the main fire-extinguishing system.

Fire-Resistive Equipment

In the event of a fire, specially insulated files and tape cabinets protect records and programs from a severe fire. However, the quantity of tape and records needed has led to the practice of operating the tape library from a fire-resistive records vault. If a tape "safe" or cabinet is used it should carry a three-hour UL rating for fire-resistance, as should the door of the records vault. Always remember, however, that many tapes are necessarily exposed in the operations area at any given time.

It is important, too, that you determine the fire-resistance of materials in the computer area. A $6.7 million loss was sustained when an overheated light fixture ignited a supposedly fire-resistant ceiling, wiping out a tape library and a computer room.

Internal and External Vandalism

Computer centers have been identified as prime targets for acts of protest vandalism because of their key role in company operations. Politically motivated attacks have been directed at this core point time and again. In 1969 rioting students of Sir George Williams University in Montreal destroyed the school's computer center. Cost? $1,-600,000. A mob attacked a computer center of the Dow Chemical Company and scrambled 1,000 reels of tape. Dow was lucky. Their damage only amounted to about $100,000. At the University of Wisconsin, bombers destroyed the Mathematics Research Center. Losses of $1.5 million included computer equipment and 1.3 million man-hours of research.

These are dramatic events headlined around the world, but there are more acts of destruction in computer facilities than we ever hear about: Among others, the disgruntled programmer who thought he might be fired, and programmed the computer to destroy its data base if it did not write a salary check for him when the payroll was made up; the three striking Honeywell technicians who managed to cause a tape backup in 600 offices of the Metropolitan Life Insurance Company which strewed miles of tape over computer center floors; the tape librarian who carefully wrote a naughty word on the computer room wall and then scrambled the labels on otherwise unidentified program tapes; and the fired programmer who erased a program she had worked to develop over three years. And let's not overlook the incidents of tape head filing, physical tape destruction, cable cutting, disc scoring, and so on.

To prevent these losses we must "case harden" our computer installation. To begin, we must establish strict access control to computer facilities. In some high-risk instances this might also include installing magnetic detection equipment through which personnel and packages would pass into the facility. Our perimeter defense must also be extended to protect air vents; many substances thrown into the air intake system could cause damage to tape and equipment.

Access control is further effected by use of a single two-way facility entrance/exit. This arrangement would ideally consist of a riot door, a corridor, and a second riot door, with both doors electrically controlled and under guard around the clock. Corridors leading to the entrance of the EDP center as well as those on its perimeter and adjacent storage areas should be kept under protective surveillance, usually by closed-circuit television. Corridor walls adjacent to computer centers are usually no more solid than other office partitions, and equally blast-prone.

All unused approaches should be alarmed, including any passage or vent of 64 square inches or larger; it is important that you not overlook cable channels, manholes, air ducts, and emergency exits, or any other opening that could provide a means of ingress.

A final precaution, if necessary, is screening of the computer room. In the Westinghouse EDP center in Baltimore, which is located next to the airport, operating personnel discovered that the airport's radar was interfering with equipment operation. The machine room was shielded, solving the problem. Such shielding can protect against nearby portable transceivers which also may interfere with operations. Even low-power transmitters near the equipment may cause a problem.

Fortunately, shielding a room against the disruption of radiation also stops the VHF radiation put out by computer remote display units. This radiation can be monitored (although not very readily or easily) by electronic intercept.

Off-Premises Protection

Whatever countermeasures are taken to protect the computer center and its operation, nothing is invulnerable; the investment in data, and the company's dependence upon its ready availability, is such that extraordinary measures must be adopted to protect data.

Off-site storage is an effective safeguard of operating programs, payroll, data, etc. which are vital to a company's operation. This is done by storing off-site duplicate tapes updated according to various schedules. Some of the data stored may be of a sufficiently static nature to require revision only once a month, whereas others should be updated more frequently. How these duplicate tapes are created is a matter between your pocketbook and your data manager. Whether they shall be the product of simultaneous operation, or created through the use of journal tapes, only your needs can determine. Suffice it to say that off-site storage of duplicate data *could* be the best investment you ever made. Remember the company that stored backup data on equipment inventories and, after a disastrous fire, had a precise list of hardware that existed nowhere except among the liabilities of their insurers. In no other manner could they have proved their loss so quickly.

Back-Up Computer Operations Facility

It is customary to locate a computer of the same model and having similar peripherals in order to form a "mutual assistance" pact in the event of disastrous loss. Contrary to popular belief, however, a virtually identical "hardware" system may *not* be compatible with yours. In locating potential back-up facilities, actual tests must be made periodically to positively prove that your company's critical programs can still be run at the "back-up" installation. This could mean contracting with more than one other data center, but in any event it is a reciprocal arrangement whereby either will support the other in the event of computer loss. The periodic tests are necessary to verify that the other installations are still compatible and their schedule capable of providing time to you should it become necessary. Equipment and program changes by either you or your back-up installation could alter emergency support arrangements. For these reasons, technical communciation between you should be maintained. A mutual aid pact is not only an economical security agreement, but in all probability it is the only feasible arrangement for both parties against disaster contingencies.

Magnets

Before we leave this discussion of computer physical security, let us touch on the damage potential of a magnet.

Almost everyone has read stories of how someone with a dime-store magnet in his pocket wiped out the data of a major corporation just by passing through the tape library, or by putting a magnetic flashlight near a tape drive. Some of these stories have been dignified by publication in respectable newspapers. In a way, it's a shame the stories aren't true, because there's no question but that they add to the ever-growing mythic atmosphere surrounding the computer. The facts, though less amusing, are more comforting for EDP personnel.

Tests have shown that a distance of about 12 centimeters between tape and a magnet is enough to prevent erasure. Other tests have shown that almost half of that distance is still safe. In fact, it was not until a pocket magnet was moved over the entire surface of one side of a tape reel that marginal erasure occurred. This is not to suggest that you can afford to be careless with magnets. You can't. If someone were able to smuggle in the components of a fairly sizable electromagnet and assemble it within the protected area, even your problems would have problems. The point is that care must be taken to avoid not only undue exposure to magnets, but also the hysteria which has been generated in some quarters regarding magnets and computers.

Above all, become well-acquainted with your data processing manager and the specialists of your computer manufacturer, for they know methods of damage and data loss so simple and effective as to be unsuitable for publication.

Computer Espionage

Much has been written about the aura of cloak-and-dagger that surrounds the complex operation of a computer. We are regularly exposed to television programs that deal with incredible data thefts accomplished with ease by instruments too sophisticated to detect. By and large, this is another amusing fantasy of the entertainment world. Industrial espionage exists, certainly, and it requires strong countermeasures to prevent it, but it rarely takes the forms that we see on TV programs.

Electromagnetic or acoustical eavesdropping are both possible but they are difficult techniques to bring off successfully. A central processing unit cannot be monitored in this manner, but a typewriter terminal or a remote terminal printout or display could be. There is usually so much interference from these terminals, however, that any data intercept is difficult. Most industrial spies know that a well-placed bribe is far more effective than the stealthy installation of equipment. Monitoring devices are glamorous, but they are usually quite unneeded; indeed, the information sought is probably being thrown out in the trash as an unneeded copy.

When an industrial spy does resort to hardware, he is more apt to use the old-fashioned "bug" in some form on data communication lines. The information which is transmitted over lines from machine to remote terminals, for example, is in a digital form and, although it may sound like nothing at all to the untrained ear, it is recognizable to anyone with computer expertise. Since this data can be reached by wiretapping and other forms of monitoring (and can then be printed out on any compatible terminal), more and more companies are going to scrambling or encoding techniques for sensitive data in their files, as well as in the transmission of such information. These techniques are one more way in which access to information is denied to unauthorized people, whether internal or external. Computers have a "natural talent" both for encrypting and, it must be said, for decoding the less sophisticated ciphers. Whoever is "zeroing in" on your computer knows computers. For any code to be most effective, you should alter your code variable with some frequency, as well as take expert cryptographic advice in setting up your information encoding system.

Above all, don't overlook the obvious. Many companies get so interested in the 007 aspects of counterespionage that they forget the little things that are even more likely to do them in. Things like all those cards and read-outs in the trash barrels, and the ribbon on the printing mechanism after printing out an important program.

There are ways that spies can get at the data in your computer, ways that range from monitoring your computer traffic, to buying your EDP center trash, to bribing an employee. There is even a case of theft of data by one computer from another.[3] But it is important that you keep the problem in perspective; you cannot afford to be casual about the possibility of such theft, and yet you cannot panic into supposing that you are surrounded by electronic super-spies.

Only you can really determine whether your data base in any given area is worth stealing. Some part of it probably is. It's valuable to you, or you wouldn't have it in a computer, but you must determine its worth in terms of anyone else's time, trouble, expense and risk. And only after this determination, and an effective determination of the *degree* of value, can you decide how far you should go in setting up protective counterespionage measures.

Data Access Control

Any computer system must have routine safeguards, mainly procedural, which are primarily designed to protect the system from misuse by carelessness or ignorance. Such safeguards limit computer access to those people who are familiar with its operation and know what they are doing. These rules and procedures, if strictly administered, will go most of the way toward providing the security you need, even though security is not their first objective.

In most applications it is also important to take additional steps to prevent unauthorized users from obtaining services from the installation, and to keep authorized users from getting to data which they are not permitted to have.

In today's technology, some system of authorization and user identification is necessary to protect computer programs and files. A few years ago sensitive business information could be protected at the computer itself. Physical access to the facility could be limited, and authorized persons could be supervised in such a way as to review all machine accessing. Today companies are operating on so-

<hr>

[3]*In this case ("Computer Theft by Computer," Security World, May 1971), the victim data processing center had taken the precaution of encoding clients' proprietary information. Unfortunately they had not protected their own proprietary programs.*

called management information systems in which consoles, teletypes, and transmitting and receiving devices of various kinds are remotely located, some of them thousands of miles away. Some of these remote stations will include visual displays which could be viewed by unknown persons. It is evident that a tight system of security must be established over these remote points or their access, in order to control the flow of proprietary data.

There are three ways to "identify" a user who wishes to access the system from a remote terminal or telephone: by a password, by a key or card, or by a physical characteristic which is, in theory, unduplicatable.

Password

The most common system is the use of a password or identifying phrase. Upon a remote station signaling the computer, the user would be asked to declare his name and the system password. The software could then identify the individual and verify his access authority.

The problem with such a system is that passwords are readily picked up by unauthorized persons. They are also frequently written out, if only to avoid forgetting and, in general, they tend to become known. Variations on the fixed password system are used in various installations to overcome its difficulties. The one-time password system can be based on a series of passwords. The series is sent by registered mail to authorized users. Other systems use algebraic variations of an assigned random number often involving the date. Another system employs an extended check and cross-check over a series of questions.

The problem with a password system is that it can get totally out of hand. While it is relatively simple to restrict a system to a handful of specially cleared employees by this means, its wide application drastically restricts the potential of the technology at hand, hampering a sizable number of employees who should have some machine access. Over-involved identification procedures can be time-wasting, and the more complex they become, the more time will be uselessly expended in simply accessing the system. At some point we have begun to encounter the point of diminishing returns.

Finally, there is no way to know if a password system has been compromised until the damage has been done and that fact verified.

Cards and Keys

Systems have recently been developed whereby a user is issued a card similar to a credit card, which enables him to access while recording the card's use. Such a system speeds up the entry procedure and provides a cross-check *if* the card or key is lost or stolen. If such a card is used after its loss has been reported, the computer can be programmed to block access and give the alarm. More elaborate equipment at the remote console can "trap" the stolen card.

Physical Characteristics

Systems also exist which identify personal physical characteristics in order to allow access. These systems, generally used for sophisticated physical access control, are still in the process of development. As yet they are not foolproof and, until certain bugs are ironed out and there is further development, they will not be found in wide use.

One system tested in operation by IBM is a voice identification device. These tests are said to have indicated that normal changes in the vocal characteristics of a user could make identification impossible. A cold or abnormal huskiness could cause the system to reject authorized users.

Also in development is a fingerprint identification device for use at terminals. Devices already exist which will verify the identity of fingerprints or palm prints, but there is not as yet any application of these systems to computer-user access verification and activation.

Terminal Security

Any system of data access control should limit the accessibility of remote terminals. Here we return to solid ground from the more rarified atmosphere of the computer. We secure the rooms that house remote terminals and/or we secure the terminal itself. Keys or combinations to release these facilities are distributed as necessary.

In addition to the physical security of a remote terminal, data security at the terminal must also be considered. Any system governing access must consider the location as well as the user. Certain data might be denied to certain locations. As an example, the personnel manager would be permitted to retrieve payroll information but not from a location outside the personnel department. If he were in some other part of the building, and sought payroll information from some unauthorized terminal, the information should be automatically denied him by programmed controls. Executive system controls must monitor each data access performed for a user to insure that such data is authorized for release to that person and place. Unfortunately, many systems have no means of identifying the remote terminal in use, except by the code supplied by the user.[4]

Multi-Level Access

In order to get the greatest use possible out of the EDP operation, it is usually necessary to specify differing levels in various programs which personnel are permitted to access. It is possible, even probable, that only a limited number of people should be permitted full access to an entire program. Even fewer should be able to reach the computer's basic instructions. On the other hand, there may be many people whose work would be considerably more productive if they had access to use (not change) a part of such programs. A rigid and inefficient system which would simply deny them access is not in the company's

---

[4]*"Computer Theft by Computer,"* Security World, *May 1971.*

best interest. The more rational approach is to encourage access up to some cut-off point. This is a "permissions" system which takes over after an authorized user has accessed by password or other entry device. The names of valid system users can be explicitly stated to have certain very specific access to the file, such as *read, write, append only, execute only*, etc. In this way a file can be put to its maximum use by allowing differing and restricted use simultaneously to users at various levels of authorization.

Carelessness—the Great Enemy

The computer is invaluable to a company because, among other things, it can store an incredible number of pieces of information which are almost instantly available for retrieval in virtually any desired form or combination. It is important to remember that this information is recorded as a digital quantity. If the integrity of that number is compromised in any way (and it happens all too often) the information in the computer gets more and more out of control. In many cases the information is permanently lost.

This breakdown of information control is usually the result of inadequately trained personnel. Ignorance is probably by far the greatest "security problem" in EDP centers. It is responsible for greater and more serious problems, and constitutes a greater potential hazard, than all the criminal activities to which companies may be subjected.

Storage

Careless storage of tapes can be a very serious problem. Excess heat or humidity begins to destroy the tapes by flaking off the metal oxides. Tapes too tightly wound print through from one layer to the next. Tapes that are roughly handled lose data.

The lesson here is obvious. The data on these tapes is the very reason your company is involved with a computer operation, and the tapes containing it must be handled with the greatest respect by competent personnel.

Crime by Computer

The crimes that have been committed by imaginative souls playing games with a computer catch the public's attention in part because it's a new method of criminality. The crimes—embezzlement and theft—are those committed long before the introduction of computers, but the mystique of the computer, the apparent ease of the theft, and (usually) the dollar value involved, capture the imagination. For example:

- A programmer in a department store set up the computer to divert all his and his friends' charges into a rarely audited floating account.

- An executive of a brokerage firm managed to have company funds transferred to his personal account. Between 1951 and 1959 he made off with $250,000.

- Another brokerage employee, the firm's data processing manager in fact, made off with $81,000 by having dividend checks mailed to his home. He was able to operate nicely at this rate until caught quite by chance four years after he started.

- A 21-year-old deduced from discarded printouts how warehouses ordered equipment. Using an ordinary touch-tone telephone he had run up $1 million in stolen equipment (apparently without detection) before an accessory "blew the whistle."

There is no end to these accounts. And we can only wonder "who" and "how" and "how much" of all those who have never been caught.

It is not easy to combat computer embezzlement. Audits are complex and necessarily incomplete, and control over authorized users is limited. Certain steps can be taken, however. As in all accounting functions, duties and responsibilities should be separated. Programmers should not have direct access to the computer, as their superior knowledge of program construction constitutes a severe temptation. Software (programming) safeguards must be "built in," allowing the computer to "recognize" very specific responsibilities and authorities in various operations.

In some companies it may be found that outside computer security specialists operating independently of computer line management may be desirable. Many large auditing firms have developed a formidable expertise in auditing for (and against) embezzlement. In either case, the outside experts should be responsible to top management for audit and verification of all security procedures.

Personnel

In the last analysis no system of safeguards can prevent internal theft by computer unless you are able to recognize those people who are in a position to do the company harm, and take steps to protect company assets from them.

And in order to protect against them, you must first understand them

Let us state categorically that you cannot "protect" your company against these people by guards or access systems or validations of any kind; they are your EDP personnel and related service persons. They set up your systems and they can destroy them. And your entire company in the process. You must understand them as people and as professionals in order to set up defenses.

Let us quickly interject that these people are probably the least likely, as a group, to align themselves as "the enemy." As a group, they are not inclined to criminality, but if you fail to recognize who they are, and what they do for your company, they could be nudged into an attitude of indifference, or even of active hostility. When either of these attitudes develop, you've got trouble in EDP.

In addition, allowance must be made for the fact that programmers are mathematicians, mathematicians play games, and computers—and frustrating over-control—are great games. It has been said that the Massachusetts Institute of Technology computer must be the most secure in the world, because it has long been the ideal of virtually every student there to outwit the computer controls. Benign, vigilant control and generous access to smaller, noncritical computers are the safety valves that protect against computer "games-playing."

Screening

We will assume that you have screened personnel very carefully before hiring. We will assume that you have followed the procedures proper to filling any sensitive position. You've double-checked previous employers in person if possible. You've satisfied yourself that the background and training of each employee is up to the standards set for each position. You've properly indoctrinated each employee in the peculiarities of your operation.

During this period you've kept the new employee busy, but your indoctrination program doesn't push him into operation too rapidly. You now have a computer operation staffed with high-grade professionals who meet your specifications and who, having had ample opportunity to see what they can expect and what is expected of them, find the company meets their specifications.

It is now important that the company, especially at the upper echelons, recognize the special status of the computer group. They are a special group, a kind of elite. If they are to work effectively, they must feel that they are special and that others feel the same way. The computer group has a very special job to do; in order to do it well they frequently work 36 or even 48 hours straight. Programmers frequently want to see a job through before they go home and collapse in bed for a day or two. In rigid 9-to-5 companies the irregular hours of the computer group are sometimes misunderstood, and become a source of management irritation. They shouldn't be. Management must understand that computer technology necessarily introduces different work routines.

Computer people must be adequately paid. In this day when the technology is growing faster than intelligent, trained personnel can be turned out, your people will—at the least—leave for richer fields if your salary scale is not adjusted to both the industry level and the work load of your office. Unintelligent computer personnel, as we have pointed out, are worse than useless to you.

Adequate salary, recognition, and understanding are the watchwords when it comes to management's attitude towards the computer group. If your company has a "hard-nosed" approach to employees and you feel that this attitude toward computer personnel would be too soft, too conciliatory, then you have a problem. You would be well-advised to swallow hard, clench your teeth, and go along with the situation. There's too much at stake up there around that funny machine for you or your associates to play drill sergeant.

Once you have established a positive attitude about your computer people, you must take a look at each position and evaluate the harm that each could do.

There are three basic functioning positions: the maintenance-repair man (who is usually on the hardware supplier's payroll); the computer operator; and the systems programmer. There are sweepers, librarians, messengers (some of whom are knowledgeable trainees), as well as middle management people, but although all of these people can represent very real security problems, they do not have—or should not have—the unique one-to-one intimacy with the computer.

The maintenance engineer must from time to time "dump" the system to correct problems that appear. A "system dump" is trade jargon for an image of a computer memory at a given moment. It's not the entire data base or all of its information, but it is a copy of everything the computer is working on at that moment. It's purely a matter of chance how much information is revealed, but the possibility of exposing confidential data always exists. In addition this technician flips switches to check out circuits, and is generally into most of what the machine is doing. Techniques have been developed to keep engineering personnel away from program material under specific circumstances, but in the long run these measures are meaningless. Many malfunctions can occur on a computer and, in accordance with Murphy's Law, they frequently do. The technician will eventually be in every part of the machine, which means he has virtually unlimited access.

The computer operations men run the machine. They work around the clock and on weekends. They are usually alone at 3 A.M., which means they can do anything they want to. Naturally the operator logs all operations—but there's no one on hand to certify the log's accuracy. There's almost no action that he cannot reasonably explain.

The last and most dangerously able is the systems programmer. If his authorized access is virtually unlimited, he is in a position to alter the system. This ability is potentially the most damaging of all, since he knows how to change any program in the system and then change it back again—undetectably. Too, he can "dump" any information in the system, and easily cover it as a routine operation.

You cannot eliminate those opportunities for crime; all three of the positions we have dealt with must, in order to function, be in a position where they can do you harm. They could, in fact, put you out of business, and there are no ultimate controls that can both prevent it and still allow the EDP center to function. A totally theft- and espionage-proof computer would be an unusable machine.

Your best security measure is in an enlightened relationship with your computer people, and topnotch security-conscious leadership. If your computer personnel feel they are properly appreciated, they will be your strongest allies. If they feel unappreciated or taken for granted, they can be dangerous enemies.

Insurance

Insurance is your final security defense against disaster. Even though we have provided a security program for our EDP facility, we cannot completely eliminate the elements of risk in an EDP system. As a result, we must provide the final shelter of financial insurance.

In purchasing electronic data processing insurance you should consider an "all risks" policy. Besides insurance against embezzlement, including "catastrophic" losses, you will need a policy that includes:

- Coverage for all equipment losses.
- Coverage for data losses.
- Coverage for reconstruction of data files.
- Coverage for cost of back-up operations.
- Coverage for loss of income.

Obviously much professional advice will be necessary in choosing the proper insurance coverage. The costs of such coverage may well be influenced by the effectiveness of your EDP security program. There is profit in protection, and it is frequently evinced in reduced insurance premiums.

THE SECURITY FUNCTION

Chapter 9

THE LINES OF DEFENSE

In preceding sections of this book, we have seen that certain forces are always in motion, alert to any opportunity to overwhelm the office. We have seen how robbers, burglars, rapists, muggers, arsonists, bombers, mobs and industrial spies are pressing at the perimeter—while embezzlers and employee thieves are boring from within!

For each potential danger, we have tried to present appropriate countermeasures but, as we have already pointed out, uncoordinated "solutions" developed on a problem-by-problem basis simply aren't effective. Neither is the philosophy of meeting problems after-the-fact, which at best only results in a massive effort to "lock the barn" against a loss that has already occurred.

As company policy, reaction is too risky; there just aren't that many businesses that can survive several or, in many cases, even one major loss. No, management must be defense-minded—security-conscious—on an overall basis, defending not just against losses already incurred, but planning against potential losses which present methods could allow.

What should the size and scope of your defenses against crime be? In the last analysis, only you can answer that. Each building, each office, and each office's exposure to crime, is unique. Although there are many problems common to all, when we get "down to the nitty-gritty" *you* must determine your own formula for the defense of your office, building, or tenants. And it's not a simple formula to arrive at.

You will have to make your evaluation in terms of the potential risks, including the loss of employee productivity and morale. This evaluation is necessary for the large and the small business office alike. Obviously, the very small office operator does not face the complexities the larger offices are heir to, but he may still be a tempting target for external or internal attack, or fire. The smaller operator is obliged to both set up a security routine and to discipline himself to follow it faithfully, since in most instances he will be at once the administrator and the sole member of the security force—in addition to all his other duties!

The Role of Office Security

In setting up your defenses, remember that, unlike a military installation, a business office is essentially a public place. Since it is either selling to or servicing the public, its offices must be open to that part of the public with which it deals.

The office must be secured, but it can't be a fort. The security system must include only as many checks and as much equipment as is necessary to prevent loss without reducing productivity by over-controlling. While your security must protect against external assault, the methods used must not unduly restrict customers, vendors, and others necessary to the profitable operation of your business.

The balance is a delicate one. While you must have some protection against even subtle and sophisticated attack, you most certainly must avoid the creation of strangling red tape that might eventually suffocate your operations, a loss equal to or exceeding any loss you are trying to protect your business against. It requires careful judgment, but then we never said it was easy—few worthwhile things are.

The Role of Employee Cooperation

An effective security system requires a lot of hard, thoughtful work, and the cooperation and concern of all your employees. With their support, your system can be an effective, virtually impregnable defense, indeed.

Employee support should consist of willing cooperation in all anti-loss systems, and an awareness of the need for security. This awareness, this security-consciousness, can result in a maximizing of all security efforts. At the same time, it is important that you do not give the appearance that you encourage informing by employees on other employees; it is important that, in developing an attitude of security awareness in the office, you do not create an atmosphere of suspicion. This, too, is a matter of balance requiring your best judgment.

Cooperating employees will report doors unlocked or tampered with, suspicious visitors, minor thefts, and the many other incidents which keep the security operation effective, but which wouldn't be reported by an indifferent or uninformed office staff or building population. They will more readily go to the slight extra trouble of keeping personal and company property under lock and key; they will be more careful and concerned about fire hazards, and about perimeter integrity and unauthorized visitors, and thereby materially assist in reducing fire and general security hazards.

In short, an informed staff is invaluable in the war against office crime and loss. Any office or building that enlists the aid of its personnel, which creates an atmosphere of intelligent awareness of the potential dangers, has taken a major step toward crime and loss control.

The Role of Insurance

Since no loss prevention system can be absolutely invulnerable, insurance is vital to protect against losses that may occur in spite of the best planned and most vigorously administered loss prevention program. But insurance cannot pay for the loss of productivity in an office shocked by some crime of violence, it can't pay for the drop in morale (let alone the losses) due to repeated theft, it can't replace customers lost due to business interruption and the destruction of valuable records, and it rarely can begin to pay for the man-hours required to piece together data lost by computer damage. The possibilities of irreparable loss are almost endless, and yet there is still a significant number of managers who feel that their security problems are under control because they "have insurance."

And let's not forget that incredible number of offices which have neither insurance *nor* any overall security program. There will always be a long-shot player, but *no* security program and *no* insurance? That's really pressing your luck.

If you, like Candide's tutor, Dr. Pangloss, believe that "everything's for the best, in this best of all possible worlds," then maybe you should risk those astronomical odds; but if you are living in today's world you will want to set up reasonable defenses against the enemies who lurk outside and within your office. They are there. Maybe they haven't gotten to you yet—but they will. Just be sure you'll be as ready for them as they are for you.

Chapter 10

DEVELOPING THE SECURITY FUNCTION

How the security function is to be administered, whether by an administrator having other responsibilities, or by a security professional heading a security department, will depend upon the needs and goals of the organization —office or office building—for which security is needed.

The final solution is rarely the result of a single planning decision; even where management intends from the first to establish a formal security operation, the eventual organization will vary withexperience and circumstances.

In some cases, creating a security staff to which is delegated the security function has occurred much more by accident than by planning. Each reaction to a crime took the company or building management further toward a security program. While some companies (and the management of newer high-rise buildings) evaluated their problems and organized their security departments into existence, most office security departments "just grew like Topsy." This "gradual" security began, in some cases, with the installation of better locks, then improved lighting, then alarms, and so on. Eventually the hardware was supported by manpower—or manpower was supported by hardware—and a security operation was born.

While this gradual or reactive approach may eventually develop into an effective security operation (and may not), it can present very real dangers. Until a complete security effort is in effect, you are exposed to all the risks you have not yet recognized. You may be feeling secure because you are guarding against minor risks while you have little or no protection against major risks. Experience has shown that management is well advised to plan, organize, and complete the development of the security function, rather than to just let it evolve as reactions to problems that have already occurred.

Once the need for an all-around security function is recognized, management needs to begin with an understanding of the nature of a private security force and how it relates to the operation of the company as a whole.

The Role of Private Security

What is needed is a definition of private security. While private security has been defined in brief as "the business of protecting business," in the office the following definition might be more helpful:

Office security is a staff function, an integrated service department whose main purpose is to protect and defend company personnel and company assets.

This definition, however, is still incomplete. It does not incorporate the factor of employee cooperation. Employee participation is both an essential of security, and an index of the success of the security department, judged on the degree of involvement and cooperation demonstrated by company employees in general, for without cooperation throughout the office, security cannot succeed.

Security Is Not Law Enforcement

Proprietary security and public law enforcement are two quite different things. While the public tends to confuse the two, their scope, their objectives and their methods of operation are necessarily quite different. Usually operational only within the confines of its own building or office, private security is charged with the responsibility of crime prevention, of creating and supervising systems to protect employees and property. Security rarely apprehends criminals. On the other hand, security departments can and do investigate speculatively, unlike law enforcement, which investigates only identified crimes, and then only to the extent necessary for prosecution.[1]

Law enforcement acts on the premise that detecting, prosecuting and confining the criminal frees society of this undesirable element and thus, in the long run, will prevent crime and protect persons and property. Private security is interested in direct, before-loss protection of persons and property, and has little or no interest in prosecution. The direct protection of private property by police—beyond alarm response (which may take three hours), and the passing of an occasional patrol car—is beyond the capacity of today's hard-pressed law enforcement, and no improvement in this situation can reasonably be expected. On the other hand, the well-planned presence of private security, backed by well-considered and supervised systems, prevents crime, protects property and personnel, and insures an atmosphere in which business can profitably be conducted. This role cannot be expected of law enforcement.

In addition, private security enjoys a somewhat greater legal latitude. In the eyes of the law, any representative of security, from a guard to the director of security, is simply another employee, a "private citizen." Court decisions have continuously affirmed this over the years. Miranda and Escobedo, "reasonable cause," the admissibility of voluntary admissions are legal requirements only applicable to sworn law enforcement. And the policeman is held to be a law enforcement officer at all times—even when

---

[1]As previously noted, insurance recovery depends upon extensive proofs; for the purpose of prosecution, only proof of a few thefts, or even just one theft, is needed. Police cannot investigate inventory shortages or the "mysterious disappearance" of stock or equipment. Security can and does fill these needs.

"moonlighting" as security personnel. Only when deputized or acting at the request of law enforcement are private security personnel held to be subject to the laws governing law enforcement personnel.

As a "private citizen" a security officer may not coerce, intimidate, or make any material promise in return for an admission. As an agent of the company, his interrogations must not accidentally constitute an arrest within the widely-construed meaning of the law,[2] and his searches of employee property on company premises must be accomplished within local or state law.

The Importance of Nothing

In security the best news management can get is that "nothing happened." Unfortunately, the problem of evaluating such good news is difficult indeed. Money has been spent and energy expended to result in a "nothing." All too often management may forget the origin of the security function and decides, "See, we don't need security after all."

Actually, the security function tends to have been established only after a sizeable loss, or a significant series of losses. This, of course, contributes to the patchwork development of the security operation. That some security is needed in every office should be beyond question. How extensive this function should be must be determined by an evaluation of the crime rate of the area, the history of loss or mysterious disappearance, the potential for loss, and the known or suspected risk to assets and personnel.

In security, half a loaf is worse than no loaf at all. When management knows there is no security, it tends to conduct itself accordingly. Where a fractional security function has been established, even though management *knows* it has merely hired "doorknob shakers" to make limited

---

[2] *The right of any suspect being questioned by a "private citizen" is to refuse to answer and to leave. If the suspect is detained, or believes that he cannot leave, a citizen's arrest has occurred.*

rounds of inspection, the delusion gradually develops that the company now has genuine protection and somehow that warm glow of security seems to embrace even those risks management knows do not have security protection.

This is why many contemporary offices and building managements are moving toward establishing the whole security function at one time, or to rapid upgrading of existing security functions presently too limited to offer adequate protection against the true range of risks.

The Security Professional

Today's security director is a man not only already competent in his field, but always capable of growth, for it is vital that he have the ability to adapt to changing circumstances and to grow as the business he protects is growing. In the past, security directors have almost invariably been drawn from the ranks of retired law enforcement—police, FBI, and military—and this is still true to some degree. While many of these men have been highly successful in adapting to their new field, perhaps an equal number have not. Those that were not successful in adapting were those who tended to be rigid in their attitudes. They brought with them the quite different mission and attitudes of police officers, and tried to apply the adversary techniques familiar to them to these new circumstances. Except in rare instances, this doesn't work.

The security man must be cooperative, innovative, and flexible. He must seek out the best solutions for his assignment without depending upon tradition—and in office security there is very little tradition. It's a brand-new field; so new, in fact, that communication between its professionals is hampered by their inability to identify their opposite numbers. As in other new security fields, this inevitably leads to "re-inventing the wheel," to developing by trial and error systems that have already been developed and tested in practice. It is unfortunate but understandable that many of the men in office security feel isolated and alone.

For this reason, it is of great urgency that, while each security administrator or executive must be involved with all the security problems within the office, he must at the same time be becoming involved with, and maintaining, outside security contacts. These outside contacts consist of security directors of as many offices as possible, particularly in his community. They include regular informal communications and cooperation with local police and fire department officials. They may also include professional and trade associations, trade publications, and state and federal bulletins. In short, outside contacts and information are vital to a competent security operation. They afford the security director the opportunity to continually update his approach to his job, as well as apprise him of new dangers or new criminal techniques that might endanger his company. And the ability to work cooperatively and constructively with these outside contacts is as essential as is the need to develop and maintain such contacts. Even the "part-time" security administrator of the smaller office will need these contacts and cooperation.

Security Attitudes

Within the office, the security professional must show the same ability to communicate. Even though his job necessarily precludes the image of being "everybody's pal," everything the security staff should be must be apparent in the conduct of the administrator. He must be friendly without being intimate, conscientious, able to lead and act independently, a man of obvious integrity and ability. Given this kind of example, these qualities will be seen in the security personnel; without it, the best security staff will disintegrate. With these qualities, the security mission can gain the cooperation of all personnel; without them, security will be disregarded, if not disliked.

The Formal and Informal Organizations

It is important for the security manager to be aware of, and sensitive to, relationships within the organization. Too many office administrators prefer to maintain the fiction that the office operates on the basis of the formal table of organization and within the strict confines of company policy as outlined by management in announcements, memoranda, and handbooks. The competent security manager, like the effective office manager, knows better. He knows that there is a formal organization and that there is also an informal organization which, though not often in opposition to the organization charts, is created by the alliances and antipathies inevitable in any society. Both know that it is this informal structure that creates the day-to-day operational processes, as well as the office "grapevine," which is the route of unofficial communication and an important index of company morale. Given a sensitive appreciation of the informal organization, as well as solid knowledge of the formal organization charts, the security manager is in an excellent position to keep abreast of the state of the office, and to spot problems as they develop.

Only time on the job will fully tie your new security manager into your unique informal organization but, if the security director is to be really effective, his indoctrination should include a briefing on this "shadow" organization.

Role of Management Philosophy

It is above all essential that security maintain a specific and uniform approach to its job, an approach consistent with the job to be done and with management policy or attitudes. The development of this approach is not always easy. Many managers find it difficult to verbalize their general philosophy. They may want a free and easy, open atmosphere while still recognizing that too much openness can be an invitation to criminal attack. Other managers may prefer a strict, by-the-numbers operation, and yet recognize that too rigid a policy can result in low morale and high employee turnover. In many ways it is up to security to strike the proper balance between what is said and what is meant, and to proceed on an approach appropriate to the climate of the particular office. It is always essential that the security approach be in harmony with the overall atmosphere, for in such harmony—or the lack of it—lies the difference between positive and negative in security's contribution.

The Security Professional

As we can see, the security function has passed far beyond the lone roundsman or watchman isolated from the work of the company. The security professional expects to be, and should be, "up front where the action is." He must be able to speak to employee groups on employee safety and the response to fire and bomb threats; to develop and implement contingency programs for emergency response; to know the capabilities and limitations of security equipment and staffing; to construct and supervise an appropriate training program for his security people; to develop procedures for the protection of confidential information; to set up a review program to regularly re-evaluate all security systems in the office; and to educate management in security's role in loss prevention. And these are only a sampling of the areas in which the security professional should be able to move with confidence.

Clearly we are describing a kind of professional new to office management, though well-established in retailing, colleges, and hospitals, as well as in manufacturing. Further, we are recognizing that there is no single yardstick for office security programs or for the responsible security officer; growth is inherent in the responsibilities of the position, and much must still be learned on the job.

Security is largely a self-taught field; though at least two colleges offer a baccalaureate degree in security (and one offers security as a major in a master's degree), not only does the most relevant training come through experience, but no real substitute for experience has been found. The rare security executive who feels he has nothing to learn is understandably regarded with extreme skepticism by his peers in security, as he should be by management.

Security in the Table of Organization

Because of its vital importance, the contemporary security function should be the concern of company management at the highest level, for experience has amply demonstrated that if security is to be effective it must have—and must be *seen* to have—the support of top management. Without this support, security cannot possibly command the respect and cooperation necessary to the success of its protective function.

While the visible support of top and middle management is a *sine qua non* of competent security, opinion differs as to the level of management at which security should report. There are many advocates of having security report to the president of the company, or to the highest-ranking financial executive, in order to avoid the common experience of having adverse information blocked or diluted in transmission. On the other hand, carried to extremes such an arrangement could burden an already-overworked top officer with excessive detail. Whoever the responsible executive may be, it is important that he be genuinely involved and familiar with company risks, in order to evaluate whether the security operation is controlling and reducing those risks. In many offices, this role simply cannot be squeezed into top management's portfolio.

The solution, it would seem, would be to tailor the decision to the specific instance, to seek the best choice for the particular situation. Where the top executive *can* be involved, and where the risk of loss is recognized as great, the responsibility for security supervision may be placed there; where the risk is believed to be less and top executives are already fully occupied, the responsibility should logically be placed on the highest-ranking executive available whose other assignments are most compatible with evaluation of security administration and its results. In situations where there is a particularly high risk, or where there has been a high incidence of loss, it might be wise to delegate other responsibilities away from the top in order to make room for security supervision at the highest level. In any event, security's access to top management must *never* be wholly blocked.

Security Administration

In small offices, the direct administration of the security operation, as well as its supervision, is often assigned to executives or administrators having other primary responsibilities; treasurer, controller, head of administration, office manager.

In larger offices and in large buildings where there is a security staff (and particularly a guard force) requiring supervision, where security administration is clearly a full-time position, the operational responsibility is assigned to a security administrator. Titles for this position range from Executive Security Officer and Director of Security down through Security Manager, Security Supervisor, Chief of Security, or even Sergeant, depending upon the structure of the particular office and company organization, and the degree and kind of responsibility delegated.

In any event, the top security administrator, whatever his title, should have the following kinds of access—among others:

- be aware of, and have access to, the operation of every department.
- understand and have access to company statistics.
- be aware of company planning *prior to implementation*, particularly building plans and alterations, and office relocation.
- understand and have access to computer operations.
- be involved in, and knowledgeable about, personnel

department operations, and have access to personnel records.

- be knowledgeable about, and have access to operations such as purchasing, equipment and equipment replacement, petty cash handling, mail room operations, and the various company accounting procedures.
- be involved in management discussions and policy decisions in all areas which may affect, even marginally, office security and safety.

While access to some of these areas may seem unusually liberal to the executive unfamiliar with the function of security, professionals in the security field can illustrate from known cases the need for every one of them. For example, smoke towers were designed and the building virtually ready for occupancy before it was observed that no provision had been made to provide a railing or barrier in the open portion of the tower on any floor—the first misstep on the top floor was a 24-story drop! The cost of adding railings after construction was $60,000. A multi-million-dollar computer center processing virtually irretrievable corporate data was placed behind ceiling-to-floor plate-glass windows at sidewalk level at a major downtown intersection. Firms handling negotiables in the millions of dollars have unwittingly (and carelessly, to say the least) hired ex-convicts to deliver them. And so on, apparently endlessly.

A Challenging Task

Obviously, the development of an effective, operations-integrated security function is almost as great a challenge as is security's assignment of loss prevention. However, without the necessary access, information, authority, and contingency planning, the goal of security will never be truly fulfilled.

BETTER SHRED - THAN READ!
WHEN DISPOSING OF COMPANY
CONFIDENTIAL
DOCUMENTS - USE THE
PAPER SHREDDER
NOT
YOUR
WASTE
BASKET
SECURITY

Chapter 11

THE SECURITY SURVEY

Before you can set up an effective defense against crime, you must have a clear idea of where the danger points are. In order to set up systems to protect against your risks, you need a systematic and specific picture of your security requirements in every part of your office and in every aspect of your office operation. This "total view" can only be developed by a complete and painstaking survey.

Survey Responsibility

In small offices already having a security program, the senior officer responsible for security is usually either the treasurer, the controller, the head of administration (whatever title he may hold), or the office manager.

In larger offices, where the security function necessarily covers a wider area and where it employs a staff whose sole function is security, there will usually be a security officer in charge of the operation. He, in turn, will report to one of the company officers listed above.

As we have noted throughout this book, it is vital that the company officer having the ultimate responsibility for security be as highly placed as possible. Beyond the expression of management's commitment this represents, a top-ranking executive as the officer to whom security reports brings to the responsibility a broader base for evaluating decisions involving security. The higher the executive, the greater the overview. It is to an executive having a company-wide overview, and one who regularly sits in on staff meetings with the chief executive officer, that the reporting level of security must be assigned, if the Executive Security Officer (as we will now refer to him) is to have the access necessary.

Whether the Executive Security Officer personally makes the security survey on which planning is to be based, or whether he employs an outside security consultant specializing in surveys, will depend upon the complexity and extent of the survey needed, and the time he has available to do such a job. Whatever the decision, the Executive Security Officer must have the background and the special knowledge of your company necessary to evaluate the survey results and to develop from it the best recommendations for your office security program.

The Survey—General Outline

If you hire a qualified consultant to conduct your security survey, your major decisions will be on the degree to which his recommendations can or should be implemented. However, for your evaluation of his survey, it would be well to be familiar with the elements of a useful security survey, in order to assess whether your consultant has adequately covered every base in his findings. On the other hand, if you plan to conduct the survey internally, the following outline will be equally helpful, by enabling you to handle it in a systematic manner.

This survey guide is divided into three parts:

- The building.
- The traffic.
- Company departments.

Each part includes a number of areas that will require your attention. The extent to which you study each area will depend upon your potential for loss in that area and, therefore, your need to reduce that risk. As previously mentioned, the very small office will have fewer requirements, but as the size of the office increases the needs increase in multiples. If you have any doubts about the survey capabilities of your own personnel, or if you wish to make doubly sure of their assessment of your risks, you would be well advised to call in a qualified security specialist.[1]

The Building

Although most office workers spend a third of their waking hours in the office, few of them are genuinely familiar with any part of the building other than their own work area. On the other hand, the thief who has picked your building as a target knows it well. He's gone over it from roof to basement to find all the security weaknesses. He may well be a professional in his business; you'd better be one in yours. You cannot afford to do less than a reasonably diligent thief would do in pursuit of his trade.

In evaluating your office space and the building in which it is located you must:

- Consider all building entrances and exits as security problems. (This includes rooftop access, an important point frequently overlooked.)
- Consider all building windows adjacent to, or a story above or below, other rooftops as security problems.
- Check all building receiving and shipping docks, basements and lobby freight elevators for accessibility, and as to the procedures followed in receiving and shipping.
- Check to determine if other tenants in your building have Gate Pass systems.
- Does your building have a properly supervised sign-in log for off-hours workers?

---

[1]*The term "qualified" means both knowledgeable and experienced in the specific or major area of your risk. Reputable consultants will not hesitate to give you, in confidence, the names of companies for whom they have conducted similar surveys, and the names of persons you can contact there for confirmation of these activities.*

- Do elevators switch to manual, or can floors be locked against access, outside of normal business hours? When are they switched over? By whom can they then be operated?
- Are there late night or early morning deliveries? (This is often the case if there is a restaurant or employee cafeteria.)
- Who collects the trash, and how and when is it removed from the building?
- Where are the fire hoses, what is their condition, and how far into your office could they reach?
- Are there fire extinguishers in or near each of your offices? Of what type are they?
- Does the building have exterior fire escapes, enclosed fire stairs, or "smoke tower" fire stairs? Can floors be re-entered from the fire stairs?

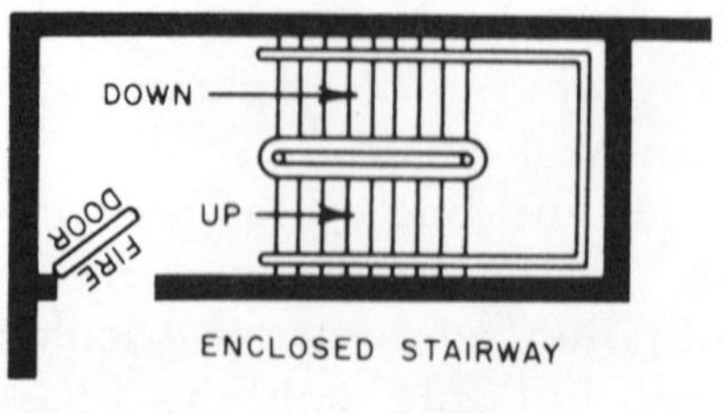

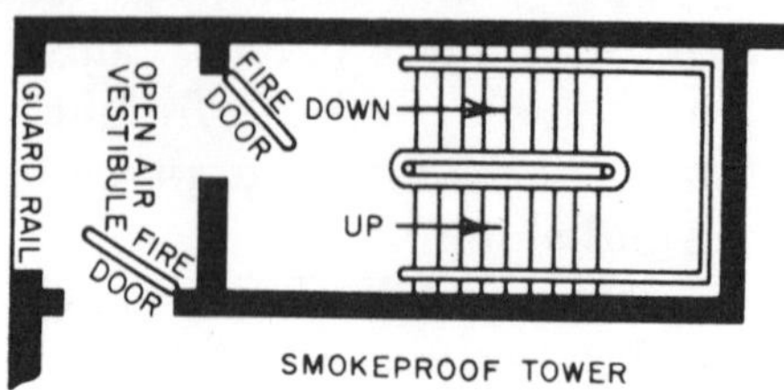

PLAN VIEWS OF TYPES OF EXITS

Stair enclosure prevents fire on any floor trapping persons above. Smokeproof tower is better, as opening to air at each floor largely prevents chance of smoke in stairway. (Fire Protection Handbook, 13th ed., National Fire Protection Association, Boston, Massachusetts, 1969.)

- In what direction do your fire stair doors open? (While all codes appear to require that fire exits open out from the interior, a fire in New York City claimed the lives of several people trapped against a fire door that opened in, rather than out.)
- Are washrooms open to the public? Can a key system be arranged for tenant personnel? Are equipment rooms locked?
- Do fire stairs open into the building lobby or to the exterior of the building? Can anyone exit unobserved by use of these stairs?
- Are hallways adequately lighted? What provision is made for emergency lighting?
- Is a master key system in use? Are issued keys cross-referenced? Have locks been changed when keys were lost? How are keys controlled and secured?
- What alarms are in use in the building (exit alarms, tenant alarms, etc.)?

These checklists of questions can be used to record the physical security of the office and building. Their answers become a reference for future planning, and a record which can be used to compare old locks, alarms, doors, etc. to later installations.

The Traffic

A careful evaluation of traffic patterns within, to, and from your office is critical to establishing an effective security system. Depending on the type and volume of business your office does, this traffic can be very heavy or quite light in the course of a normal business day. You have no wish to reduce this traffic, but you probably should control or channel it. In any event you must be thoroughly familiar with it, its peak periods, who it consists of, and what its condition is at various times of the day. External traffic consisting of visitors, customers, vendors, servicemen, messengers, deliverymen, etc. will probably be of first interest to you, but in the interest of personnel protection, as well as company security, you need to be familiar with established internal traffic as well.

External Traffic

- Who delivers the mail in the morning and at what time? What happens to empty mail sacks?
- Do you have a vendor who brings in coffee for coffee breaks? Is the wagon inspected before it leaves your offices?
- If you or other tenants have a cafeteria, there will be night or early morning deliveries by a number of vendors. Who are they? What time do they arrive? How are they admitted? What equipment do they bring with them? Do they leave with the same equipment? Do they have access to other parts of your office? Of the building? Are they inspected when they leave?
- Do you send records out for storage? How are they picked up? By whom? When? Is an inspection made of boxes so picked up?
- Do you authorize certain people or organizations to sell or solicit contributions in your office? Who are these people? How do they carry material in? Are they inspected when they leave? Are their bona fides checked periodically?
- Who does the cleaning in the building? In your offices? Are they given keys? Who is accountable for keys given cleaning personnel? Do they have access to master keys? Are cleaning personnel bonded?
- Who does the painting in the building? How does he operate? Under whose supervision?
- What construction company does most of the interior work? How do they operate?
- Who are the servicemen, the water cooler men, the machine maintenance men, the air conditioning people, the phone people, the electricians, etc.? Are

their tool cases inspected when they leave? How are their bona fides established? By the building? At the office? Are alarm company servicemen allowed unlimited access?

- How is furniture moved into and out of the building? When is this done? What security is provided when such moving takes place at night or on weekends?
- Do you or other tenants have substantial messenger traffic? Are messengers handled by a receptionist or other coordinating person, or are they free to go directly to the person requesting or receiving the messenger service?
- How are job applicants handled? Is one person responsible for receiving all job applicants? Could someone posing as an applicant "case" or steal from your office?
- How are visitors received in your building? At the lobby? At the elevator? By your office receptionist? Are visitors met and escorted in your office space? Are there precise, published instructions for handling all visitors?
- Which departments of the office (or which tenants) have the heaviest incoming traffic? Who does this traffic consist of?
- Who can use the freight elevator? Does it operate automatically? Does it have an operator? When is it secured against operation? Does it open into your office space?
- Do you permit a shoeshine man to operate in your premises? Is his box inspected on leaving?
- Are people claiming official status, such as building inspector or fire inspector, permitted free access within your building or office or are they escorted? Are their ID's checked? By whom? Is there a policy for handling this type of visitor?

Internal Traffic

- Do building and office personnel use public stairs and/or fire stairs, as well as elevators, to go from floor to floor, or only elevators?
- What comprises the heaviest traffic through your office or through your building? Where do they go? For what reason?
- Do you use messengers internally? Have they access to offices which may be temporarily unoccupied? Are these messengers your employees?
- How is mail delivered throughout your office?
- Do secretaries carry cash in hand or do they carry it in an envelope?
- Who is authorized to open your reception area doors in the morning? At what time? Who closes it at night? At what time? Who verifies this? What provision is made to insure that this area is never unattended?
- Which floors have the heaviest traffic flow?
- If you have a cafeteria, who uses it besides your employees?
- Do you have a "bookie" in the building? In the office? How do people place bets with him? Are there signs of loan-sharking?
- Are office machines moved from floor to floor (or from office to office on the same floor)? Who can authorize such moves? Are office machines secured in place?
- Is someone selling hard or "soft" drugs? (This should be considered. Drugs are sold in schoolyards and factories, and there sure isn't anything sacred about your office.)

An interesting point to keep in mind when making a security survey is the knowledge of the maintenance crew. Maintenance personnel (whether your own or the building's) have more first-hand knowledge about the personnel, the building, and the normal traffic than anyone else is apt to have. They get involved with every tenant or every department. They are aware of the movement of goods and materials into, through, and out of the premises, and probably hear as much behind-the-scenes gossip as any group in the building. They usually have keys to more areas than a tenant or office manager. Keep the maintenance people in mind when you evaluate your security needs; their cooperation can be a big help in your survey and in the security program itself.

Weekend Traffic

It is essential that you have a sign-in log—preferably in the lobby of the building but, failing that, at least in your own premises. Such a log will soon identify weekend traffic patterns. Authorized weekend workers normally prefer working on Saturday, arriving around 10:00 A.M. and leaving by 3:00 P.M.

Night Traffic

There is necessarily a certain amount of traffic in every building after hours—cleaning, maintenance, elevator operators, watchmen, alarm company servicemen, etc. There are also deliveries by vendors in certain buildings and in all buildings housing a cafeteria or restaurant.

This schedule of night traffic should be analyzed by study of the sign-in log. A pattern will probably emerge from which you can predict the events and possible trouble spots of the night. Such records can be valuable in investigating night crime in your building.

The Departments

Each department within your organization should be evaluated separately in terms of its particular security risk. Consider each one from the viewpoint of the potential for loss.

- What equipment can be stolen from the department?
- Are there any special problems relating to theft of personal belongings?
- Is the department function such that it is vulnerable to embezzlement?
- Can fraud or confidence routines be perpetrated against the department either from internal or external attack?
- Does the department have cash funds or negotiable instruments on hand (i.e. petty cash, customer accounts, company safekeeping, etc.)?
- Does the department house confidential records?
- Does the department house computer equipment, including tapes?
- Does the department have "attractive" items in it, such as drug storage, jewelry samples, valuable art, etc.?
- Does the department have heavy external traffic?
- Would a fire in this department cripple your operation? Is it near a fire hazard area?

Vulnerable Departments

In the following pages we will discuss those office departments that are most vulnerable to crime. We will also discuss a method of evaluating the degree of vulnerability.

Personnel Department

- Can the department area be locked off from the rest of the floor after hours?
- Are files kept locked when not in use?
- Who has the keys to doors? To file cabinets? (Night access to the department is tantamount to file access.)
- What system is followed in adding new personnel to the payroll? In terminating employees from it?
- What are the working relationships between

members of personnel and of payroll departments?

- Does the department make applicant reference checks with past employers, schools, etc.? Are these checks accomplished by letter, phone or personal visit?

Security of personnel files are of extreme importance. Normally these files will contain information on every employee, past and present, from Chairman of the Board on down. This information is confidential[2] and must be handled that way.

The Accounting Department

The Accounting Department has full functional supervision of your company's money and will almost always be the area most vulnerable to major loss due to crime. Even though some protective systems undoubtedly are already in operation in this area, you will benefit from re-examination and re-evaluation of the security of the accounting operation. For convenience, let us break it down into petty cash, accounts receivable, accounts payable, and company bank accounts.

Petty Cash, Cashier, and Check-Cashing

- How accessible is the cash operation to hallways, stairs, and elevators?
- Do posted signs clearly announce to everyone, including external traffic, where the cashier is located and what the operating hours are?
- Is cash on hand ever enough to tempt an employee to abscond with it? To attract an armed robbery?
- Study the existing system of cash disbursements and consider what constructive changes could be made in forms, controls and audits.
- What procedures prevent the cashier from forging vouchers and pocketing the cash?

[2]*It is not generally recognized that there is enough information in the average employment application to make possible a full-scale investigation of personal matters not relevant to employment.*

- Have you examined all the possibilities of collusion in the petty cash operation?
- If employees are paid in cash, or checks are cashed as a service to employees, is the security provided equal to the risk?

Accounts Receivable

The Accounts Receivable section processes payments received. The most common fraud in this area consists of "short-stopping" these payments. In the event an account pays in cash, as when delivery is C.O.D., that payment is clearly subject to theft. More difficult, but nonetheless more common, is to destroy the billing and cash the check.

In evaluating this possibility you should:

- Consider the billing procedure in accounts receivable, with particular attention to the forms used and the separate authorizations required.
- Try to determine how difficult it might be to cash a check payable to your company.
- Is it remotely possible for one person to destroy all records of billing while personally receiving and cashing the incoming check? For two people?
- Is it possible to alter invoices (and supporting documents, if any) to show a lesser amount payable? To destroy shippers so that there is no billing?

Accounts Payable

This area is extremely susceptible to attack, usually from within. The standard fraud is the phoney invoice from a dummy corporation. The company check is mailed to a post office box or other drop, where it is collected by the embezzler or an accomplice. This fraud is difficult but not impossible in a computerized operation, since payments are authorized by individuals.

- Re-examine the forms and the system of checks and balances on a careful step-by-step basis.
- Do you check the authenticity of new accounts? Are

all receivers double-checked against their authorizing vouchers?

Payroll

This area, along with Accounts Payable, has most often been attacked in today's office. The usual method has been to insert a fictitious name into the payroll records and collect checks drawn for that employee.

Here it is important to review the entire procedure of making up the payroll, drawing checks, and distributing them.

- What is the system for introducing a new employee into the payroll procedure?
- Are there corresponding records in personnel and in payroll and are these cross-checked to verify employment?
- Is it possible to conceal fictitious employees by collusion between an employee in payroll and one in personnel?

Company Bank Accounts

- Can one person transfer unlimited company funds?
- Is there a ceiling which limits withdrawal of company funds?
- What instructions have been given to the bank? By whom?
- Are two signatures necessary for large single withdrawals or transfers? Can either or both be machine-written? Who controls the signature blocks?
- Who audits the company bank accounts? How often?
- Could the treasurer or controller leave with your company's bank accounts?

If this last question is annoying, keep in mind that desire and opportunity comprise all the conditions necessary for embezzlement. If your financial officer could, in a moment of weakness he might. It is your responsibility to protect your company, but it is also axiomatic that no one man should bear the temptation of having all the company's funds at his disposal.

The Data Processing Department

- Check all your financial programs and determine if adequate audit procedures are used in conjunction with such programs.
- Check on the manner in which printouts of secret or confidential information are handled.
- Are there duplicate tapes? Where are they stored? Are they up-to-date?
- Who can enter the computer operations center? Where can they go within the center? Can messengers enter the computer room?
- What are the fire prevention and fire protection procedures in the center? What training is given employees in fire prevention, location of hoses and fire extinguishers, and fire extinguishing systems?
- How well can the computer area be physically secured against overt attack? Against unauthorized acquisition of data? Unauthorized access to operating programs?
- Check all entrances to computer areas, including tape storage. Who has authorized keys, combinations or other access? When was the list of authorizations last audited? Who has access during off-hours and how is this recorded?
- Do you have a fail-safe indicator of actual computer use and a concurrent log of authorized use? Are these cross-checked?
- Re-study your program accessing controls.

Purchasing

In considering the purchasing function we will confine ourselves to the purchase of material for the office itself, such as supplies, equipment, furniture decorating, cleaning contracts and the full range of services from car leasing to computer maintenance. We are not here concerned with the more sophisticated buyer of raw goods and materials in a fabricating operation, which presents somewhat similar problems with considerably more complex possibilities.

In today's office, the buyer of office materials is frequently the office manager, the service manager, or the administrative manager. Whatever his title, he is frequently responsible for a number of areas in addition to the purchasing function. In larger offices, especially in highly volatile businesses, the volume of purchasing is usually such that a position or even a department is established to perform the purchasing duties.

The purchasing agent is faced with every possible temptation. If he is responsible for any appreciable volume of business, he will be catered to by unscrupulous vendors. Besides excessive entertainment, temptations in the form of kick-backs, trips to Europe, and other inducements are regularly offered by vendors seeking an advantage. While this is not a matter that should directly involve security, security may be called upon to investigate unexplained affluence. Certainly purchasing should be carefully administered and management should be constantly aware of the potential problems.

There are some areas in purchasing that must be evaluated from a security viewpoint:

- Study the possibility of the fraudulent invoice. This device is the same in purchasing as it is in accounts payable, or as it is, in effect, in payroll. What audit procedures check authenticity of vendors? Of receipts? How frequently?
- Can a system of competitive bids be established for all major office purchases?
- Check out purchase forms used, authorizations to purchase, authorizations to pay, delivery receipts, etc. Can copies be destroyed or altered without detection?
- How often do you inventory and test-audit office

equipment, furniture, supplies, or other physical assets? Are there unexplained "shortages"?

- Selling is often a part of the purchasing function. Who negotiates for the sale of paper or other waste from your office? Do you verify the actual amount carted out? How are used furnishings or equipment sold or traded? How are they removed from the premises? What records are kept on the sale or trading of such material? Is the system audited?

Miscellaneous

- What guards against theft of stamps? Unauthorized use of postage meter? Theft of funds allocated to postage? What records do you keep of postage meter usage? Can it be cross-checked?
- What system do you use to control office supplies? Do you have a requisition form? Declining inventory? "Sign out" record?
- Since certain documents may not be reproduced on your office copying machine, either for legal reasons or because of company policy, have you posted a list of these proscribed documents and copying practices at the copy machine?
- If you have a large graphics department with plate-makers and offset presses, have you taken steps to prevent its possible use for counterfeiting money or documents, for photographing company confidential documents, etc?
- Do you exercise control over availability of all forms that can order merchandise, verify receipt of merchandise, or authorize payment in any way? Are these forms always numbered and their sequence maintained?

And More

This brief tour through areas of your office where you may be particularly vulnerable should serve as a guide to your own all-important survey. We cannot include, or even identify, every sensitive spot in your organization; only you can do that, by painstaking point-by-point inspection and consideration. You must omit nothing possible, because you cannot afford to only protect against the probable.

Set Up Your Security Files

As a result of your evaluation you now have records describing doors, windows, trouble spots and other parts of the building. You will have a description of both internal and external traffic. You will have a thorough breakdown on the operations of each department. You should have a useful profile of the company's daily activities.

But don't stop there. To be effective these records must be accurate, kept up-to-date, and reviewed and modernized on a regular basis. You should also collect the latest information on drugs and drug distribution, demonstrations, criminal methods, arson and bomb threats, con games, and fire prevention and safety. You should develop a library of texts and files for relevant articles from newspapers and magazines.

In short, you must develop as much data as possible on crime as does, or might, relate to your office, in order to at least stay even with the ever more sophisticated crook.

As you create and broaden these files they will become increasingly useful in your security operation. You will be able to determine and thus prepare for many kinds of assault on your office, many of which are predictable if you have the data on which to base your prediction.

For example:
- You will be able to predict which days and seasons will be the busiest for the security operation.
- You will soon see what areas attract the most criminal attention, and are therefore the greatest risk.
- You will have a "picture" of the type and number of crimes occurring.

- You will be forewarned by emerging patterns of crimes against personnel on pay day, or the holiday weekends which seem to be most attractive to the criminal, or the internal patterns which predict (or, perhaps, encourage) criminal activity.
- What manner of entrance and exit is most used by thieves.

The careful and thoughtful use of the data obtained is not only helpful in your defense against crime in the office, it is essential if you are to have any hope of success.

Chapter 12

THE SECURITY OPERATION

With the results of your security survey in hand, you should have a thorough overview of your security problems and be able to identify most of the "soft spots" in your defense against crime and loss.

You may be pleasantly surprised to discover that your physical and procedural defenses are already strong—that you need install only a few new systems. But you probably won't find that. If yours is like most offices and office buildings, and if the survey has been carefully done, you are almost certain to have discovered that several new security programs will be needed to achieve any real degree of security. If this is the case, you have basic decisions to make.

How to Implement

First you must decide whether to implement your entire security program or reformation at one time (or within a short period of time), or whether you will set up systems, step-by-step, on a pre-determined priority schedule.

The Gradual Approach

This "step-by-step" approach is still the most widely used method of installing or upgrading a security program. It has its advantages. It allows you to get into programs "on the installment plan," so to speak. You pick the trouble spot, develop your protective system for that problem, and implement it. In this way you can buy your systems one at a time. The initial cost is less, you can concentrate on the particular system, and you can devote more of your efforts to making the system operate smoothly.

On the other hand, this step-by-step approach has obvious flaws. It's essentially a reactive approach. It parries criminal thrusts as they occur, or as you believe they will occur. It must guess where the greatest dangers lie. If you are wrong, you may incur a catastrophic loss from an unexpected direction.

Another flaw inherent in the step-by-step method is management's flagging interest in the security problem once the major hot spots have been cooled. It is a common reaction for management to feel "Why fix the roof when it's not raining?" This apathy frequently appears where the initial results of the first security systems have been very successful. In these cases, a satisfied management has frequently failed to support the installation of further systems, leaving the organization in some ways even more vulnerable than before, because of the false sense of security generated by the partial success. Security personnel for such organizations, continuously frustrated in their efforts to fulfill their professional responsibility, often lose interest in their jobs; it is almost impossible to remain vigorous and creative in administering the security of the assets of a company which is plainly indifferent to security.

The Total Approach

The creation of a complete security system—a total apparatus—on a short-term schedule is therefore the best way to move under most circumstances. Your decision, however, must include consideration of the following:

- Total cost of implementing the entire program.
- Availability of such sums.
- The existing degree of risk.

The major problem in installing a total security system (assuming it is economically sensible and feasible) is that the administrative load in the early months of the system's development and implementation can be very heavy indeed. However, this difficulty can be largely overcome with proper pre-planning.

In the following pages we will discuss some elementary systems used in office security today. Every security-conscious office has systems of its own devising, systems that work in that particular business, or in that particular place under its particular circumstances. You, too, will develop systems that suit your own needs; however, there are a few basic systems that should be incorporated into every security program. These systems deal with access, the most significant area in crime control.

Every organization, large or small, must have systems to control traffic into or within its building and/or office. This necessarily includes control over the movement of equipment or supplies, both for crime prevention and for after-the-fact crime detection.

Enforcement Key to Success

Before taking up these basic systems, let us once again emphasize the importance of vigorous management of each aspect of the security program. If, for example, five doors led into your office and one of them was regularly left unlocked and unattended, whatever you did with the other four doors would be irrelevant. You could lock them, alarm them, watch them via closed-circuit television cameras, and it would still be wasted effort as long as the other entrance was available to the thief; one entrance is all he needs. Security can be compared to a boat which is in trouble because it is only 99 percent watertight.

It is equally essential to the success of your program that systems be maintained. If your security people fail to enforce sign-in and sign-out procedures, if they don't check passes for packages, boxes, etc., then you have no security for company property; an unenforced system is a useless function.

It is the security administrator's responsibility to see that systems are adhered to, and that security personnel carry out their responsibilities with due diligence. If you let up, then your people will let up, and their performance will soon become perfunctory and mechanical. This is the death of any system. In fact, worse than death, because behind the illusion of security this indifference invites the thief to circumvent the minute degree of security remaining.

Basic Systems

The following are systems which are basic in any security operation.

Building Package and Access Pass System

All office buildings should employ this system, but unfortunately many plead limited funds and do not implement this integral part of access control. Where it is used, it has proven highly effective in reducing office equipment theft. A properly administered pass system will go a long way toward defending against intruders and reducing the "shrinkage" in company property.

Policy

Before or after normal working hours or on weekends, visitors, vendors and servicemen should not be allowed to enter a building without an authorizing building pass. No one, regardless of rank, should be permitted to leave the building with packages, boxes, equipment, etc. without surrendering a pass describing the items and authorizing their removal.

Method

A list of tenant and company personnel authorized to issue access and package passes should be available in the security center. A specimen of each authorized signature, in alphabetical order, should be provided to building management guards at entrance checkpoints. The distribution of blank passes to these authorized persons should be controlled by office security, and a log used to record this distribution. Used passes should not be returned to the authorizing office but held by security for comparison when questions arise. Employing a two-part consecutively numbered form protects the integrity of the system in the event a pass is not surrendered or is unused. Test transactions should be made periodically to verify the effective application of the system by entrance guards. Updating lists of authorizing personnel regularly is also essential.

Building In/Out Log System

A supervised sign-in and sign-out log should be maintained by building management to record the coming and going of building and tenant employees and of visitors on weekends, holidays, and before and after normal working hours. Such a log can be a valuable reference when a crime has been committed. It will tell who was in the building during the time in question and where in the building he should have been.

Policy

Building and tenant employees, and emergency servicemen (alarm service personnel, particularly) should be required to sign an entrance log when entering or leaving the building before or after normal working hours, including weekends and holidays. Periodic checks should be made with tenants and supervisors to verify their knowledge of the employees' and visitors' entries.

Method

The log should be placed in the lobby of the building at 6:00 P.M. and removed the following morning at 8:00. A uniformed guard or elevator operator must always be on duty to receive off-hours traffic, and witness the signing in and out of such individuals. All elevators should be taken off automatic, and the remaining elevator operated manually by the lobby attendant or a second employee.[1] If secured fire stairs restrict floor-to-floor movement to the elevator, visitors' access will be restricted to the floor they sign in to visit.

Identification Card System

In larger organizations and/or where security problems justify it, an identification card can be employed. This system is far superior to the in/out log system alone. There are many kinds of ID cards. Some carry only the owner's name, affiliation, and signature, while others incorporate a photograph laminated into the card. If the card is properly designed, it will be difficult to alter the card without the change being instantly detectable.

Automatic equipment capable of "reading" the identification cards, admitting the cardholder, and recording the use of the card, is a labor-saving extension of a card system. Such automatic access systems can also control entrance to restricted areas within a building. A system having a recording capability has secondary values such as clocking employees in and out for payroll purposes, and recording who entered an unattended entrance at what time. Individuals joining or leaving the company can be immediately added to or deleted from the more automatic systems, whether or not the employee surrenders his card when he leaves the company. This system has particular value for a volatile office having a high turnover in personnel and irregular hours, because the system is extremely flexible and easily up-dated.

As a comparison, a closed-circuit television access system with a guard or receptionist remotely monitoring and releasing the door lock relies heavily upon the present knowledge, memory and recognition of the individual on duty. Of course CCTV access systems can also include the use of an identification card. This adds a higher degree of

---

[1] *If the lobby attendant must operate the elevator, the lobby of course should be locked during his absence, if it is not always kept locked during these hours.*

security than card-only systems which can be used by persons with stolen cards. While the cost of the dual camera system with video tape recorder back-up is more than a simple CCTV remote-access installation, it does not approach the cost of the computer-linked time-recording, card-reading systems.

Policy

Company personnel should not be permitted to enter or leave the office or the building outside of regular hours without producing an identification card. Where additional security is needed, this requirement should be in force at all times. Personnel who do not have their cards would be escorted to the Personnel Department for a temporary ID card. Such a system requires employees to cooperate in what is often considered an annoying and time-consuming routine at least twice a day. It will require all of management's skills to convince employees that this system is necessary and is in their and the company's best interest. Security personnel must make every effort to avoid any implication of indignity or harassment of the employees while still maintaining the integrity of the card system.

Method

The method will vary depending on the type of system installed, but the essential difference is between visual, remote, and electronic inspection and acceptance of cards.

Crime Information System

Reports

In spite of all precautions, some incidence of crime is inevitable. When such incidents occur we must make every effort to not only detect the criminal, but to record the event in such a way as to develop data that may help us improve our security procedures so as to prevent a recurrence. To this end, a crime or missing property reporting procedure is essential. Over a period of time this file will provide a profile of losses and their circumstances that will be most valuable in the evaluation and updating of your security program.

Security reports should be typed or written in ink on pre-printed forms. For speedy reference they should be consecutively numbered. Completed reports must be treated as Confidential and safeguarded accordingly. If possible, access to the file should be on a "need to know" basis in the Security area itself, and the file unknown outside the area.

Where insurance or a possible insurance claim is involved, a different form must be completed for the necessary distribution and reporting. Remember that, for insurance purposes, missing items must be considered as being missing or misplaced until they have been *proven* stolen.

Information Gathering

In support of your own information gathering and collection, the experience of other tenants and neighboring companies and buildings with similar security problems can be most valuable. Contacts with them should be maintained in order to exchange information, discuss new techniques, etc.

It is important that you establish active lines of communication with local law enforcement and fire authorities. You should know, preferably from actual test runs, how quickly they can respond, and how helpful they are able to be in various situations. Most police departments are understaffed and are necessarily perfunctory in investigating what they must classify as petty crimes. On the other hand, the police will appreciate prompt, thorough and accurate reports of crimes by you. When new criminal operations develop in your area your local police will know about it and, if your lines of communication with them are open, you will know. And as long as you are able to anticipate the criminal's moves, you are a long way toward checking his attacks against your company or building.

Photo File System

Taking pictures and maintaining a file of photographs is a highly effective system which should be used more in the office. The few companies who utilize such a system do so only after they have apprehended an intruder or a thief. My experience has been that the more you use photography, the more effective it becomes. When photographs are taken "after the fact," they are useful as part of the information you need to collect, but when photographs are taken at random of external traffic (visitors, vendors, messengers, servicemen, etc.), you have a defensive weapon. An individual is less inclined to attack when he knows you may have his picture on file. Using such photos we have, on occasion, enabled victims to make positive identification of thieves seen. The reaction of visitors to having their pictures taken has been generally good. Occasionally there is a hostile reaction, but this may have been from someone who felt he now could not operate. With photo files of this nature—even if they are only random candid snaps—your information-exchange association with local authorities, other tenants, and neighborhood companies becomes more effective, especially when others are using a similar system.

Implementation of Security Systems

The more complicated a security program, or a system within the program, the more difficult it will be to implement. Advance testing—"dry runs"—will give you a strong indication of applications problems and should assist in the de-bugging of the new system.[2] All equipment involved should be tested completely over substantial periods of time, in order to be sure it is and will be functioning properly. When a system is activated, sufficient supporting supplies should be on hand for continuing operation of the system, such as receipt and records forms for systems in-

[2]The term "de-bugging" is used here in the colloquial sense of "get all the bugs out" of a new program, design, or procedure through testing in practice.

volving keys or identification cards. As part of the introduction of programs, security personnel must be thoroughly trained in, and completely conversant with, the systems they are to administer. Supporting systems and procedures should be equipped and supplied to work with the main system. A target date should be chosen. While every effort should be made to meet the target date once it is set, no system should be activated until everything is ready—a blundering introduction may permanently hamper acceptance of a system or program.

Notification

Since systems almost always involve people, their indoctrination is necessary to insure success of the systems, not only before, but also during and after implementation. Where a system has been pre-tested, you will be further along in that at least some employees will have seen the system in operation. Even the simplest system such as an in/out log in the lobby will require some personal supervision for its introduction. A memo to all employees is necessary, but insufficient by itself. An extra man temporarily stationed with your lobby guard or elevator starter can help remind people of the need to sign in and out. Within days the system should be operating smoothly. On the other hand, the introduction of ID cards to be used with access control and identification equipment will require more preparation. Here pre-testing is particularly important. The test should be of a part of the program, as in a small area where access is limited and the number of people involved is small enough to be readily managed. A staff memo should be issued well in advance, a second shortly before implementing the system, another on the day it is activated, and follow-up memos as needed to correct misapprehensions or to re-affirm the need for cooperation.

Temporary signs or instruction posters are helpful as additional reminders of new procedures. Support personnel should be deployed and used freely to help explain where necessary. Department heads should be asked to help by reminding their people of the need and reason for such a system. Having senior security management very much in evidence helps to impress upon employees the importance given to the new system. For example, when introducing an identification card system involving equipment, a senior manager should be present at various key locations during heavy traffic periods in the initial phases and until both the procedure and the equipment are working smoothly.

Modifications

In the testing and in the follow-up process, you will discover the bugs in your program. Every system will need some alterations or adjustments; even if it is an exact duplicate of one used by another office, it will still need tailoring to fit your company's needs.

When necessary, modifications should be made as quickly as possible. Explanatory memos should be precise as to the changes being made and, whenever possible, as to why they are being made. Retraining may be necessary and new equipment may have to be installed. This should be done on a crash basis, if possible. Speed is essential in any system modification, since any interruption will mean more retraining, more explanations, and more resistance.

Follow-up

Follow-up of any new system is an absolute necessity. Without it weeks or months of planning may be wasted.

Follow-up consists of checking all operations and procedures. Operational personnel should also get reactions from personnel of each group affected by the system, for employees are less candid in responding to management inquiries. Follow-up should pay particular attention to equipment performance and system efficiency at peak periods.

Memos

The best memorandum you can write will always be none at all; however, as we have discussed, there are occasions when a memo can't be avoided. On such occasions remember to write your memo in simple language, in short sentences, and in as positive and precise a manner as possible.

Demonstration

Obviously, a live demonstration of the system is the most effective form of communication and instruction. To show, by demonstrating, how a system works is both the simplest and the most effective teaching method. When an on-site physical demonstration is not possible, a visual presentation in an auditorium or conference room is an almost equally effective alternative. Slides, films, art cards, or a blackboard chalk talk can all be useful to the clear presentation of the need for, or the basics of, a security system.

Keep the meetings small to encourage discussion, short and informative. Train enough security personnel to conduct such meetings so that your entire organization can be reached quickly by scheduling a number of small groups simultaneously. Be sure each speaker is well prepared for questions; nothing can be more discouraging to listeners than a speaker who doesn't seem to understand his subject fully. Any speaker, however, is bound to get an unforeseeable question or two for which he doesn't have the answer. In that case don't fake it; tell the group you don't know, but you'll find out. And then follow through. Find the answer and be sure each member of the group who had been present is notified.

Even if the question and the answer are inconsequential, it is important to show that you care, and that you are willing and capable of researching your subject as far as may be necessary.

Maintenance

Equipment is faulty or becomes defective or obsolete. Systems are "streamlined" or short-circuited. Personnel can become lazy and enforcement complacent. Unless your program is dynamically managed, all of this erosion of security can take place. You must inject a sense of daily challenge—an atmosphere of innovation—from the top down. As we know, security requires active, minute-by-minute participation to be effective, and it is your job to keep that participation alive in your organization.

Maintenance and renewal of equipment and systems is vital. New equipment should be evaluated and kept in mind as potential replacement for current equipment in the event it becomes obsolete in the face of increasingly sophisticated criminal techniques or a changing office environment. It is important that you keep abreast of the latest in security techniques and equipment by keeping in touch with security organizations, trade publications, and vendors. While you may find that a great deal of the material doesn't apply to your situation, if you find only one new technique or one effective piece of crime prevention equipment a year, your continuing attention to the security field will have been worthwhile.

The erosion of a security system can begin with forms being bypassed or improperly filled out. If this continues without immediate and firm remedial action, personnel will lose confidence and respect for the system. While system modifications are frequently necessary and you must be flexible enough to make them whenever and wherever necessary, these changes must be made by management in response to the need, not by employees for reasons of convenience or indifference.

Security, of all departments, can least afford the luxury of lowering standards. To be the guardian of the office, security must always be on guard—even of itself.

Security Personnel

All of the diverse elements of an efficient and effective security program are designed to function within a specific environment. Each element is important to the operation of the whole, but if we were to rate all factors in the order of their importance, we would have to agree with the majority of security experts that the most important element in any security program is a good security man. Machines, equipment, techniques, and systems—some of enormous sophistication—are available to us, but it is the security man who will select and—even more important—operate them. Their effectiveness is in his hands. It is essential, then, that security personnel at every level be given all our support and cooperation, and all possible help to increase their understanding and skills in the difficult and, all too often, thankless job they perform. It is equally important to begin with the best; to seek out young men interested in security as a career, rather than recruiting only retired police or servicemen. We need balanced teams of veterans and rookies backed by a reasonable pool of applicants in order to phase in new personnel on an orderly basis.

In order to create and operate an effective security department, personnel must be a matter of first concern. Let's take a brief look at those elements of security personnel management with which we must be concerned: Procurement, development, compensation, integration, and maintenance.

Since security presents unique problems in terms of employment, management will be very much involved in the security personnel function. Our discussion here will be limited to the special needs of security personnel and will not apply to the broader personnel needs of the company as a whole.

Procurement

In the past, we have all too often hired a retired man to fill the post of "guard." Today, as we have discussed, every effort should be made to balance our force with both young and older men. We should be alert to the degree of interest an applicant shows in his interviews. We must look for applicants who show signs of an innovative turn of mind; who are sufficiently flexible in their approach while firm in their principles. We must feel that our candidate is an active performer, not a passive automaton. He must be capable of following orders, but he must at the same time be self-motivating. He should be familiar with general company policies, especially in regard to prevention, detection, apprehension, and prosecution and be able to accept them without any reservation. Finally, he must be thoroughly checked out.

It is particularly important that reference checks be made as far back and as completely as possible on all applicants for jobs in security. Where it is at all possible, these checks should be made in personal interviews with past employers. Phone calls should be made only if personal interviews are not possible. Checking by mail cannot possibly be adequate. As we have mentioned in another context, checking a reference by mail misses every nuance, every hesitation, every tone of voice which can be so important in evaluating the previous experience and performance of a prospective employee.

If you do not make thorough multiple reference checks of potential security personnel you might as well close this book—you cannot possibly have a security program you can depend on.

The initial procurement process should be handled by the personnel department, with security management entering the picture when a prime candidate has been discovered. The process might be something like this:

Personnel Department:
1. Recruitment through:
   Advertising (newspapers and trade magazines), employment agencies, recommendations of present employees, labor unions, schools and colleges.
2. Reviewing application
3. Preliminary interview
4. Testing

5. Reference checks
6. Refer to security management

Security Department:

7. Final interview or interviews
8. Physical examination
9. Further reference checks
10. Employment

Development

Development and training of your security people must be a continuing concern of management. Development in security is largely accomplished by regular training to improve the security man's skills and knowledge, and to keep him constantly up-to-date with the latest advances in the field. The merits of such training will be reflected in each person's attitude toward his job. In almost all cases the result is a more positive attitude, better morale, and increased incentive. Naturally, each individual's background will determine the amount of training he will need. Above all, never believe that a former law officer does not need training; he definitely does. In order for him to be successful in security, he must develop certain new skills and override some of his previous training.

Your training program should consist of some of the following:

- Company indoctrination
- Company and security department policies, systems and procedures
- Basic operation of departments
- Background in applicable basic law (individual rights, citizen's arrests, rights of search and seizure, etc.)
- First aid
- Self-defense, including use of weapons if armed
- Methods of surveillance
- Fingerprinting and photography
- Indoctrination in equipment in use by security

- Professional standards, including attitudes toward fellow employees and other departments

Security personnel must be cheerful, cooperative and tolerant in all their dealings within the company, for they—and the company—need the cooperation of every employee. They must be patient when faced with excessive inquisitiveness, flip remarks, or irritation from their fellow workers. They must understand that they are not members of a law enforcement agency, but employees who have the job of helping to provide office security. If they are good-humored, patient, tactful, and professional, their fellow employees will soon come to hold them in the highest respect. It won't happen overnight. They may have to hang in there for a while. But it will happen.

Security personnel should be reminded that they are professionals in a new but growing field. They should be encouraged to keep themselves informed by reading security texts and publications, joining security associations, and taking formal security courses where these are available.

Advancement

In the process of developing, an individual expects to be told how he is progressing. He is interested in advancement; therefore, definite levels of seniority and rank must exist in order to satisfy that interest.

Titles and Ranks—Most companies have used military or police designations to delineate rank and authority of security personnel. These designations have been: Corporal, Sergeant, Captain, Chief of Staff, Security Manager, Director of Security.

These military ranks may be appropriate for industrial guard and security forces, but in the office they are not suitable; they tend to create a barrier between Security and the rest of the company. This is the very barrier that Security must break down. We should create titles without the military connotation, since we cannot afford to have the office security force considered a paramilitary operation distinct from the business of the office. Security must be considered as much a part of the organization as Accounting or Sales.

Possible titles that blend in with business titles in general use might be:

Top Management: Security Executive, Security Operations Analyst, Executive Security Director.

Middle Management: Security Manager, Security Supervisor.

Operational Level: Senior Security Agent, Security Agent, Operations Agent.

Because office security is new, it has the opportunity of establishing an original image rather than being saddled with inappropriate stereotypes. It is important that this image be a positive one, rather than one which creates an almost instinctive resistance and has to be changed eventually in any case.

Salary—It is poor economy indeed to skimp on the wages paid to your security personnel. A poorly-paid security man is a poor operative, and a resentful security man can be doubly dangerous. Better to have a smaller staff adequately—even generously—paid, than a larger staff of under-compensated personnel who feel, with some justice, that they are being asked for more loyalty than they are given.

Salaries should be kept above the average for your area and periodically reviewed. Each position should have a sufficiently wide salary range to allow considerable flexibility in your management of the department. Periodic performance appraisals will often dictate salary increases when promotion is either not indicated or impossible because of your table of organization. A wide salary range for each position will make this possible.

Integration

The integration of a security man into the security organization is more involved than the integration of new employees in other departments. Where other employees will simply receive the personnel department indoctrination and be introduced to their nearest neighbors in their new department, the security man must be familiar with the workings of each department in the formal organization and conversant with the informal organization.

By way of review, the formal organization of a company is that of the organization chart, which shows the lines of authority, reporting, responsibility and control. The informal organization is created by friendships and association, and will cross and bypass the formal lines.

Both types of organization are real and operate concurrently in every company. Good management uses both. It is part of the security man's job to know both intimately.

Obviously a tour of the building from roof to basement, including every setback and crawlspace, must be included as part of the integration program. Personnel should be given or have access to simplified and reduced floor plans as part of their training.

Evaluation—The new man should be closely supervised and evaluated on the basis of how he reacts to different situations as well as on his over-all performance. Suggestions and changes in his approach should be made as soon as possible, as it will be more difficult to accomplish at a later date. All new security employees should be on a 90-day probation or trial basis.

Follow-up—After your new man has been on the job for a couple of weeks, and at intervals thereafter, you should check with him to see that his training, indoctrination, and equipment have been provided as scheduled. Without this follow-through, you can't be sure that he has been properly integrated into your operation. Additionally, he will be impressed by your concern and will usually react with increased confidence.

Morale—We need to be more concerned with morale in security than in many other areas of the company. Security personnel are constantly dealing with daily visitors and vendors as well as with fellow employees; what they do and how they do it has a negative or positive effect on the image of your company as well as on your security force.

Morale, of course, is more than just helping to solve employees' problems. It involves dignity, respect, and considerate treatment. The harmony you create among your people and, as an extension, that they create among the people they deal with, is a playback of your actions and attitudes in working with them.

Maintenance

Uniforms

Although there are many plainclothes operatives in the world of security, it is highly desirable that you outfit most of your men in a recognizable uniform, whether formal or informal. The appearance of the uniform at key points in your office or in the building indicates to the would-be criminal that he is faced with a professional opponent, and may persuade him to do business elsewhere. It also inspires confidence in the employees.

However, it is necessary that your uniformed men be dressed properly. That means a good-looking, well-made uniform that fits. All too often we see men in obvious hand-me-downs that were cheaply made to begin with, and clearly don't come close to fitting. A man so uniformed looks ridiculous and projects the same image. Once you put a man in uniform you identify him—which is the reason for doing it. It should follow that you will want to identify him as neat and carefully dressed. A "spit and polish" appearance suggests a competent and efficient operation, and furthers the sense of confidence and strength.

The company should bear the cost of uniforms and accessories as well as having uniforms dry-cleaned on a regular basis. If this is not possible for some reason, a less desirable way of handling cleaning is to provide an allowance for cleaning to each man.

Equipment

Since security personnel will wear uniforms or plainclothes as need dictates, a locker should be assigned for each man. The locker will be used for securing other items of his equipment.

Watch: We live in a clock-oriented world. A security man must know when to report, when an incident occurred, etc. This is a personal item not provided by the company.

Flashlight: A necessity for night patrol and emergency situations. Company-provided.

Pocket pager or two-way radio: Can be vital to any coordinated effort. In emergency situations you must be able to round up your people and instruct them immediately. Company-provided.

Nightstick: Carried for self-defense. Company-provided.

Pen and pad: Needed for taking notes for later transcription. Company-provided.

Handcuffs or detaining device: A necessary item for controlling persons resisting arrest. Company-provided.

Firearms and other weapons: This is a basic policy matter which will require much consultation and consideration. In the event such weapons are to be carried, they should be provided by the company, to assure that they are of the correct type and in good condition.

Routines

Make it a practice to change assignments and vary routines. The movement and change will keep your people mentally active and interested. As your force becomes more effective and the rate of incidents is reduced, such changes may be the only exciting events that occur. You should also alter your routines frequently enough to make them unpredictable to a thief. Building rounds, for example, should never be made on an exact schedule.

Communications

Security, like so many special fields, uses its own language, a language derived from police usage. A sentence like "the perpetrator of the aforementioned act was apprehended while he was intent on escaping from the scene of the crime" might be considered proper securityese, but it won't enchant management. Since management must be sold if security is to succeed, it is best that security learn to communicate in the manner management prefers.

Management is not fond of bombast or oratory. It is the simple stuff that makes it. Management likes concise and positive answers—even when it is a quick NO. In writing reports use the so-called six "W's": Where, When, What, Who, How, Why. Be simple, direct and positive about what you know and what you don't know. Don't try to fake an aura of professionalism by the use of specialized language.

Sell Your Program

Now that you have evaluated your security requirements and decided what your needs are, your next step is implementing the program. This means committing your company to what could be substantial expenditures. In order to move management to okay this commitment, you must submit a budget and a specific plan of attack. Most managements need little selling to accept security; they recognize the need and want it. They are, however, frequently ignorant of the elements that go into an effective program and the cost of those elements. They are also, as we have mentioned, frequently unaware of the potential cost of an inadequate security program. It is important to recognize that although management rarely needs to be sold on the need for security, it very often must be sold on *your* security program. It is not easy to get management's blessing of a considerable cash outlay. Additionally, many companies, expecially highly competitive sales-oriented firms, find it difficult to generate any enthusiasm for expenditures which cannot be directly related to income. Remember that the company's energies are largely directed toward maintaining or improving the level of net income, and not on the reduction of losses. It will be your job to refocus some of your company's attention on this aspect of profit-making, by means of a thoroughly professional job. You will have to sell your proposal. You should use every tool at your disposal such as slide projectors, charts, graphs, films—any device that will support and dramatize your presentation. Be brief, but above all be accurate. You are engaged in a business which is effective insofar as it is direct, specific, efficient and accurate. Your presentation must reflect these qualities throughout.

The Budget

Certainly the bottom line in any presentation of this nature which touches on basic company policy is the budget. Its preparation separates the men from the boys, because once you've made your basic decisions you are on the firing line. Every sharpshooter in management will take a shot at it, and you will need a stout heart and a cool head to stand up to it. It can be a tough job to create a virgin budget. But it's your job to do, and your job to do it accurately. Many department managers over-budget to protect themselves against unforeseen contingencies and to protect themselves against the cost-cutting attack of a sharp-eyed controller. Don't get into this game. Security of all departments must make every effort to remain aloof from this kind of gamesmanship. Be accurate.

In your budget include:
- The cost of equipment including maintenance.
- The cost of systems including supplies.
- The cost of personnel including miscellaneous expenses and projected increases.
- A designated contingency figure.

NIGHT OWLS (BLESS U)

WHEN WORKING LATE · CALL
FOR ASSISTANCE IF YOU SEE
OR HEAR ANYTHING UNUSUAL

SECURITY

Chapter 13

EQUIPMENT FOR SECURITY

As the crime rate and crime losses rise, so does the development of equipment for security applications. Almost daily we are offered new and more sophisticated devices to prevent or detect criminal activity. A similar but slower "equipment explosion" is occurring in the fire protection field. Before us is spread a dazzling array of equipment much of which, if properly used and supported, could be invaluable in our security programs. But the essentials are the selection of the right equipment, its proper application, and its intelligent use and support.

In this chapter we will deal with the considerations of choice, the equipment available and its applications.

Timing in Equipment Selection

Security equipment and fire prevention and detection devices installed in a five-year-old building are five years too late, since this equipment should have been included in the original plans and incorporated in the construction of the building. Not only does post-construction installation cost considerably more, but these costs may be prohibitive. Buildings on the drawing board or even under construction today should include provisions for fire and security equipment to specifications developed in consultations with *independent* (non-vendor) applications experts from the security and fire protection fields.

If necessary, walls, fences, gates, lights, locks, and mirrors can be installed after construction and even during normal working hours. Alarm industry practice for alarm system installation is to lease the equipment to the user and to install after construction. This is unavoidable where high-risk tenants must have UL-certified central station alarm systems. On the other hand, proprietary (building) central alarm reception equipment and closed-circuit television systems are best designed at the planning stages and incorporated in construction. More and more prestige high-rise buildings are incorporating proprietary central reception of fire and intrusion alarms from throughout the building, as well as central monitoring of CCTV surveillance of key areas.

Publicizing Equipment

Where security equipment does not restrict or affect the normal activities of employees, there is no need to notify personnel of the installation of such equipment, though news of the installation of safety devices could give morale a boost, and might be publicized for that reason. The installation of local alarms on doors or stairwells, or of evacuation alarms, should of course be carefully explained to employees. Notification should be shortly before installation and then a brief follow-up on the day such alarms are to be activated. Signs are particularly advisable. Alarms are installed on fire stair doors to prevent their being propped open and to signal possible misuse.[1]

This is an example of local alarms that would concern all employees. Uniformed people should respond to such an alarm, unless the door is observed by closed-circuit television and the alarm can be restored from the control center.

---

[1] *In New York City a recent code change requires that it be possible to enter any floor from the fire stairwells. To prevent this safety measure from becoming the security risk it is, alarms are being installed which signal if the door is opened from the stairs. This is done by an adaptation of standard fire exit alarms usually applied only at street level.*

An "all hands" memo may be enough to explain any new equipment that you want to publicize, but of course a demonstration is more effective.

Follow-up

Once equipment has been installed, tested, and put into operation, it is important to be sure that it continues to work properly. Checking equipment will require physical inspections, regular maintenance, trouble reports, checking to see that it is properly used, and on-going tests according to a pre-arranged schedule. Where equipment affects employees, their reaction to the equipment is important.

Innovate

Do not hesitate to be innovative in equipment usage. The professional thief is familiar with many of the common "hardware" solutions and, unless you surprise him, he may evade or overcome your equipment.

Think for a moment of the suburban office building, the kind of commercial structure seen more and more often outside our major cities. It's usually a low glass and steel structure surrounded by expertly contoured landscaping. The beautifully planted and meticulously cared-for grounds seem more suited to a country club or university setting than an office. The hedges and trees outline the property and at night the lights accent the beauty of the surroundings. To the passing motorist it is a lovely scene. The thief may or may not find it attractive. The hedges and the trees may conceal a fence or a trip-wire alarm. At any rate, his vision will be substantially reduced by the glare barrier of the lights while the inside security man can have a clear view of the building's perimeter grounds. But are the lights, the fence, the pressure wire alarm useful only in applications such as this? Of course not! They are part of the equipment arsenal, and can be used wherever and however an imaginative security agent wishes.

Consider your own location. Wouldn't illuminating rooftops next to your building or the space between your building and its neighbors eliminate the shadows so convenient for the thief? And suppose that chain link fence were inside, installed floor to ceiling to encase the supply room or highly pilferable merchandise, and locked and alarmed? The trip-wire alarm stretched across a key office area at night is an effective alarm defense against the burglar who hides-in or evades the alarms on doors and windows.

The more unorthodox you are in the selection and placement of protective equipment, the more difficult you may make it for the thief. On the other hand, equipment without competent personnel for operation or response is, of course, virtually useless. And innovation requires an above-average knowledge of the equipment, its normal applications, and its special vulnerabilities.

The Equipped Building

Imagine an office building equipped throughout with the latest and best security equipment. At night every door except the main entrance is doubly deadlocked, and checked periodically by guards. The main entrance is bathed in light. All the building's locks are highly pick-resistant. The interior corridors are "mined" with pressure-sensitive alarms. Additionally, hidden closed-circuit television cameras are scattered throughout the office. Most interior doors are locked. Consider, then, how all these devices were defeated in one masterful stroke by the thief who came into the building before closing time, and hid in a closet in the room in which the company safe was located. That night his only obstacle was the unalarmed safe itself. He had evaded all the other defenses. The next morning he strolled out of the office with his loot as the building prepared to begin another day in the market place. This is an actual case history of a crime committed against a major corporation's home office.

In a comparable case, a New York firm placed expensive locks on the doors entering from the fire stairs after a rash of thefts of office machinery. The locks permitted exit to the stairwell from the inside office space, but once the door closed it locked behind you; there was no place to go except to leave the building. This was very effective in eliminating floor-to-floor movement except by elevator.

For a while, this stopped the theft of the machines, but then it started up again. Management could not fathom how the thefts were being accomplished. Close observation revealed that the employees on the second and third floors preferred to walk down to the street level at lunch and quitting time—it was faster than waiting for the crowded elevators. The thieves had spotted this. They waited in the stairwell and, when an employee opened the door from the interior, these well-dressed gentlemen thanked him and entered the office. After selecting a machine, they would leave by the same stair.

The moral of both of these stories is that good equipment alone cannot provide solutions. In both cases a system was needed. In the first case, what was needed was a practice of checking all spaces before locking them for the night; in the second, an employee trained not to permit entry from the stairs would have balked at admitting strangers, however polite. Both are simple systems which were overlooked. Many buildings have "traffic" alarms and closed-circuit TV observing the lower portions of the stairwells. Such an arrangement would have spotted the "upstream" traffic.

The "Paper Wall"

In today's modern office building, many private offices have metal doors with a three-hour "A" fire rating. Such a rating means the door will hold up against the pressures and temperatures of fire for approximately three hours. This door, fitted with tamper-resistant hinges and a reasonably pick-resistant deadlock with a one-inch bolt, would certainly stump any amateur bent upon forced entry, and might hold off a professional. Of course, if the attacker happens to be carrying a chisel, he could simply cut through the wall beside the door; it takes little effort to penetrate the type of wall construction found in today's office. To regard the expense of the door as wasted is to forget that the door is designed for fire-resistance, not security, and that no equipment can be totally effective so long as a "weak link" exists in the security chain.

Fences

The majority of perimeter fences installed today are of the chain link type. By themselves, they can only prevent people from straying on to the property. Obviously, anyone intent on climbing the fence can do so. Installing supporting devices such as perimeter alarms and increased lighting will improve the security of the perimeter, provided the fence is in good condition. A fence with a hole in it, or which can be pried up, simply is no fence at all.

Metal Gates

The accordion-type gate (and, less often, the roll-down grille) is used to protect store fronts though it is seldom used to secure office building entrances, where smash-and-grab attacks are much rarer. A freight entrance, on the other hand, may very well need such a device. These gates should have top and bottom slide tracks and be locked with a strong pick- and force-resistant lock, and the hinge pins should be non-removable. Roll-down steel doors can be even more effectively secured, but if the freight entrance is not overlooked or frequently patrolled, it might be well to alarm the freight area at night and on holidays.

Lighting

For technical information on external lighting you should contact the Illuminating Engineering Society, which publishes the American Standard Practice for Protective Lighting. Parking areas and all entrance points should be well-lighted, especially rear and side alley doors. Shrubbery should be kept low and well-illuminated, so as not to conceal muggers and thieves.

Doors

Of the various doors, steel doors or wooden doors of the solid core type offer the greatest protection against forced entry. Unless lined with sheet metal, hollow-core doors cannot be recommended. Doors having glass panels should not be used in side or rear of building entrances, where they can be quietly attacked. When doors with glass are used, they should be fitted with locks that are "keyed both sides," to use locksmith jargon; that is, cannot be opened by breaking the glass, reaching in and operating a handle or a thumbturn.[2]

While glass doors are often used at entrance locations, they are rarely attacked through the glass. Exterior door hinges on steel exit doors (which are necessarily exposed) should all be of the non-removable type and preferably should not yield even though sawn. Where door frames are weak, as is true in the aluminum frames of glass doors, special long-bolt, pry-resistant locks and cylinder guards should be used.

Overhead doors should be solid and the interior bolts secured with padlocks. Remember, the thief is as interested, or more interested, in an unhampered rapid exit as he is in getting into your building. Where elevators cannot be secured from operation, a second door requiring a key should be installed at the floor to be safeguarded to prevent easy access.

Fire tower and fire stair doors should be fitted with panic bars. These panic devices can sound an alarm when operated and are used where fire doors are not to be opened except in a genuine emergency. If your fire stairs

---

[2]*The one exception is interior fire stairwell doors. In the event of a fire, firemen break the glass and open the door in this manner. Further, local fire codes make it illegal to secure any fire exit (and many building entrance doors) in this manner.*

are used as a convenience by your personnel, door or stairwell alarms which can be activated at night and turned off during the day would be more appropriate.

Windows

All ground floor windows should be secured with alarms, bars or expanded steel mesh which cannot be removed with ordinary tools. Ground windows on an alleyway or in the rear of the building should be fitted with barrier protection and alarmed.

Windows opening onto fire escapes and windows opening onto rooftops should be considered emergency exits and should not be key-locked. Alarms should be installed in such windows. Air conditioners set into accessible windows should also be alarmed, since removing the unit creates access. Transoms are not features of newer buildings with central air conditioning, but where they do exist in older buildings they are a danger and should be permanently sealed.

Don't overlook other openings in the perimeter of the building which could pose a security problem. Any opening greater than 64 square inches should be protected by grilles or bars. These openings include air and water intakes, exhaust tunnels, heating ducts, culverts, etc. Check all manholes within the area for means of entering the building. These tunnels might require fencing or alarming. Sidewalk elevator doors should be securely padlocked from the basement.

Locks

Lights burn electricity, personnel require salaries, dogs must be fed, and most equipment has maintenance expense, but heavy-duty locks once purchased seldom require costly maintenance. Locks are by far the cheapest security investment you can make and yet, in an effort to make even greater savings, companies often buy—and architects even oftener accept—cheap locks. This is sometimes justified by that tired old saw, "any lock can be picked by a pro." This is essentially true, but a top-quality six- or seven-pin lock cylinder can gain you time by stalling even a pro. (If surreptitious entry might be a problem, choose pick-resistant cylinders for critical doors.) Don't save pennies on locks; most attacks are direct "jimmying" efforts. The lock you buy should be of top quality, deadlocking, and have at least a one-inch bolt. Locking hardware is usually a one-time investment and it could return your investment many times over.

It is important to know that the relative security factor of any locking device is measured in time; the purpose of the lock is to delay unauthorized access to an area or to a container. Most locks (but not all) will buy you time, but they are simply delaying devices and should never be considered to be more than that. Of course, if the door is secured by a latch that can be pushed back (that is, non-deadlatching), there's little point in even closing the door.

In order to get the best protection from a lock, be sure that it is rated with a high resistance to force (jimmying), to picking, and to cylinder-pulling.

Padlocks

Padlocks should be hardened and strong enough to resist prying, and the shackle should be close enough to the body to prevent the insertion of a tool to force it. The lock cylinder insert should have no less than five pins if it is to be used for a security purpose. Padlocks should never be left in place unlocked because of the risk of substitution.

It is important to remember that the hasps or the locking bar may be attacked to evade the necessity of forcing the padlock; therefore, all the hardware involved with the padlock should be of hardened steel. The locking bar should have no external rivets and should be bolted through the door to the inside and through a backing plate with the bolt ends burred over.

Special Door Locks

Beside the standard door locks there are some which have special interest for security. These are:

- Lock cylinder with multiple angled pins—operated by a non-reproducible key with indentations or varying angles of cuts.
- Pushbutton—no key required, combination readily changed.
- Electronic locks—with computer link, can record entrance and exit time of visitors. Not highly secure unless alarmed, but offers other advantages such as code operation, rapid access, remote operation, etc.

Door lock cylinders should have beveled guards making it impossible to pull the cylinders out of the door. All locks should be of the deadbolt type, and spring latches without the deadlatching feature should never be used.

If your office has substantial personnel turnover, you may be faced with the need to change locks frequently to deny access to departed key-holders. Obviously, you will make every effort to regain keys so issued, but this is not always possible and in any event most keys can readily be copied. You are faced with evaluating the risk involved in the possibility of having a floating key beyond your control, and the cost involved in changing all locks the missing or compromised key can access. You may find that it will be cheaper in the long run to install removable-core locks (allowing rapid unskilled key changes) or pushbutton combination locks of one of the various types available today. Code combinations can be changed almost instantly with any change of personnel or policy.

In reception areas, where doors are kept locked primarily to thwart unwelcome visitors, a remote control "electronic lock" is normally the most effective solution. With such a system, the receptionist can open a door by pressing a button at her desk.

Most pushbutton-operated "electronic locks" are actually standard locks released by activating an electric strike in the jamb of the door. Many of these strikes can be tampered with, and are only secure if electronically monitored to be certain the lock bolt is in the strike and the strike is in the closed position.

Safes

If you occupy space in a building on more than one floor, your safe should be located as far from the core of the building as possible; force a thief to take greater risks to get to your cash. Remember, fire safes can be easily entered by burglars, while burglary-resistive safes cannot protect your records against fire. Your best solution is a fire-resistive vault containing a burglary-resistive safe.

The recent penetration of the modern vault of a bank in Laguna Niguel, California, is simply proof, if any is needed, that no vault is proof against expert attack, and that "party-line" alarm circuits are easily "beaten" by experts. Fortunately the few experts seek high-dollar targets.

The better the safe and/or vault, the more time you gain for your alarm system to bring help.

Safes are rated alphabetically. Fire resistance is rated up to "A," resisting external temperatures up to 2,000° F. for four hours. A Class "B" safe can protect against exposure of 1,850° F. for two hours; and a Class "C" safe, one hour at 1,700° F. Fire safes are also tested for their resistance to building collapse in a fire.

Burglary resistance is theoretically rated down from "A," but the "E"-rated safe provides the first significant protection in the ranking of money chests. It has a 1″ steel body with a 1½″ steel door, and its door is tested against ripping or cutting with ordinary hand tools.

A safe rated burglary-resistant by Underwriters' Laboratories must include a UL-listed combination lock, UL-listed relocking device, cast or welded-plate body, and door(s) of special metal alloys which resist carbide drills.

Higher safe ratings indicate tested resistance to torch,

tool, or explosive attack for varying periods of time (e.g., 15 minutes for an "F" rating, 30 minutes for an "H" rating, 60 minutes for an "I" rating).

UL testing for burglary-resistance in safes does not include the use of diamond core drills, thermic lance, or other sophisticated attack devices.

Whatever safe you have selected must be further protected. As we have pointed out, a fire safe can be burglarized faster than an alarm can bring help, so if you are protecting valuables, cash or negotiables, we will assume you have an "E"-rated money safe or equivalent vault. Safes should be bolted securely to the floor. No safe means anything if it is light enough to be carted away to be worked on at leisure. And "light enough to be carried away" covers a wide territory; burglars in Fresno, California, removed a 2,000-pound safe from a first floor office.

You should establish a ceiling on the amount of cash you will keep in your safe. (In fact, your insurance may spell this out.)A safe is invaluable in securing cash which you accumulate or must keep on hand for the day's business, but it's no substitute for a bank. There's no point in offering too much temptation to a thief, external or internal.

While it is true that money or negotiables stolen from a safe by a burglar is reimbursed (to the amount insured and the extent to which its presence in the safe is documented) you have no insurance to cover the sharp increase in premiums which subsequent years will bring. If you feel that your insurance is the main body of your security effort, you might check out the various premiums you pay at various "experience" levels, as well as the premium advantages of vaults protected by UL-certified alarm systems with line security.

Keys

The issuance and control of keys should be the responsibility of your office security operation. This vital responsibility is frequently handled in a surprisingly off-hand manner and yet the potential loss resulting from the misuse of keys is overwhelming.

In the Do's and Don't's of key control you'll find a preponderance of Don't's, so we'll start with a few Do's.

- *Do* keep your key cabinet and record files in order, current and cross-referenced. *Do* secure your key cabinet with a dial combination lock.
- *Do* make a visual inventory of all keys on hand or in the hands of employees from time to time. (You not only find keys have been lost, but also keys not authorized to the holder.)
- *Do* review your list of authorized keyholders regularly.
- *Don't* issue keys to anyone unless they absolutely must have one. For temporary access, have a keyholder or security agent admit them.
- *Don't* carelessly leave your keys lying around during the day, and warn all keyholders against this. Do not leave your office keys in your car when parking at restaurants. (They are likely to make an impression on someone who is waiting for the opportunity to make an impression of them. Such an impression is costly in theft or lock changes.) The "pro" can identify the use of every key you have; to him they are as "readable"as a book—especially master keys.
- *Don't* forget to change the key cylinder when an authorized key holder is discharged for cause.
- *Don't* use anything but highly pick-resistant key cylinders where surreptitious entry is a particular risk. Unfortunately, these cylinders are quite expensive to buy and to replace.

Paper Shredders

There is a full line of paper shredders on the market today ranging from wastebasket size to large industrial types. In the office they can be purchased and deployed according to need. A chief executive's secretary should make it a habit to use one constantly in place of a standard wastebasket. A centralized duplicating department could pass all day-end confidential waste paper through a large shredder. Smaller shredders should be placed beside decentralized copiers. Departments such as research, sales, advertising, personnel, and engineering, to name a few, should have shredders.

Once installed, a continuing effort should be made to motivate employees to use them. Wastebaskets should be checked occasionally for papers which should have been shredded—after all, someone else may be checking the wastebaskets if you aren't!

Mirrors

The threat of an attacker lurking around the next corner or out of sight in the elevator can be very real. This can be the source of considerable anxiety to employees working late at night or on weekends. A mirror facing the turn of the corridor and other blind corners would alleviate this situation. These inexpensive reflectors "pay off" in increased protection of your workers. Additionally they avert collisions where mail carts, hand trucks, coffee carts, etc. are used. Such mirrors can also be used in reception areas where one girl should be able to see a relatively large area while operating a switchboard.

Signs

Since office security is basically defensive in nature, we are constantly trying to prevent attacks from without. With that thought in mind we busily go about the task of creating traps and heavily fortified barriers to capture or deter a thief. If you consider the real function of office security, you realize you neither want to apprehend nor frighten away a thief—you simply want no part of him.

Having created a balance of power and perhaps a deterrent force, your next step is to make it public. Tell your adversary, the thief, through the use of signs and posters, that you have the means and determination to capture and prosecute him. Create and install signs that tell him that.

A word about signs. If you do put up informative security signs, keep them clean and, if possible, well-illuminated. All too often I have seen such signs caked with dust and sign lights burned out. A natural reaction to a well-kept security sign is that the company must have a well-organized security program. Also, put the signs where they will be read and have them say something. I agree we don't often put them in expensive executive suites or reception room areas, or even in the company cafeteria. But there are many places for them, such as by your elevators, your fire stairs, on the backs of doors, side doors, in loading docks, on perimeter fences, and entrance gates, to name some.

Next, say something! New language is needed. The old lines have lost their effect: "Violators will be prosecuted"; "Trespassers will be prosecuted"; "You will be prosecuted to the fullest extent of the law." Each has lost its punch.

In taking a page from some of the most successful advertising agencies in the world, "Write good copy. Give enough facts." As a sample of this concept, the following is offered: "Any person or persons attempting or completing a criminal act against this company, its employees, equipment, or property will have charges preferred against them by this company. We make no exceptions"—XYZ Company's Management.

Advertising agencies' research departments will tell you, "Well-written and interesting copy, although long, is usually well-read."

Lock-Down Devices for Office Machines

In an office having only a few typewriters, adding machines, calculators and the like, it is definitely worthwhile having those machines locked to the desk or the stand they are used on.

In larger organizations the problem takes on a different

dimension. The cost of bolting down every machine is considerable and, in those cases where a machine is bolted to a desk or table, the mobility of the machine is decreased. (But then, that's its purpose!) On the other hand, experience has shown that where machines have been secured with lock-down devices, theft of equipment has been drastically reduced and, in some cases, halted altogether.

Your job is to evaluate your current rate and risk of loss compared to the costs involved in securing the machines. You may find that it's not worth the expense, but if it's close, or if certain machines are more exposed to theft, then do it and eliminate one more lure to attract the criminal.

Alarms

Integral to any effective security program is an alarm system of some kind. These systems generally economize on manpower by permitting mobile security personnel to respond to a large number of points as needed, rather than establishing a similar number of fixed posts or patrol rounds. They "back up" physical security, your first line of defense. They are also used where more positive security or physical barring of an area or position is not possible because of building layout, costs, appearance, or some other reason. Most commercial central station alarm systems are required by insurers. Any alarm installation must be supported by response, either by building security personnel or alarm company guards or both.

Elements of an Alarm System

The elements of an alarm are:
- The activating or detecting element, which can be anything from a broken light beam to an interrupted circuit to a Doppler shift.
- The wiring from the detectors to the control unit which signals.
- The alarm. Aside from the conventional local bell, an

alarm can be a flashing light, a dialed phone, turned on lights, a signal to a central alarm console or panel in the building, or sent over telephone wires to a central alarm service company or police station, or any combination of these.

Types of Alarm Systems

There are four basic types of alarm systems.

- The simplest system is the "Local" alarm. These trigger a bell or siren which creates a loud noise in the immediate area of the intrusion. The system usually frightens away amateurs but has very little effect on a pro who knows how to handle it—or to ignore it. In selecting a local alarm, you must determine who is to answer it, how long it will take them to do so, and whether the alarm can surely be heard by your designated respondent.

- The company or proprietary alarm center. This is a company-owned, operated and staffed system employing a central control board, usually on the premises. Company security personnel respond to signals received at the control center.

- The commercial or central station alarm system. This type of alarm system is the only remote-signalling system recognized by insurers. These systems signal over a leased telephone line to transmit a signal to a central station owned and operated by a commercial service organization. When burglary alarms are received by such a station, their armed alarm servicemen are dispatched to the sending location as promptly as possible. The central station company can also receive and identify opening and closing signals.

- Police-connected alarm system. In small towns an alarm system can often be connected to an alarm panel in the local police station. Police respond as rapidly as possible, but the high number of false alarms and other police responsibilities tend to delay response except to robbery alarms. Police-connects can be combined with a proprietary system for additional security. Police connects are rarely possible in large cities because of the number of potential users and the burdens of an already overworked police force.

Types of Burglary Alarm Devices

Since an alarm is designed to detect the intrusion or the proximity of any unauthorized persons, it must be triggered by that person's presence.

Metallic Foil Strip

This is the type that can be seen on so many store windows and doors. The foil is part of a continuous closed-circuit loop connected to alarm relays. Breaking the foil activates the alarm.

While tiny cracks in the foil undetectable by the eye can interrupt the circuit, this type of alarm system is one of the most stable and least subject to false alarming. It can be circumvented by cutting the glass without disturbing the foil by means of a glass cutter and glazier's suction cups, but this is rare.

Contact Switches

These are normally used on doors and windows; when the door or window is opened the alarm is activated by the breaking of the alarm circuit.

Traps

This type employs photoelectric or infrared beams, or trip cords. These cross interior aisles or paths to intercept the intruder within the premises. Any interruption of the light between its source and the receptor will activate the relay. The simplest photoelectric beams are easily compromised, while the pulsed infrared beams cannot be compromised and must be avoided. The light beam can be extended and "bent" by the use of mirrors.

Capacitance Sensors

This type of sensor is used on metal objects such as safes and file cabinets. Creating an electronic field a few inches or more around a metal object, this type of device creates an electronic shield. When a person comes close, the alarm is activated. The situation is similar to the interference that is sometimes induced in a television set when one walks up to it.

Motion Detection

Ultrasonic—Generates a very high frequency sound pattern which fills a closed area; movement in the area causes a change in the frequency that will trip the alarm. In the right application and under proper conditions this detector can be very effective, since it completely protects the entire interior of a given space. It is affected by air currents and vibrations, and if used in areas subject to such disturbances has a high rate of false alarms.

Microwave—This type is similar to the ultrasonic motion detector except that it operates on what might be thought of as a sight rather than a sound pattern. Any movement within the protected area is perceived as a frequency change. It has a much wider application since it is not affected by air currents, or light, and covers a wider area, but it can penetrate glass and walls, and is subject to a high rate of false alarms.

Acoustical Detector—This is, in effect, a big ear. It is a listening device which is activated by a number of sounds of an intruder approaching or making an entrance. Although sensitivity can be adjusted, a high rate of false alarms can be triggered by unexpected harmless interior or exterior noise.

Vibration Detector—This device is, in effect, a switch in which contact making a closed electrical circuit is most delicately made. The detector can be placed on or in specific objects such as cabinets, files or safes. Any movement or vibration will activate the alarm.

This type of detector has a limited use because of the high incidence of false alarms, but in the proper application is very effective.

Alarm Transmission Lines

All remote-reporting alarm systems should have protected transmission lines. A method of checking these lines *must* be included in your system. There are a number of ways of doing this which can be explained to you by your alarm system consultant. Be certain your method of circuit is as fail-safe as possible and set up a strict system for its use.

If a professional has your office picked out for a hit, he will have to circumvent your alarm system somehow. This is frequently done by "jumping" the transmission lines to isolate the alarm circuit. Cutting the transmission line creates an alarm, but the cause may be assumed to be in the telephone company circuits. You must have an arrangement which insures that a guard will be on the premises if the line is "out" for any cause. The burglar often causes alarms to see what the response will be. Always check alarm line connections whenever you have had an unexplained false alarm.

Psychology of Alarms

Office security is essentially a defensive operation. Its role is not primarily the detection and apprehension of criminals. True, it is important to root out the bad seeds in the organization, but its real mission is to prevent attrition of company assets.

Since we have the assignment of defense we must make every effort to keep intruders out of our office space. We will fit perimeter windows and doors with alarms which at least make loud, unpleasant sounds which frighten away all but the most dedicated criminal. Internally we take a different approach. These alarms are silent. They report to a switchboard or panel located where they will be seen by security personnel. If a burglar has entered the office, he may already have his loot by the time he trips an alarm. We wish to recover that loot. A loud alarm would put him to instant flight—with company property. A loud alarm could cause him to panic and fight. This could be lethal to someone. Additionally, although our role is not primarily apprehension, if an intruder manages to make it into the building it is desirable to catch up with him before he starts making a habit of it.

It is suggested then that you consider the following procedure:

Noisy local alarm (supported by central station or other remote back-up) installed at the exterior to scare off intruders; silent alarm inside.

Cameras

Although they have many different uses and capabilities, mechanical visual protection devices boil down to these three:

- Closed-circuit television (CCTV)
- Motion picture cameras
- Sequence cameras

Closed-Circuit Television and Video Tape Recorders

The cameras are usually used on a continuous basis with transmission to a monitoring center in the building. Various cameras keep corridors, entrances, and sensitive areas of various kinds under constant surveillance. Video tape recorders are frequently used for file and reference, for identification, and for a review of suspicious or significant events.

Motion Picture Cameras

Using 16mm high-speed film with fast lenses good, clear pictures are available under normal lighting conditions. This system is activated by a button or pre-arranged alarm sequence. Film cameras are limited as to the length of the situation to be filmed.

Sequence Cameras

A sequence of still pictures can be very effective in providing a visual record of events. The camera can be set to take pictures at regular intervals or it can be activated in an emergency to take a pre-arranged number of pictures by a button or alarm. The time intervals between pictures can be pre-adjusted to lengthen the period over which photos are taken or it can be shortened for a more precise record of the sequence of events.

Filming can be accomplished in the dark using infrared film and an infrared emission source. This method is seldom used in the normal office but is available to those officers having a problem which this technique could help solve.

In using any of these photographic methods, be sure that the cameras are out of reach and well secured. If necessary, they can be alarmed against tampering. They are desirable items and it can be very embarrassing to the security department if these protective devices are stolen.

Summary

New equipment, improved equipment, and more sophisticated equipment is being manufactured and marketed each day. Deciding what is useful and where it might be employed in your company will be a continuing function of office security. From time to time equipment will fail due to inadequate maintenance, or accident, raising the question of whether or not we need back-up equipment. Many security people feel that it is difficult enough to justify basic equipment without endangering such proposals by including back-ups. In most normal offices I agree. I think security must first show that it can walk before it attempts to run. If, by installing equipment, we can show savings by reduced losses, then perhaps we can justify expenditures for back-up equipment. Even so, where company security personnel are employed, back-ups should not be necessary. Instead, security personnel should be deployed until equipment is functioning again. Manpower should be as capable as the equipment it employs.

Finally, equipment can best be installed, and most economically so, when a building is being constructed. If you are ever involved with a new building, then that is the time to "go for broke." You will never have a better opportunity. Above all, remember to take special pains with your computer area, reinforcing walls, floors, and ceilings. You may one day sub-lease the floor above or below to a potential bomb blast tenant, or your company itself could be the intended victim.

TM
TH NK
SECURITY

Chapter 14

MANAGEMENT'S RESPONSIBILITY

Every office in the United States is faced with an ever-increasing danger of crime from every side. Not only is the rate and cost of crime increasing at an alarming rate, but the nature of crime against the office is becoming more serious and more sophisticated. The situation has developed to a point where the business community has begun to look at the problem from a different perspective. Only a relatively few years ago the great majority of companies took only a few basic precautions in their daily conduct of business, and wrote off the losses they suffered as the "cost of doing business." This attitude seems to be on its way out.

With increasing operating costs, greater competition from abroad, and less availability of capital funds, the profit margin and the profit potential are shrinking. No longer is it reasonable to feel that as long as income can stay ahead of costs, the company is in good shape. Today the business community has recognized that losses from criminal activity are not only out of hand, but they can no longer be tolerated in today's competitive and costly operations. Any number of approaches to aid or protect the profit margin must be studied.

Certainly security and loss prevention techniques have come into increasing prominence, and more and more offices have come to recognize the need for some system in their security. Security, of course, exists in every office. The doors are locked at night and the cash is deposited in the bank, and checks are countersigned. And so forth. But this kind of security is no more than the kind of routine precaution that any homeowner would take. Many offices have established systems whereby each department protects itself against assault. This is a step in the right direction, but misses achieving the overall protection every company needs.

The job of security is a big one and getting bigger. Real security requires a specialized task force. There should be a specific function within the company that deals with all matters pertaining to safety, crime prevention, and the protection of company assets from fire, theft, or fraud. Industrial plants, universities, large retail outlets and the like have had security departments for many years, but offices have not. But that picture is changing and today businesses are recognizing, in increasing numbers, the need to establish a specific entity responsible for office security. This entity takes many shapes and is incorporated into the organization in many different ways, but for better or for worse it's a security department and its single mission is to provide security.

All this is fine, and it's a giant step in the right direction, but we still have a problem. The word "security." We've talked about security all through this book and no one choked on it, so why is there a problem now?

Well, up to this point we've used the word in its broadest sense, which is fine because that's exactly what we've been talking about. Unfortunately, most people *think* of the word "security" in a much more restricted way. The word frequently carries a stigma. It conjures up images of badges, clubs, handcuffs, jails and whatever else is thought of as repressive and negative in today's society. The name "security" suggests to too many uninformed persons that the department's goal is the apprehension of criminals and the detection of dishonest employees. This is neither adequate nor correct. The real goal is, and must be recognized to be, the prevention of loss or attack on profits.

We find this goal expressed more and more frequently in our increasingly systems-oriented business community. The emphasis seems to be swinging to the concept of "loss control" instead of "security." Saul D. Astor, who writes extensively on inventory and systems control and on employee dishonesty, has for several years crusaded vigorously to change the name of the security department to the loss prevention department. He takes the view that such a change of name, in itself, would be a giant stride toward different, more beneficial goals; that the security department tends to be comprised of emergency-motivated trouble-shooters, while the loss prevention department takes on the challenge implicit in the belief that most losses can be prevented. It's an interesting notion and it certainly wouldn't be the first time that changing the title changed the function and the performance.

Obviously, the goals of this loss prevention function, whatever it is to be called, are a matter of management decision which cannot be casually arrived at. If the decision is to establish a loss prevention program, management must make an all-out commitment to make its effective operation possible. This is not an easy decision. It requires study. And to begin with, it boils down to a question of authority—how much authority loss prevention requires to do the job.

Any evaluation of the scope of authority required by loss prevention must examine the organizational framework of the company and the proper role of loss prevention within that structure.

It must be recognized that in the concept of loss prevention with which we are dealing here, the department must cut across all departmental lines to enter into virtually every function of the company. Loss prevention should permeate the office—not as a repressive presence, but in the role of cooperative specialist. Even so, this role will inevitably lead to conflict.

On paper the relationship between loss prevention and other departments is ideal. They are working in concert to solve common problems. In practice, however, there is frequently some resentment and a feeling that loss prevention is interfering in the efficient performance of operational routine.

Loss prevention must have authority to accomplish its mission. It must have direct authority to deal with establishing or correcting systems, with auditing system performance, with evaluating and re-evaluating risks anywhere within the company. It must have direct authority to handle these and hundreds of other problems that fall within the scope of loss prevention.

Management must clearly establish the *degree* of authority the department may exercise in given situations. In increasing increments on the authority scale the department might exercise: advisory authority, compulsory advisory authority, concurring authority, or final authority.

Advisory Authority

Voluntary acceptance of the advice of a security professional may be adequate to cover the needs of some companies. This will depend on the nature of the business. Even in companies where the security function operates at a high level of authority the advisory approach is common, especially in matters concerning the welfare of employees. In other matters, the security executive should advise the concerned supervisor of the situation and work with him (if the supervisor desires) to develop corrective measures. Obviously there will be many instances where the supervisor will reject the advice thus offered to him. In such a case the security executive must be able to take his case to much higher authority.

In an active company with a number of high-risk areas, a security function limited to advisory authority would be inadequate to the responsibility. Since security would have no motivating authority it could neither implement nor adequately audit protective systems. There is, additionally, the danger that security would be put in the position of having to constantly run to management to arbitrate in matters that should be within its own scope to resolve.

Compulsory Consultation

If consultation is compulsory, the security function must be called in before any action is taken by operating personnel. This plateau of authority at least keeps the loss prevention department advised as to contemplated changes throughout the company. Since, in most cases, the contact between departments will be initiated outside of security, security's role in the discussion and in the eventual decisions will be strengthened.

This level is still below the authority required in companies with an appreciable number of high-risk areas.

Concurring Authority

In this situation security has the authority to over-rule any action that touches on its areas of responsibility. It may not necessarily motivate the action but it can cancel it. This means that new files may not be ordered unless security approves of locks; that a new elevator system cannot be approved until security agrees that it satisfied certain standards of safety. At the same time, security may disapprove the purchase of individual office shredders as unnecessary.

Final or Functional Authority

This is the ultimate authority. In cases where this degree of authority is granted, the security official may exercise direct authority over any employee activities related to security in any way. This kind of authority could result in a directive from a security official ordering a revision in the receiving process, or ordering structural changes in certain offices for reasons of security. Obviously such authority should be used sparingly and with the greatest of discretion. It is rare, indeed, that a security function has such authority and when it does it must protect it with the greatest care. Management, too, must exercise judgment in granting this authority and should probably restrict its application to very specific areas.

It is likely that a well-run security function in a well-run company will have some combination of these authorities, but whatever the level in whatever circumstances, it is vital that this authority be spelled out in the clearest possible language by management. With such an understanding, management can go a long way toward avoiding the conflicts that would otherwise arise.

It is almost invariably the case that management turns its attention to security problems only after the office has been beset by a series of crimes. We can sagely observe that this is not very smart, however human it may be. High-salaried executives are not paid to be human in the sense of being subject to human frailty and error; they are paid to administer the affairs of the company in such a way as to contribute to its growth or well-being, and to anticipate and forestall those elements that might interfere with the essential health of the corporate body. Crime committed against the company is a most unhealthy and costly adversary, and proper security against such attack is a high priority requisite in the company's scheme of things. This security must be incorporated into a long-sustained, effective loss prevention program.

All too few companies today show enough sustained interest in the never-ending problem of crime. Even after initiating an effective program in response to a wave of crime against the office, management often loses interest in security matters as crime declines. And, as management loses interest, procedures, systems and controls erode and deteriorate. This situation is particularly dangerous because it engenders a false sense of security. In the belief that controls and anti-crime procedures are protecting company assets, management is lulled into an unwarranted complacence.

It is essential that management recognize that the security function must be a dynamic instrument in the war against crime. It must be as alive, as innovative, and as alert as the criminal. It must be renewed and refreshed regularly if it is to be equal to the enormous job it has to perform. It must be supervised! It must be administered! It must be important!

It is curious—but true—that in security matters there is frequently a reluctance on the part of top executives to think past retaliation. They will commit elaborate funds to track down a thief and they will look for uncommon heroics in response to a fire, but they can find a lot of reasons not to spend money to prevent the theft or the fire. Unless the management of your company can be educated to a broader, more enlightened view you are doomed to a purely reactive security function and you will certainly never make it to loss prevention.

If you do educate your management to the extent that you have been designated as the loss prevention department (or at least have the scope implicit in that name) you had better be sure that you are prepared for the job. Ask yourself if you are law enforcement oriented. If you are, are you willing to broaden your base of expertise through additional training and study? Does your staff consist largely of uninformed guards whose duties are essentially access control? If so, you will need to take immediate steps to expand your departmental capabilities by staffing with professionals with broad backgrounds including systems, accounting, training, administration, and research. This is a big step for a function that only yesterday was performed by a few door-rattling ex-cops, but if security is to serve the ever-growing needs of today's embattled corporation, that step must be taken.

In sum, management cannot ignore the rising tide of crime in the office. No matter how true it is that the countermeasures may be seen as unattractive, expensive, and occasionally restrictive and inconvenient, the problem must be faced.

A firm, decisive attitude and effective measures fulfill the obligation which management owes its stockholders, its employees and, in a larger sense, society in general.

It may well be that this participation in the war against crime by the business community may be hastened by legislation—legislation which sets certain minimum standards for security for all kinds of enterprise. If the notion sounds far out, you might try to project yourself back a few years before there were codes specifying minimum standards of construction and safety to combat fire and injury or death from fire. In a way it is strange to realize that we had to enact legislation insisting, in effect, that people protect themselves from the ravages of fire. Similar legislation could go a long way toward consolidating the business world in a united front against the destructive onslaught of the criminal.

But it should not be necessary, nor should the situation be permitted to deteriorate to the point where inflexible regulations replace management's most efficient response to dangers which threaten profits and assets.

BIBLIOGRAPHY

Books and Pamphlets

Auchincloss, Lewis. *The Embezzler*. Houghton, 1956.

Bomb Threats: Suggested Action to Protect Employees and Property. New York: National Association of Manufacturers.

Brodie, Thomas G. *Bombs and Bombings*. Springfield, Ill.: Charles C. Thomas, 1973.

A Check List for Plant Security. New York: National Association of Manufacturers.

Code for Life Safety from Fire in Buildings and Structures. Boston: National Fire Protection Association, 1970.

Cole, Richard B. *The Application of Security Systems and Hardware*. Springfield, Ill.: Charles C. Thomas, 1970.

Cole, Richard B. *Protect Your Property: The Applications of Burglar Alarm Hardware*. Springfield, Ill.: Charles C. Thomas, 1971.

The Considerations of Data Security in a Computer Environment. New York: International Business Machines Corporation, 1970.

Curtis, Bob. *Security Control: External Theft*. Chain Store Age Books, 1971.

Drug Abuse as a Business Problem. New York Chamber of Commerce, 1970.

Factory Mutual Approval Guide: Equipment, Materials, Services for Conservation of Property. Norwood, Mass.: Factory Mutual System, 1969-1970.

Federal Bureau of Investigation. *Crime in the United States*. Uniform Crime Reports, 1970.

Fendrock, John J. *Managing in Times of Radical Change*. New York: American Management Association, 1971.

Fire Department, City of New York. *Annual Report*, 1969.

Fire Extinguishing Equipment. Bureau of Facilities. Washington, D.C.: U. S. Government Printing Office, 1970.

Flippo, Edwin B. *Management, A Behavioral Approach*. Boston: Allyn & Bacon, 1970.

Flippo, Edwin B. *Principles of Personnel Management*, 2nd ed. New York: McGraw-Hill Book Company, 1966.

Gocke, B. W. *Practical Plant Protection and Policing for the Security of Business and Industry*. Springfield, Ill.: Charles C. Thomas.

Greene, Richard M. Jr. *Business Intelligence and Espionage*. Homewood, Ill.: Dow Jones-Irwin, Inc., 1966.

Haacke, Harry H., and San Souce, William B. *How to Reduce Embezzlement Losses*. New York: Royal-Globe Insurance Companies.

Hamilton, Peter. *Espionage and Subversion in an Industrialized Society*. New York: Humanities Press.

Healy, Richard J., and Walsh, Timothy J. *Industrial Security Management: A Cost-Effective Approach*. New York: American Management Association, 1971.

Hemphill, Charles F., Jr. *Security for Business and Industry*. Homewood, Ill.: Dow Jones-Irwin, Inc., 1971.

Inbau, Fred E. and Aspen, Marvin E. *Criminal Law for the Layman*. Philadelphia: Chilton Book Company, 1970.

Industrial Defense against Civil Disturbances, Bombings, Sabotage. Washington, D.C.: Department of the Army, Office of the Provost Marshal General, 1971.

Jaspan, Norman. *Thief in a White Collar*. Philadelphia: Lippincott, 1959.

Kaiser, Julius B. *Forms Design and Control*. New York: American Management Association, 1968.

Loss Prevention Check List. New York: National Retail Merchants Association.

Management Guide on Alcoholism and Other Behavioral Problems. Chicago: Kemper Insurance Company.

Martin, James, and Norman, Adrian R. C., *The Computerized Society*. Englewood Cliffs, N.J.: Prentice-Hall, Inc., 1970.

Momboisse, Raymond M. *Industrial Security for Strikes, Riots and Disasters*. Springfield, Ill.: Charles C. Thomas, 1968.

Oliver, Eric, and Wilson, John. *Practical Security in Commerce and Industry*. 2d. ed. London: Halstead Press, 1973.

Pike, Earl E. *Protection against Bombs and Incendiaries*. Springfield, Ill.: Charles C. Thomas, 1972.

Post, Richard S., ed. *Combatting Crime against Small Business*. Springfield, Ill.: Charles C. Thomas, 1972.

Post, Richard S., Kingsbury, Arthur A., and Buckley, Charles L. Jr. *Security Administration*. 2d ed. Springfield, Ill.: Charles C. Thomas, 1973.

Pratt, Lester A. *Embezzlement Controls for Business Enterprises*. 2d ed. Baltimore, Md.: Fidelity and Deposit Company.

Public Buildings Service. *International Conference on Fire Safety in High-Rise Buildings*. Washington, D.C.: U. S. Government Printing Office, 1971.

Reeves, Elton T. *The Dynamics of Group Behavior*. New York: American Management Association, 1970.

Stoffel, Joseph. *Explosives and Homemade Bombs*. 2d. ed. Springfield, Ill.: Charles C. Thomas, 1972.

The Thief You Pay. Los Angeles: Security World Publishing Co., Inc., 1969.

Thirty-Third Annual Report of the National Labor Relations Board. Washington, D.C.: U. S. Government Printing Office.

Underwriters' Laboratories. *Building Materials List*. Northbrook, Ill.: Underwriters' Laboratories.

Underwriters' Laboratories. *Fire Protection Equipment List*. Northbrook, Ill.: Underwriters' Laboratories.

Weber, Thad L. *Alarm Systems and Theft Prevention*. Los Angeles: Security World Publishing Co., Inc., 1973.

Articles in Periodicals

"The Anatomy of a Con Game." *Purchasing Week*, February 19, 1968.

Astor, Saul D. "An Investigator Talks of Embezzlement and Robbery." *The Office*, September 1971, pp. 55-57.

"Bankers Advise on Office Security Precautions," *The Office*, September 1971, p. 28.

Bond, Horatio. "Sprinkler Protection for High-Rise Buildings." *Fire Journal*, November 1968.

Buzby, Walter J. II. "Arson and the Security Officer." *Security World*, June 1971, p. 35.

Carroll, Leslie H. "Bomb Scare: A Medical Center's Program." *Security World*, December 1970, pp. 29-32.

Cramer, William L. "Mr. Jones? A bomb will go off in your building in just seven minutes. But you don't know where it is, do you, Mr. Jones." *Professional Management Bulletins*, Administrative Management Society, August 1971.

"Crime Is Cancerous." *The Office*, August 1969, p. 118.

Doe, Everett. "Fire Loading in Retail Stores." *Security World*, June 1968, p. 22.

Donovan, Bob. "Anatomy of a Demonstration." *Security World*, Part I, July-August, 1966, pp. 12-15; Part II, September 1966, pp. 24-28.

"Drive to Halt Terror Bombings." *U.S. News and World Report*, March 15, 1971, pp. 17-19.

"The Drug Addiction of Business Personnel." *The Office*, December 1970, p. 49.

Elliot, Raymond W. "Computer Embezzlement Prevention and Control." Unpublished presentation at the International Security Conference, February 1971. Security World Publishing Co., Inc.

Faulstich, W. L. "Anatomy of a Demonstration, Part III." *Security World*, October 1966, pp. 26-31.

"Fire Hazards in New Buildings." *The Office*, October 1970, p. 32.

"Fire Is A Full-Time Menace." *The Office*, October 1970, p. 32.

"Fortifying Your Business Security." *The Office*, August 1969, pp. 39-52.

French, Harvey M. "Current Arson Problems." *Security World*, February 1971, pp. 14-19.

French, Harvey M. "Investigate that Fire!" *Security World*, February 1969, p. 19.

Goering, George B. "Basics for Bomb Emergency Planning." *Security World*, June 1970.

Gohr, Phillip R. "Exercising Security Authority." *Security World*, January 1972, p. 14.

Golden, Arthur J. "Empire Crash Fire." Fire Department, City of New York, October 1945, pp. 4-7.

"The Greenest Are Ripest for Plucking." *The Office*, September 1971, pp. 49-51.

"How Paper Shredders Protect Business Data." *The Office*, September 1971, p. 58.

"How Security Does Pay Off." *The Office*, September 1971, p. 22.

Imberman, A. A. "These Executive Traits Cause Personnel Problems." *The Office*, December 1971, pp. 12-16.

"In-Office ID Systems Aid Company Security." *Administrative Management*, April 1969, p. 24.

Johnson, Don S. "Office Executives Have Long Been Fair Game for Fraud." *The Office*, December 1968, pp. 41-45.

Klein Schrod, Walter A. "Crisis in Office Crime." *Administrative Management*, November 1971, pp. 24-27.

Lefer, Henry. "How to Preserve Your Business Lifeblood." *Modern Office Procedures*, April 1971, pp. 21-27.

"The Major Property-Loss Fires of 1970." *Fire Journal*, May 1971, pp. 28-39.

McCollum, David Jr. "Some Points on Bombs and Bomb Threats." *FBI Law Enforcement Bulletin*, April 1971, p. 13.

McGuire, Patrick E. "Targets for Terrorists." *The Conference Board Record*, August 1971.

McGuire, Patrick E. "When Bombing Threatens." *The Conference Board Record*, September 1971.

Momboisse, Raymond M. "Management and the 'Ad Hoc' Committee." *Security World*, June 1967, pp. 12-16.

"The Moral Power of Shareholders." *Business Week*, May 1, 1971, p. 76.

Morris, Sid. "My Vendors The Spies." *The Office*, December 1968, pp. 46-49.

Parr, Edward M. "Some Basics of Sprinkler Protection." *Security World*, February 1969, p. 54.

"Pre-Riot Retail Planning." *Security World*, June 1966, pp. 34-36.

"A Push-button Lock for Computer Room Security." *The Office*, March 1971, pp. 161-163.

"Riot and Premise Protection: A Summary of the Los Angeles Experience." *Security World*, September 1965, pp. 10-14.

"The Rising Wages of Fear." *Time*, May 24, 1971, p. 80.

Ritz, Richard E. "A High-Rise Fire-Resistive Office Building with Automatic Sprinklers Installed Throughout." *Fire Journal*, September 1969.

Rubenstein, Sidney S. "Your Safe Can Save Your Company." *Security World*, January 1965, p. 10.

Sampson, Arthur F. "Life Safety Systems for High-Rise Structures." *Fire Journal*, July 1971, pp. 8-10.

Stevens, Richard E. "The High-Rise Building Dilemma." *Fire Journal*, July 1971, pp. 5-7.

"Stolen Stocks and Bonds for Sale." *Changing Times, The Kiplinger Magazine*, February 1971, p. 28.

"Theft: Is This What It's Coming To?" *Special Report*, National Office Products Association, February-March 1971.

"There Is a Bomb Planted in Your Office." *Administrative Management*, August 1970, pp. 18-25.

Toepfer, Edwin. "Lock Security: Cylinders, Keys and Keying." *Security World*, July-August 1965.

"A Unique Premise Protection Squad Surveys and Studies Security Techniques." *Security Product News*, November 1971.

Wackenhut, George R. "Business Is the Target of Bombings and Bomb Hoaxes." *The Office*, September 1971, p. 14.

Wilson, Ralph. "Will an Office Thief Strike Tonight?" *Modern Office Procedures*, June 1964, p. 19.

Zalkind, Joseph G. "Is Your Office Part of the Drug Scene?" *Administrative Management*, October 1970, p. 40.